Contents

Foundation GNVQ Information and Communication Technology

Second Edition

Jenny Lawson

In this book you will find helpful icons showing which key skills the Activities can be used for:

 Communication

 Application of number

 Working with others

 Problem solving

 Improving own learning and performance

Pearson Education Limited
Edinburgh Gate
Harlow
Essex CM20 2JE, England
and Associated Companies throughout the world

First edition published 1997
This edition published 2001

ISBN 0 582 35708 X

British Library Cataloguing-in-Publication Data

A catalogue record for this book is available from the British Library.

Set by 3 in Humanist, Rotis Serif, Caslon

Produced by Pearson Education

Printed by Henry Ling Ltd, at the Dorset Press, Dorchester, Dorset

Introduction

This book is written for Foundation level GNVQ Information and Communication Technology students and covers the nine units specified by the QCA (Qualifications and Curriculum Authority) available through any one of the three awarding bodies that examine GNVQs: AQA, Edexcel and OCR.

This book is also suitable for Foundation level Part One students of GNVQ Information and Communication Technology.

What is Foundation GNVQ Information and Communication Technology?

GNVQs were designed to offer students a one- or two-year full-time course as an alternative to GCSEs. There are two qualifications at Foundation level GNVQ:

✪ The six-unit GNVQ qualification is equivalent to four GCSEs at grades D to G or NVQ level 1

✪ The three-unit Part One GNVQ qualification is broadly equivalent to two GCSE grades D to G

GNVQs are vocational qualifications related to broad areas of the world of work, such as information technology (IT). A GNVQ qualification in Information and Communication Technology helps you to develop an understanding of IT and introduces you to some of the skills and knowledge you will need to go on to work or further study.

For Foundation GNVQ Information and Communication Technology, there are three **compulsory units**:

✪ Presenting information

✪ Handling information

✪ ICT systems

Together, these three units cover all the material you will need to understand how ICT is used at work.

There are then six **optional units**, which give you the opportunity to choose areas that you find particularly interesting. You may also choose a unit from another GNVQ area, e.g. Leisure and Tourism, so long as the units do not have similar titles.

How do you achieve an award in GNVQ Information and Communication Technology at Foundation level?

The three-unit Part One GNVQ ICT involves about half the work of the full award, but you are tested on each unit. For the six-unit award of a Foundation GNVQ in ICT, you must complete six units:

✪ **Three compulsory units from the ICT area**

✪ **Three optional units from any GNVQ area, including ICT**

You will be tested on two units: one compulsory unit and one other chosen from the optional unit suite.

Because each awarding body offers only one tested unit within the set of optional units, this effectively changes your choice to four 'compulsory' units (the three decided by the QCA plus the tested optional unit for your awarding body), plus two optional units. Which units are tested by each awarding body is shown in the Examination Guide on page 447. This means that two-thirds of your work will be assessed as you work through the course (continuous assessment), and one-third will be tested at set times of the year (January or June), after you have worked on a particular unit.

These two methods of assessment appeal to different types of student. Some students do not like tests; for them, continuous assessment seems less stressful. Others may prefer a single test, perhaps because they think they can leave all the learning till just before the exam. Having both methods of assessment in the one course, you are encouraged not to leave things to the last minute, and, although there are exams to face, your work is assessed in the least stressful way.

For Part One students, all your work will be assessed, and all three units will be tested. For both awards – the six-unit award and the three-unit Part One award – evidence of your work will be kept in a portfolio. Details about how to prepare your portfolio are given in the Portfolio Guide on page 429.

While studying for your GNVQ course, you will also have the opportunity to gain the key skills qualifications. As far as is possible, evidence of key skills may be seen in your portfolio of work, and your teacher will advise you on how you can build evidence of key skills into your assignments. The Key Skills Guide on page 439 also provides useful information about key skills.

What is a unit?

A unit covers one area of study. Foundation GNVQ ICT Unit 1, for example, concentrates on presenting information. Each unit specification has four main headings:

- ✪ **About this unit**

- ✪ **What you need to learn**

- ✪ **Assessment evidence**

- ✪ **Guidance for teachers**

Although the final section is written for teachers, because your success on this course depends on you, rather than your teacher, you should find it quite useful. It explains how you can work hard to achieve a good grade for the unit and what key skills you might achieve while doing the unit. With GNVQs, you are expected to take responsibility for your own learning, so it makes sense to find time to read this section very carefully.

How to read a unit

The **title of the unit** gives a broad description of what the unit covers. e.g. 'Handling Information'.

The **About this unit** section introduces the unit. It explains the benefits you may expect from completing the unit and gives a broad description of what you will do. It also tells you about links between this unit and other units.

The **What you need to learn** section is the longest section. It lists all the topics you should cover for this unit, though not necessarily in the order you will learn about them. Notice that this section is called 'What you need to learn' rather than 'What you will be taught'. This is because it is quite possible that your teacher will do very little 'teaching'! GNVQ students are expected to take control of their own learning, and it is your teacher's job to guide you towards this independent approach to learning. One of the objectives of a vocational course like a GNVQ course is to prepare you for a job, and this teaching style is an important part of the GNVQ process.

You should find that you have more freedom to decide what to do. However, you will also need to make decisions for yourself. Meeting deadlines is very important, and you must put in the hours needed to complete your work on time. Otherwise, you may be given poor assessment grades. However, your teacher will help you.

How will your understanding be tested? If you are on a GNVQ Foundation six-unit course:

✪ **For four of the units, you will demonstrate your understanding by your portfolio material**

✪ **For two of the units, there are 90-minute written tests, one per unit**

If you are on a Part One GNVQ course:

✪ **For all three units, you will demonstrate your understanding by your portfolio material**

✪ **For all three units, there are 90-minute written tests, one per unit**

The obvious way to learn about work is through your work experience placement or a part-time job. However, your course should also offer you the opportunity to try out a variety of work experiences:

✪ **Working on your own as well as with others in a team**

- ✪ Doing short projects and completing long assignments

- ✪ Visiting local firms and businesses, and interviewing people such as employers, their staff and their customers

- ✪ Designing products and services

- ✪ Organising events

The **Assessment evidence** section is given as a chart with two sections, with the lower section split into three columns. The top section lists what evidence you need to produce for the unit. There may be one large piece of evidence, or the task may be broken down into a number of smaller tasks for you to complete. You will need to have covered the unit and developed an understanding of the topics in the 'What you need to learn section' to produce your portfolio evidence, but not all topics need be evidenced. This top section will also specify how many examples you need to produce for your evidence.

The first column in the lower section of the table explains what is expected for a pass. Use this column to check that your work is at the required standard for a pass.

The second and third columns explain what is expected of a merit and a distinction student. For a merit, you must do the things in the pass column as well as those in the merit column. For a distinction, you must do the things in the pass column and the things in the merit column as well as those in the distinction column!

The items listed in the merit and distinction columns are not extra tasks for you to complete; instead, they show what extra qualities you are expected to demonstrate in your evidence:

- ✪ How good you are at planning and organising your work

- ✪ How independent you are when carrying out your work – whether you can cope without a lot of help

- ✪ How much the quality of the work you are producing is improving

✪ **How much you show a greater understanding of what you have learned**

It is important that you read the assessment chart very carefully.

The portfolio

Your portfolio contains all the evidence collected as you work through the units. Mostly, this will be evidence of your work on a computer system and so will be printouts, annotated to explain what you have done. Some units may ask for a special form of evidence to be produced by you:

✪ **Unit 1 asks for a portfolio of six original documents and a review of two of these documents**

✪ **Unit 2 asks for a database and a spreadsheet to meet a given requirement**

✪ **Unit 3 asks for screen prints and printouts**

When assessing your work, your teacher is looking for the right quality and quantity of work. He or she will first look to see that you have covered everything by checking all the items listed on the 'Assessment evidence' chart. However, work of a high quality may earn you a merit or distinction award, so your teacher will be looking at the last two columns of the chart in particular.

Before handing in your work to your teacher for assessment, you should check exactly what is required for each unit and make sure that your portfolio holds all this information in an easily accessible way. Guidance on how to present your portfolio is given in the Portfolio Guide on page 429.

Grading

By the end of your course, your portfolio will contain a great deal of evidence. In deciding what grade to award (pass, merit or distinction), your teacher will consider a number of things:

✪ Your approach to learning and how you tackled your work

✪ How much responsibility you took for planning your work

✪ How you decided what information you needed

✪ How well you reviewed and evaluated your own progress

✪ The quality of your evidence

It is important, therefore, to aim high. During your course, you should receive feedback from your teacher giving you a clear picture of how you are doing, and how you might improve your performance.

The external tests

For the six-unit Foundation GNVQ ICT award, there are two tests: one compulsory unit and one optional unit. Each examination board offers different tested units, so which units will be tested depends on which board your school or college uses. The details of which units are tested is shown in a table on page 450 in the Examination Guide section.

When you have completed the work for a single unit, you should be ready to sit the external test – a written test, lasting 90 minutes. You write your answers in a booklet in the spaces provided. Sample papers are available from the web pages of the three examination boards. You can use these as 'mock' examinations.

Some guidance about how to prepare for these tests is given in the Examination Guide on page 447.

How should you use this book?

This introductory chapter explains how GNVQs work. The main part of this book is then divided into nine chapters, each one matching one of the units in Foundation GNVQ Information and Communication Technology.

The three examination boards – AQA, Edexcel and OCR – number their units differently! A table on page 450 in the Examination Guide shows which chapter matches which unit for each of them.

There are many features in each chapter:

✪ Notes on what you need to know, with plenty of diagrams and examples, mostly based on case studies

✪ Stopping points with exercises to check that you have understood what you have been reading about

✪ Activities to test your understanding and to help you to produce portfolio evidence

✪ Sets of revision questions

Towards the end of the book, there are four guides:

✪ The Good Working Practice Guide provides useful information about health and safety issues and other good working practice expected of you during your practical work

✪ The Portfolio Guide includes hints on how to prepare

your portfolio, plus some help in gaining merit and distinction grades

✪ The Key Skills Guide explains what you have to do to demonstrate your key skills in communication and application of number (key skills in IT at level 1 are automatically covered in the GNVQ ICT course)

✪ The Examinations Guide offers useful advice about preparation for the written examinations

There is also a list of abbreviations and a comprehensive index. The index lists all important words used in the book. Indexed words appear in bold in the text or in headings. The index also includes cross references to help you to find what you are looking for.

What else do you need?

As well as this book, you need a copy of the unit specifications for Foundation GNVQ Information and Communication Technology for your particular awarding body, plus sample papers and past papers for the written examinations.

All nine unit specifications are available on the websites of all three awarding bodies and can be downloaded free of charge. Access to these sites and other useful sites for GNVQ and NVQ resources is available through Pearson Education's web page: http://www.longman-fe.com

You are also recommended to visit the website of the British Computer Society (BCS) and to obtain a copy of the glossary published by Pearson Education, which explains all the terms used for this GNVQ course and in this book. Two versions are available:

✪ *A Glossary of Computing Terms*, ISBN: 0582369673

✪ *IT Glossary for Schools*, ISBN: 0582312558

Acknowledgements

I am very grateful to all those who provided material for the many examples and case studies in the book:

- ✪ Alan and Maxine Wade, Penhaven Country House Hotel

- ✪ The Green Team at Chris Lane Family Leisure Club, especially Tim Lane, Andy Harris, Simon Thorpe and David Gabb

- ✪ Peter Hawkes

- ✪ George Honour

- ✪ Martin Burley

- ✪ Kris Tynan, Nicky Givan and the team at Bodylife

- ✪ John Hore

- ✪ Lorraine Mayle

- ✪ Jason Dobson, Robert Cockerill and the team at NCI for discussion of their recruitment policy in Chapter 8

- ✪ Sailing friends who suggested ideas for the fictitious case study in Chapter 2, too many to list by name

Thanks are also due to my colleagues after many years as chief examiner for GNVQ IT: the principal examiners (Graham Redfern, Geoff Brignell and David Bittlestone) and the many assistant examiners who offered advice, or who, during discussion at our many examination meetings, raised questions that I have tried to answer in this book.

Special thanks go to my colleagues at the examination boards – everyone in the GNVQ units, the teams of setters, pre-moderators and moderators involved in the preparation and marking of external test papers.

Finally, the team at Pearson Education deserves a mention for its encouragement and support – and my family, who were as patient as ever during the preparation of this book.

The Case Studies

Many case studies are used in this book to illustrate the ideas presented, and to give you ideas about organisations you might contact for information:

- ✪ Bodylife
- ✪ Martin Burley, fuchsia grower
- ✪ Chris Lane Family Leisure Club
- ✪ Hawkes Design
- ✪ George Honour, butcher
- ✪ Lorraine Mayle
- ✪ The Met Office
- ✪ NCI
- ✪ OCC Online Cruising Club
- ✪ Penhaven Country House Hotel
- ✪ Sailing Breaks

In this section, each one is introduced, in alphabetical order, so that you have some background information on each organisation:

- ❂ Who is involved

- ❂ What product or service the organisation provides

- ❂ How ICT systems are used in the organisation

When you are trying to find users for whom you can develop projects, think about similar organisations to these case studies.

Bodylife

Bodylife is a small company that works from very pleasant offices in the grounds of a garden centre in Woking, Surrey. All the small team of hand-picked staff are keen on keeping fit and have years of experience in the health and fitness industry.

Bodylife magazine is published six times a year. It is directed at health clubs and people in the health industry and includes articles about how health clubs might be run.

Articles are received from contributors as Word files. These are copy-edited and proof-read before being passed to the designer, who uses DTP to produce the page layout.

The magazine includes lots of photos. These are scanned in and placed in the pages to create an attractive and interesting effect.

The page proofs are checked very carefully to make sure there are no errors. Then the magazine is printed and distributed to all Bodylife subscribers.

Martin Burley, fuchsia grower

Martin is a keen gardener. His passion is for growing fuchsias, and he grows as many as 30 different varieties. He is so good at it that he takes his plants to shows and sells his plants to the public. His main opportunity to show his fuchsias is at the Royal Horticultural Society's annual show, where he has a stand.

To help visitors to the stand to find out about the many different varieties of fuchsia that Martin grows, he produces a small leaflet explaining the plants. This is what the text says:

> All of the standards are between one and four years old. They have been wrapped in netting to keep the stems straight. For show purposes, a full standard is classified as having a stem between 30" and 42". A half standard is between 18" and 30".

> Some of the more vigorous varieties have grown heads of over 4 ft wide in less than one year.

> A few samples of young standards being trained have been included in the display to show how the head develops after the first pinch.

> The patio and trailing plants being used for ground cover have been grown from cuttings taken in March.

> Every plant in the display has been grown and trained in my garden at Park Cottage, Prince's Park, Irlam, Manchester.

> All of the plants are for sale. They can be reserved and collected from the stand at the sell-off time of 4 pm on Sunday. With reasonable care the standard fuchsias should flower from June to October and last for several years.

Martin also has a large sign MARTIN'S STANDARD FUCHSIAS, a numbered list of the varieties of fuchsia on display, and a 'map' showing the position of each numbered variety.

Lots of people have a 'hobby' that they enjoy as much as Martin enjoys growing his fuchsias. If they are good at it, they may 'show' or sell what they make. Think of people you know who work in this way. They may make wedding cakes, breed rabbits, make soft furnishings like curtains, or grow herbs. It is most unlikely you will find out about them through 'normal' advertising. Still, they may welcome your designing a leaflet that explains what they produce. Many people who make things only sell them at craft stalls in markets, at summer fetes, or around Christmas time, so look out for them especially then.

Chris Lane Family Leisure Club

Chris Lane opened his club fifteen years ago, initially as a tennis club with 150 members and four staff. Since then, the club has grown dramatically and now has thousands of members enjoying facilities that include indoor and outdoor tennis courts, a fully equipped gym, therapy rooms and beauty treatment rooms, studio, pool, crèche, bar and restaurant. Recently, the clubhouse has been redeveloped to incorporate KidSports, a facility for children to learn through organised activities.

The staff at Chris Lane – called the Green Team – are committed to customer care. The aim of the Green Team is to make each visit to the club a positive experience for every member every time they visit the club.

The club keeps in touch with members using the club magazine, *In Touch*. Leaflets and posters are also displayed around the clubhouse. Producing posters is a full-time job – over 250 new posters are needed each year to advertise the many events on offer to members.

ICT is used in a number of ways within the club. When members enter the club, they swipe their membership card past a sensor, which releases a turnstile and lets them into the clubhouse. The system records that they are present – useful in case of fire or if someone rings the club trying to contact a member.

Members can also put money on to their membership cards for use in the bar and restaurant. Members are given a 10% discount on any purchase made with the card. The club benefits from this positive cash flow – but it does offer the opportunity for members to leave valuables at home and to visit the club to train carrying only their membership card. In the bar, a concept keyboard is used to record purchases.

There are many similar clubs in the UK, and it would be worthwhile visiting one near you to find out how ICT is used by its staff and how it affects its members.

Hawkes Design

Peter Hawkes is a graphic designer. His clients include educational publishers, environmental organisations and local organisations. For these clients, Peter designs and produces logos, magazines, theatre brochures and programmes, advertisements and publicity flyers. Each year, he creates a one-page calendar, which includes samples of his work. He sends a copy to his clients and contacts within the publishing industry to remind them of the services he offers.

Peter is one of the many freelancers that publishers use to produce their books, and my first contact with Peter was in producing a series of maths books. Artwork briefs were sent to Peter, who drew the artwork using his software and not inconsiderable artistic talent; these final drawings were then placed in the text of the book. His work is time-consuming and requires a great deal of patience. He checks his work very carefully before sending it back to his clients for approval. The hardware and software used by Peter are explained in Chapter 3.

The publishing industry relies on freelancers like Peter. You may find details of local people with similar skills by looking in your Yellow Pages.

George Honour, butcher

George Honour appeared as a case study in the previous edition of this book, published in 1997. At that time, I included George as an example of a trader who rarely has a need for IT. Time has moved on! In the last three years, George has not changed the quality of the meat he supplies or the way he deals with his customers at all. Despite the threat of competition from nearby superstores, he still gives excellent service to the local residents and many, like me, who live further away and make a special trip to his shop. However, he has started to use a computer in the administration side of his business. He is now using word-processing and databases on a regular basis.

After the *E. coli* outbreak a while ago, the finger of blame – perhaps somewhat unfairly – was pointed towards butchers in general. To ensure that such an outbreak does not occur again, butchers have got together and agreed a code of conduct (which the best butchers like George were already following). They have studied the route that meat takes, from the live animal to George's (and other butchers') shops and then into the customers' shopping bag. Each step has been examined and a risk analysis drawn up. It is important that meat is kept in conditions that do not encourage the spread of bacteria. Apart from cleanliness, for this, the correct temperature is important. As a result of this, George has a number of checklists, which help him to monitor the conditions of meat that he sells. When each delivery arrives, the temperature in the van is noted. If the conditions are not right, the delivery will be rejected. The temperature of the fridges in George's shop is also monitored.

For health and safety reasons, so that the authorities can trace all ingredients used in the many different varieties of sausage and burger, George also keeps records of all recipes used in the shop (although George makes sausages and burgers each week and so knows these recipes off by heart). There are also procedures to do with cleaning rosters and the health records of the staff who work at George's shop.

All this information is word-processed. The checklist masters are photocopied. The data sheets, like the recipe sheets, are filed. Then if any details change, it is easy to correct the document and print out a fresh version. The information is now all in one file, instead of inside George's head – and it is there to be seen by any inspector who may need to check that the correct procedures are indeed being carried out.

George is also using databases, mostly in the run-up to Christmas, to help process Christmas orders for meat. Details of how George uses the database appear in Chapter 4.

All companies, even those that employ as few as five people, have to follow health and safety rules. This includes assessing the risks in the workplace and drawing up procedures to minimise risks and remove potential hazards. All companies will have fire regulations and written information about what to do when the fire alarm sounds. If you contact any small company, they should already have this documentation in place. If they don't, you would be helping them if your project involved setting up the necessary documents for them.

Lorraine Mayle

Lorraine is a member of the Federation of Holistic Therapists. She offers reflexology, reiki and other therapeutic massage to her clients. She has a business card, which she gives to clients so they can contact her to book an appointment. Her leaflet explains the treatments she offers, and her charges. I found her leaflet in the waiting room of a local hospital, where she regularly provides therapeutic massage to the patients.

> There are many people who offer a service like Lorraine – or a completely different service, like plumbing or decorating. These people rarely advertise in the local press because it may be too expensive, and, anyway, they rely on recommendations to find new clients. However, they all need to advertise their services using a leaflet or some other flyer and may need to have a business card to give to clients. You may find leaflets like Lorraine's in your local library, or in the waiting room of a doctor's surgery. Supermarkets may also display business cards of local traders.

The Met Office

Like many other government departments, the Met Office uses ICT in a big way! The computers used to process weather data are huge, and their use of telecommunications spans the world. They have a website on which you can find out how they work: http://www.meto.gov.uk

It is possible to arrange a visit to the Bracknell headquarters, but since this is so popular it may not be feasible within the time span of your course. However, a visit to the website will give you lots of information. You can also ask to be sent a copy of the annual report – one copy for the whole class should be enough!

> The websites of government departments are a very useful source of information. Try searching for keywords such as HSE, CENSUS and DfEE and see what information you can uncover. All limited companies are required to register with Companies House – if you look at the Companies House website, you can find out about companies that you might want to approach for your project, or for a job.

NCI

NCI provides maintenance and support services to its clients. It is a relatively new company, with a few carefully chosen employees. Its first offices were very small, but before long it took larger offices close to a mainline station with easy access to London.

Part of its work involves customising computer systems, especially networked systems for its clients. A newcomer to NCI needs lots of experience in the operating systems that its customers may choose, e.g. Windows, and an ability to learn about applications. All NCI staff are expected to be keen to learn and to attend courses so that they remain up to date with current software products. Self-motivation is very important.

It is also important that staff can mix well with clients. Some of the time is spent on client premises, trying to fix systems that have crashed or maybe replacing a defective component. If a system has crashed, the NCI technician may be asked to reinstall all the software for the client and check that the applications work to the customer's satisfaction.

Because all the staff are IT experts, there is no secretarial backup – everyone writes their own letters, and lots of work is done either by phone or using e-mail. Robert Cockerill has worked for NCI for quite a while and has recently revised the NCI logo, bringing it up to date to reflect the products and services that NCI provides.

If you are very keen on using ICT, a small and growing company like NCI may appeal to you as an employer. If so, you should make sure you learn about as many software products as you can. Read about ICT, and go on courses if at all possible. Even playing games can be to your advantage. If you enjoy playing computer games, presumably you know what makes a good game. If you can write these games, you could land yourself a prosperous career in the computer industry – as a programmer.

OCC Online Cruising Club

The OCC Online Cruising Club case study is loosely based on a sailing club of which I am a member. For confidentiality reasons, none of the data given in the examples is real. This case study was devised because it is similar to any sports club:

- **Members' details need to be kept so that newsletters can be sent to them with details of club fixtures and social events**

- **Subscriptions will be paid and recorded by a treasurer**

- **Meetings will be held and minutes taken**

- **The club will be run by a committee – usually volunteers. The committee changes each year, although some members may remain on the committee for a few years**

It is quite likely that such a club would provide opportunities for projects. Most committee members are busy with daytime jobs, and work done for the club is fitted into spare time in the evenings and at weekends. Any suggestions that will reduce their workload would be warmly welcomed.

Penhaven Country House Hotel

The level of detail given here is an indication of how much information you should try to get from users that you hope to help in your project.

Penhaven Country House Hotel was opened by Maxine and Alan Wade, who retired from the music trade before they reached the age of 40. Their lounge bar is decorated with trophies of their musical past: gold and platinum discs from groups such as the Thompson Twins, Men at Work and Musical Youth. (Your parents may remember these groups!)

At Penhaven Country House Hotel, there are twelve bedrooms – all *en suite*, with tea-making facilities, remote-control television and telephone. There are also six cottages in the grounds that can house a family of guests. The hotel is open seven days a week, 52 weeks of the year, apart from a break each January, when the hotel is redecorated and Alan and Maxine go in search of next year's wine list.

Maxine and Alan have created a peaceful atmosphere with excellent accommodation, food and wines, and want their guests to relax and enjoy themselves during their stay at Penhaven. In the grounds, there is a nature trail – useful for walking off the excellent meals. There are badgers in the grounds, and these are encouraged and protected by Alan and Maxine. A parking space is left clear in an area where the badgers are likely to appear, and their nightly visit can be watched from the lounge. Badgers are included in the graphics of several pieces of stationery: the breakfast menu and special weekend menus.

Maxine is responsible for the administration side of things. Booking enquiries are mostly received by telephone. Maxine notes the name and address and any special requirements. On the same day, she sends a letter – on headed notepaper – thanking the caller for the enquiry and enclosing a copy of the Penhaven brochure, the tariff, a booking form and copies of any 'special' weekends in the near future.

The letter heading includes the country house motif; the brochure is in full colour and includes both the country house motif and one of the badgers, as well as a map to show how to find the hotel and several photographs of the restaurant, bar and grounds. All these documents go in an envelope, which bears the Penhaven Country House logo, and are posted first class. When the caller receives the mail the next day, this envelope shows that Maxine has dealt with the enquiry immediately, as promised. This is the first indication of the level of service to be expected from Penhaven.

Confirmations of bookings may be by telephone, on a booking form in the post, or by fax. Recently, Maxine and Alan have arranged a web page at http://www.penhaven.co.uk on the Internet, so they may also soon be receiving bookings by e-mail. The details are recorded in the bookings diary, and a letter confirming the booking (and the deposit taken) is sent in the mail.

Each day, Maxine prepares the 'welcome pack' for the following day's arrivals:

✪ **A personally addressed brochure of guest information, such as meal times**

✪ **A card, which is handed to the guest with the room key and shows the name of the guest, the room number, the cost of the room and the leaving date**

When guests arrive, they complete a registration form. This includes extra details such as car registration number, whether newspapers are required and how the guest intends to pay for the stay. This information is used to update the customer record file and is used for future mailshots.

Great care is taken to produce promotional material that reinforces the impression that guests are given the 'red carpet' treatment and will enjoy their stay at Penhaven:

✪ **The headed stationery has the country house motif**

- ✪ The compliments slip has the badger motif, including a red carpet

- ✪ When guests arrive in their room, more small touches are evident: the notepad beside the phone; the complimentary toiletries, all bearing the Penhaven logo; and the freshly made biscuits

- ✪ At reception, postcards with a colour photograph of the gardens at Penhaven are on sale

- ✪ At breakfast, special menus are on display, depending on the type of breakfast available: full English or continental

- ✪ Menus for lunch and evening meals are displayed in the lounge/bar area and orders taken before guests go through to the restaurant

- ✪ At the dinner table, complimentary matchboxes bear the country house motif

- ✪ When orders are taken, these are written on pre-printed pads, which have the country house logo

- ✪ In the restaurant and bar area, drinks mats bear the Penhaven logo

Alan is responsible for the food and wine. Penhaven offers an excellent menu and has an extensive list of fine wines to match the food. Menus are planned the evening before – a lot depends on what local butchers and fishmongers have available – and individual menus are printed during each morning.

Penhaven advertises in national newspapers. The hotel is in an excellent position for anyone wanting to explore Devon, so guests could come from anywhere in the UK. Another way of attracting guests is to offer special weekends at special prices, and these are held several times a year: Christmas, St George's Day, May Day Bank Holiday, Midsummer's Day, and so on.

The menus for these special weekends have to be decided months in advance to allow Maxine time to send out a mailshot of 400 menus to past guests. For this, Maxine keeps records of all past guests: their name, address and telephone number. With the advertising and the mailshots, enough enquiries should result in a 'full house' for each special weekend.

Penhaven's home-made marmalade is served at breakfast and is so popular that it is bottled and sold to guests. The label stresses that the marmalade is home-made and that it is produced at Penhaven.

At the end of dinner, coffee is served at the table or can be taken in the lounge – a comfortable room with a huge log fire. With the coffee, Penhaven's home-made fudge is served. It too is delicious, and many guests asked to buy some. It is now sold at reception.

When guests are due to leave, an invoice is prepared showing their room charges plus any extra charges such as telephone calls or drinks. The invoice has room for details of seven days' stay, although most guests stay for a few days only.

> Hotels – even those that appear to be small – require levels of administration that can be made very efficient by introducing IT. Wherever you live in the UK, there will be a hotel near you that you may be able to visit to find out how it uses IT. You do not need to stay in the hotel to find out how it takes bookings, confirms bookings and prepares advertising material and other information such as menus.

Sailing Breaks

I first met John Hore when I attended a course run at the local adult education centre. John is an RYA instructor and gives courses to those interested in learning about sailing. His course notes were excellent – produced using a word processor and including diagrams that John had drawn or scanned in. Because they are word-processed, John can easily amend them. So, each year his course notes improve – an enormous help to his students.

John's company is called Sailing Breaks. He has a yacht called *Half Nelson*, and he takes groups out for sailing days. Apart from courses arranged to provide RYA practical qualifications, Sailing

Breaks provides fun sailing for anyone keen to try it and the opportunity to take part in races. Full information about Sailing Breaks and a photo of John – looking rather windswept – can be seen on his website: http://www.sailingbreaks.co.uk

All teachers – in schools or adult education centres – are faced with preparing class notes to give to their students. Looking at how teachers produce this material can teach you a lot about the ICT they are using. You may also be able to suggest improvements for those teachers who are not as familiar with ICT as you are. If you help them, you will also be helping their students.

Presenting Information

- Write in styles that suit your readers

- Choose and use standard layouts to present information

- Improve the accuracy and readability of documents that you create

This unit also offers the opportunity to develop good working practices. Details about these, which apply to all units in this course, are on page 407 in the Good Working Practice Guide.

This chapter looks in detail at four topics:

- ✪ Standard documents and their purpose

- ✪ Styles of writing

- ✪ Accuracy and readability

- ✪ Presentation

Several case studies are used to introduce and illustrate the ideas of this chapter:

- ✪ Lorraine Mayle, therapist

- ✪ Chris Lane

- ✪ Bodylife

- ✪ Hawkes Design

- ✪ Penhaven Country House Hotel

- ✪ OCC Online Cruising Club

Background information about these organisations is given in the Case Studies section of this book, starting on page xvii. You will look at many sample documents supplied by these organisations. You will see the writing style used and the way information is presented to their clients. For your portfolio, you will need to create a similar collection of sample documents.

Standard documents and their purpose

Here are some examples of documents:

- ✪ A **formal letter** to a company in reply to a job advertisement

- ✪ A newspaper **advertisement** for a second-hand piano

- ✪ A **note** to the milkman ordering milk

- ✪ A **formal invitation** to a wedding

- ✪ A single-page **advertisement** for a new computer

- ✪ A **letter** to a local newspaper

- ✪ A **table of results** for a sports league

- ✪ The **results** of an opinion poll

Depending on what the document is saying and who you are writing to, you must choose between formal and informal style.

Exercise 1.1

Write down three other examples of documents.

Activity 1.1

Collect as many documents as you can from home or organisations. You may try to identify some local organisations, like the ones used in the case studies, that might be willing to show you examples of the documents used in their organisation. However, it may prove easier to collect any letters or leaflets received at your home. This will give you plenty of useful examples – without having to contact the organisation concerned.

Think about the **writing style**, **layout** and **presentation techniques** used in some of these documents. This will help you to recognise how they can be used to meet different needs.

Here are some examples of needs:

✪ Attracting attention and creating interest, e.g. by using special fonts, pictures or speech bubbles

✪ Setting out facts clearly, e.g. by using bulleted lists or tables

✪ Reminding people about something, e.g. by using bold, underlines or italics

A formal invitation to a wedding needs to attract the reader's attention and set out the facts clearly (that is, the date of the wedding, the venue and what you should wear). Figure 1.1 shows a template of an invitation available in Microsoft Publisher.

Table 1.1 shows the needs met by some documents.

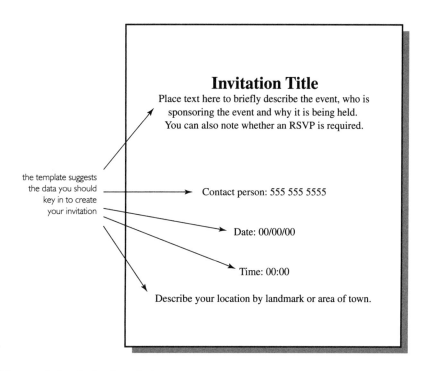

Figure 1.1 *Invitation design*

	Needs		
Documents	**Attracting attention**	**Setting out facts clearly**	**Reminding colleagues**
A formal letter			
A note			
A formal invitation			
An advert	✔	✔	
A table of results			

Table 1.1 *The needs met by documents*

Hawkes Design

Peter produces 'advertisements' that promote his services. See Figure 1.2. Peter's advertisements are intended to attract attention and create interest.

The complete publishing service from manuscript to printed book

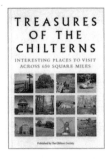

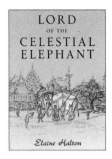

Hawkes Design, Ground Floor, The Old British School House, East Street, Chesham, Buckinghamshire HP5 1DG
Telephone: 01494 793000 Fax: 01494 776331 E-mail: Hawkestalk@aol.com

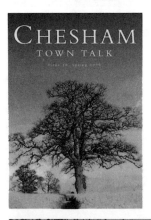

Telephone: 01494 793000

Hawkes Design, Ground Floor, The Old British School House,
East Street, Chesham, Buckinghamshire HP5 1DG
Fax: 01494 776331 E-mail: Hawkestalk@aol.com

Figure 1.2 *Two of Peter Hawkes' advertisements*
Courtesy of Peter Hawkes

Lorraine Mayle, therapist

Lorraine's leaflet explains clearly what services she offers. See Figure 1.3.

Exercise 1.2

For at least three of the example documents that you have collected, decide which need they meet.

Activity 1.2

Copy and complete Table 1.1, adding more rows for the extra documents you have thought of. Then tick boxes for each document listed in the table by deciding which needs are the most important.

Are any other needs met by these documents?

> To include a good variety of documents, you might concentrate on the needs, and think of documents that meet these needs – rather than the other way around.

Organisations design their own documents to suit their own needs, but some documents are used by most organisations. These are called **standard documents**:

Agendas and minutes

Business cards and letters

Fax cover-sheets

Memos and e-mails

Newsletters

Publicity flyers

Lorraine Mayle

I am a fully qualified and insured
Reflexologist, Massage Therapist and
Reiki practitioner.
Since completing my training at
Guildford College, I have expanded
and developed my knowledge by
attending various courses/workshops.
These include the Bristol Cancer Help
Centre.

I am a caring and sympathetic
therapist, working to a strict code of
ethics. I am a member of the
Federation of Holistic Therapists.
I respect information given by a client
and undertake to maintain
confidentiality and discretion.

Reflexology

1st.appointment and detailed consultation:
1 hour 30 mins......................£25
Follow-up appointments:
45 mins. to 1 hour....................£20

Therapeutic Massage

Full body: 1 hour.....................£20
Back and shoulders..................£15

Reiki

Approximately 1 hour.............£20

_____

* Reduced rates for courses of treatment *

Reflexology

Reiki

Therapeutic Massage

Holistic treatments for health and wellbeing.

Lorraine Mayle
Dip A&P, I.I.H.H.T.,M.I.C.H.T.

Cranleigh based therapist

Reflexology

Reflexology was practised thousands
of years ago by the Chinese, Egyptians and
early Indians.
It is a gentle therapy, which uses the feet
to treat the whole body. This is based on
the principle that there are energy zones
that run throughout the body and reflex
areas in the feet that correspond to
every part and system of the body.
By applying pressure to these reflex
points, this encourages the clearing of
neural pathways, regulating energy flow
around the body, restoring balance and
health.

Reflexology:
- Reduces stress
- Improves circulation
- Cleanses the body of toxins and
  impurities
- Balances the whole system
- Revitalises energy
- Activates the healing powers of the
  body
- Preventative health care

Therapeutic Massage

Massage is an ancient art, used for the
care of the body and relaxation of the
mind. Records show that massage was
practised in China as early as 3,000 BC.

Massage:
- Improves skin tone
- Relieves muscular tension
- Toning effect on muscles and
  tissues
- Mobilises the joints
- Increases circulation
- Increases elimination of waste
  products
- Calms the nervous system by
  reducing the effects of stress
- Relaxes mind and body

Reiki

Reiki (Ray-Key) is a Japanese system of
natural healing. The word 'Reiki' means
'Universal Life Energy'
It is believed to have originated
thousands of years ago, in Tibet. Reiki
was re-discovered a century ago, after
years of research and meditation, by a
Japanese Buddhist Monk, Dr Mikao Usui.

The treatment involves the gentle laying
on of hands, to different areas of the
clothed body. Reiki energy will naturally
flow to the areas most in need. The
Reiki 'giver' is used as a channel to
conduct the Universal (surrounding) Life
Energy. Although Reiki is spiritual in
nature, it does not conflict with any
religion, belief system or philosophy.

Reiki is a natural and safe form of
healing, which restores balance and
harmony to all levels - physical, mental,
emotional and spiritual.

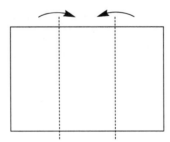

Figure 1.3 *Lorraine Mayle's leaflet: two landscape pages are printed back-to-back on A4 paper then folded into three*
Courtesy of Lorraine Mayle

Each standard document meets a particular need and has its own writing style and presentation technique.

Business cards and letters

Business cards are used by people to pass their contact details to other people they meet. Any logo and all contact details are usually contained on a card small enough to fit into a wallet. **Business cards** are usually printed on a heavy card to make them more durable, i.e. last longer.

Lorraine Mayle

Lorraine Mayle's business card includes her logo, her contact details and a description of the therapies she offers. Note her choice of peaceful background. See Figure 1.4.

Figure 1.4 *Lorraine Mayle's business card*
Courtesy of Lorraine Mayle

Chris Lane

The staff in the Beauty Room at Chris Lane do not have business cards. Instead, they can give clients an appointment card, which contains contact details and confirms the time of their next appointment. See Figure 1.5.

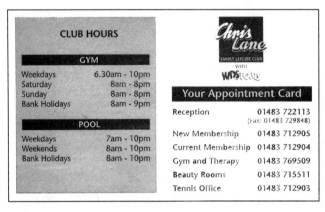

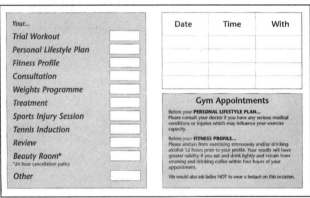

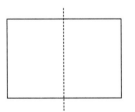

Figure 1.5 *Chris Lane appointment card: two pages printed back-to-back then folded*
Courtesy of Chris Lane Family Leisure Club

Activity 1.3

Collect as many appointment cards, business cards and similar documents as you can. Compare the styles used. What information appears on all these documents? Design your own card to give to friends.

All organisations write business letters to clients, suppliers and other external organisations such as the bank, their auditors or the Inland Revenue. The business letter is an important document, not only because of the information it contains but also because of the impression it gives of the organisation.

Chris Lane

Figure 1.6 shows an example of a business letter written by the Nursery Department at Chris Lane. Notice that Chris Lane's logo includes his signature. This conveys the very personal attention that Chris pays to all members of his club.

At the top of a business letter, the organisation's logo and contact details are shown. This will include the name, address, telephone number and any other important information.

Chris Lane's signature is part of the logo

personal information has been blurred to respect confidentiality

a clip art is used to make the letter less formal

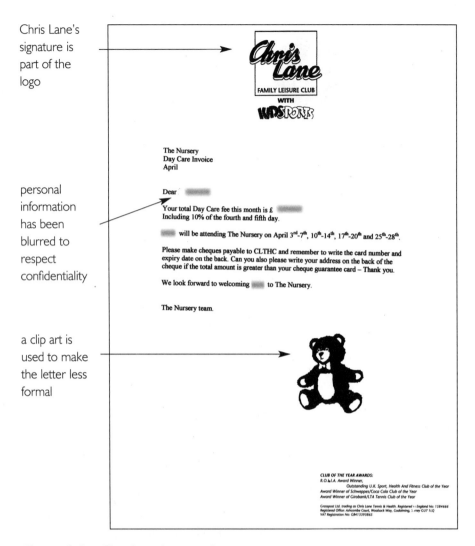

The Nursery
Day Care Invoice
April

Dear ▓▓▓▓▓

Your total Day Care fee this month is £ ▓▓▓▓▓
Including 10% of the fourth and fifth day.

▓▓▓▓ will be attending The Nursery on April 3rd-7th, 10th-14th, 17th-20th and 25th-28th.

Please make cheques payable to CLTHC and remember to write the card number and expiry date on the back. Can you also please write your address on the back of the cheque if the total amount is greater than your cheque guarantee card – Thank you.

We look forward to welcoming ▓▓▓▓ to The Nursery.

The Nursery team.

CLUB OF THE YEAR AWARDS:
R.O.s.I.A. Award Winner,
Outstanding U.K. Sport, Health And Fitness Club of the Year
Award Winner of Schweppes/Coca Cola Club of the Year
Award Winner of Girobank/LTA Tennis Club of the Year

Grasspost Ltd. trading as Chris Lane Tennis & Health. Registered n England No: 1584666
Registered Office: Ashcombe Court, Woolsack Way, Godalming, 5 mey GU7 1LQ
VAT Registration No: GB413393865

Figure 1.6   *Chris Lane business letter*
Courtesy of Chris Lane Family Leisure Club

OCC Online Cruising Club

Figure 1.7 shows the logo of the OCC as a letter head. Because the committee is elected each year the names of the people can change, so these are not pre-printed.

OCC logo

no preprinted
contact
information
because this
can change
every year

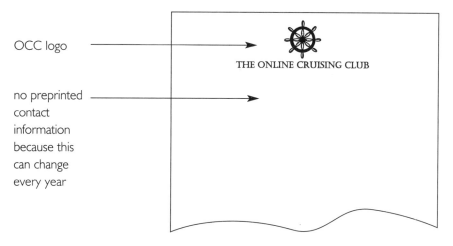

THE ONLINE CRUISING CLUB

Figure 1.7 *OCC letterhead*

What is written in a business letter is obviously important. It should meet any legal requirements and convey its message clearly and briefly.

Activity 1.4

Compose one letter to send to organisations. In the letter, ask whether they have any work experience opportunities for GNVQ ICT students. Ask if you might meet one of their staff to discuss part-time or holiday vacancies. Include your own contact details, so they can write back to you. Keep a copy of the letter in your portfolio. Send the letter to ten different organisations – with luck, you will get a positive response from at least one of them.

Try to choose organisations that none of the other students on your course has chosen. Also, if you have personal contacts within local organisations, write your letter to them.

Most business letters are produced on A4-size paper, used with portrait **orientation**.

Chris Lane's bar menu uses both portrait and landscape orientation. See Figure 1.8.

Most office IT systems have printers that accept A4 or smaller-size paper. For larger documents (e.g. plans) special plotters are needed.

Chris Lane logo →

'MENU' in landscape orientation →

'side orders' text rotated to lie on its side →

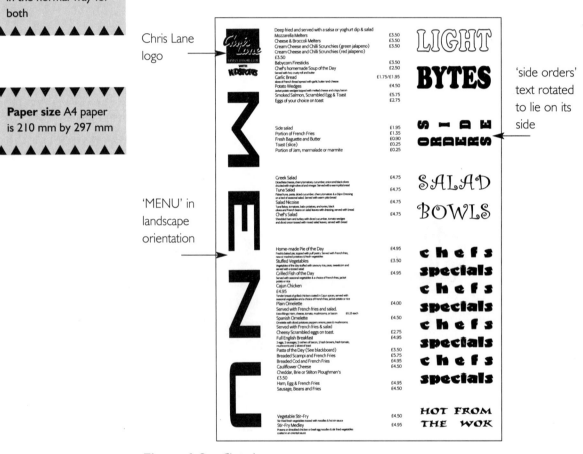

Figure 1.8   *Chris Lane menu*
Courtesy of Chris Lane Family Leisure Club

Exercise 1.3

Find out about other sizes of paper. Figure 1.9 shows sizes A1 to A7.

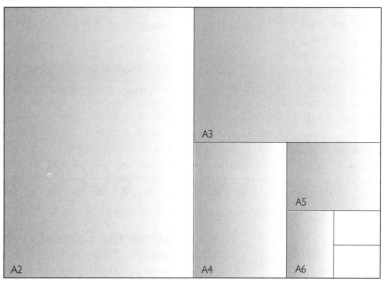

A1

A2

A3

A4

A5

A6

Figure 1.9 *Paper sizes*

You have been asked to design a logo for Gary Granger, who is setting up in business to provide a gardening service for people living near him.

Gary has not yet decided on a name for his service but has a couple of ideas: Gary's Gardening, GG Gardening.

Gary will need his logo to appear on business letters, quotations and invoices, business cards and publicity flyers.

★ Decide on a name and design the logo
★ Present the logo as it would appear on a business card
★ Choose a size of card that would match a credit card and draw your design actual size

Gary's address: Rose Cottage, Godstone, Essex CM4 1PE. Telephone: 01354 992211.
Keep the business card for your portfolio.

If you are using Microsoft software, you could use WordArt to design the name.

The layout of the information on a business letter, the **typeface** used and the **point** size all contribute to its overall impression. There are two 'families' of typeface: those with **serifs** and those without (known as **sans serif**). Sans serif looks 'cleaner' and is often used for headlines. Serif fonts tend to be used for normal reading text.

Penhaven Country House Hotel

Maxine uses an italic **serif font** on her menus.

Hawkes Design

Peter chose a **sans serif font** for text in a leaflet promoting the Elgiva in Chesham (Figure 1.11).

Figure 1.10 *Sample menu from Penhaven Country House Hotel*
Courtesy of Penhaven Country House Hotel

The following labels appear on the figure:

serif typeface → (pointing to "FIND US")

sans serif typeface → (pointing to the Mailing list / Elgiva volunteers text column)

Mailing list

Join our free mailing list and receive all our seasonal brochures and keep up to date with what's happening at the Elgiva.

Elgiva volunteers

The Elgiva has an ever growing band of volunteers who support in a variety of ways – reception, theatre ushers and backstage! If you fancy spending a couple of hours helping us – and having fun at the same time – please give us a ring on 01494 582900, or come in for a chat. A continuing 'thank you' to all those who have helped us so far, in whatever capacity.

Private hire

All areas of the Elgiva are available for private hire. For details of our excellent facilities for weddings, private parties, anniversaries, conferences and business meetings please call 01494 582900 for a very competitive quotation.

Accessibility

Level access to the front of and throughout the building. Disabled toilet facility. Four wheelchair spaces in the auditorium. Please inform the Box Office when booking if any of your party is a wheelchair user. Infra red induction loop system in the theatre. Please ask at the box office for a headset. If you have difficulty with stairs ask for rows A, B, C, D, E or F – and please book early!

HOW TO FIND US

The Elgiva is situated in Chesham Town Centre, off St Mary's Way. 5 minutes walk from the station via the High Street.

The Elgiva

The Elgiva Manager is David Roden

The Elgiva is owned, managed and funded by Chesham Town Council

P A HAWKES
DESIGN & PUBLISHING
MEDICAL · EDUCATIONAL · ENVIRONMENTAL · LOCAL

Designed by Hawkes Design 01494 793000

The information in this brochure is published in good faith and was correct at the time of going to press. The management reserve the right to change the advertised programme without notice.

Box Office telephone: 01494 582900

Figure 1.11   *Advertisement for Elgiva designed by Peter Hawkes*
Courtesy of Peter Hawkes

Activity 1.6

Collect together any replies received from the organisations contacted in Activity 1.4 and other material you have collected.

For now, try to ignore the message given in the letters. Instead, concentrate on your impressions of the organisation, based only on the overall look of the letter.   *continued*

continued

★ Make notes on the logos. Do any impress you particularly? What is it that impresses you?

★ Compare the amount of information shown in the letter headings. Is it clear how you could contact the person who wrote to you?

★ Look at the layout of the letters. What do you notice?

★ Look at the different fonts and styles used. What do you notice?

Memos, e-mails and faxes

A memo is used in a number of situations:

✪ When you want to put some information into writing, e.g. to confirm a meeting date and time, evidence of action taken, or a record of a conversation

✪ When the person you need to tell something to is not immediately available – you might send a memo, which they will then read the next time they are in the office

✪ When you need to tell lots of people the same information – a single memo can be addressed to many different people

Memos are used for **informal** communications. More formal information would be put in a letter and addressed personally to the employee, e.g. a letter advising an employee of a pay increase, or a warning letter about his or her poor punctuality record.

Organisations usually have a standard layout for memos. This includes the heading section (to say who it is going to, who it is from, and the date) and space for the message to be handwritten or typed. Memos are often printed on **A5 paper**.

Usually, a memo is printed in landscape orientation – the longer side at the top.

Chris Lane

Memos are used a lot at the Chris Lane Club. Most staff work on shift systems, so they cannot rely on seeing each other to pass on information. Figure 1.12 shows an example of a memo sent by Martin when he was busy organising one of the many social events: a dinner dance. The memo was produced using a Word wizard.

M E M O R A N D U M

DATE:	April 15, 2000
TO:	Reception / Cindy
FROM:	Martin
RE:	Deliveries on Thursday/Friday
CC:	Ted

There will be a lot of deliveries for the Dinner Dance next Friday, arriving either Thursday or Friday.

- Long tables from Spencers - to go in the corridor behind the gym
- Balloons from PartyTime - to go in the main bar area
- Table decorations from Daisy Chain - to go in Ted's office

If I am not around when the deliveries are made, please make sure everything is put in the right place.

Thanks

Figure 1.12 *Memo example*

E-mail offers an alternative to sending memos, telephoning or writing to someone. So long as the other person also has **e-mail** facilities, you can send them an e-mail note. In some organisations, staff use an internal e-mail system rather than memos. Many organisations are linked via the Internet, and now their staff have

Activity 1.7

Design a memo layout for Gary Granger, the gardener. Use A5-size paper with landscape orientation.

Produce a sample memo, using your design. The memo is from Gary's assistant, Jill, to Gary. The memo is dated 5 February 2000 and is to confirm that a new client, Mr Parsons, has a big lawn that needs regular mowing. Mr Parsons requires help for 2 hours per week at £7 per hour, starting on 1 March 2000.

Keep a copy of the memo in your portfolio.

> Look at the memo wizard layouts available to you with your word-processing software for some ideas. Don't copy the wizard layout exactly, though, otherwise your design will not be original!

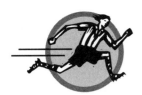

their own addresses. This means that anyone with an e-mail facility can send messages to the organisation or to individuals in the organisation.

OCC Online Cruising Club

Many of the members of OCC are on e-mail. This makes it easy to contact each other, e.g. to confirm sailing plans. It takes only seconds to e-mail members, but it would take hours to telephone them all.

E-mail addresses are made up of two main parts separated by the @ symbol:

1   Before the @ symbol comes the name of the person or company

2   After the @ symbol comes the address of the company or the service provider

Within both parts, a period (dot) is used to separate information.

> The author's e-mail address is firstclass@btinternet.com. The author works for a company called First Class and the e-mail facility is provided by BT Internet.

Exercise 1.4

Some e-mail addresses end in **.co.uk**. What does this mean?

All staff at Pearson Education, the publisher of this book, have e-mail addresses formed from their name separated by a dot, and followed by @pearsoned-ema.com. So, to write to a Mrs Janet Jones at Pearson Education, the e-mail address would be janet.jones@pearsoned-ema.com

Exercise 1.5

Find out the standard e-mail address for someone who presents a show on TV or your local radio. Look in newspapers and find out how you might e-mail your comments on an article to the editor, or to the person who wrote the article.

Penhaven Country House Hotel

Maxine and Alan Wade decided to advertise their hotel facilities on the Internet. Part of the Internet package included an e-mail facility, so they can now be contacted by, and make contact with, their guests using e-mail as well as by letter or telephone.

Exercise 1.6

Your school or college probably has e-mail facilities. If so, find out what the e-mail address is. Does the e-mail address appear on any stationery?

Activity 1.8

For some local organisations, find out whether they have an e-mail facility.

★ Do they have only internal e-mail facilities, or do they also have a link via the Internet?

★ Is the e-mail address included on any stationery?

You might decide to contact the organisations through their websites. These often include an e-mail address.

E-mails can replace non-urgent telephone calls in a number of situations:

○ The person you are trying to contact is always on the phone – you just get the engaged signal

○ The person you are trying to contact is not available – on holiday, off sick today, in a meeting, out to lunch, not in yet, or gone home already

The person you are trying to contact might also prefer to receive an e-mail rather than a telephone call:

○ If a lot of their day is spent in meetings (or teaching in a classroom), they would not want to be disturbed by telephone calls

○ If they have an urgent deadline to meet, they may need to concentrate on a particular task for the next hour or so – or they may be watching EastEnders

E-mails are particularly useful when there are time differences between the people who need to communicate:

○ Some office switchboards operate strict opening hours: say, 9 am to 5.30 pm. If you work outside these times, you may not be able to contact people working at these offices

✪ Suppose you want to communicate with friends in America or Australia. The time difference between countries means that you may want to speak to someone when they are actually asleep. It is easier to send an e-mail during your normal working day; they can then reply during their own working day

Since more people now work on a freelance basis, sometimes from home, the times when they might want to send e-mails but not accept telephone calls is increasing. The e-mail facility allows people who work from home to switch their answering machine on when they do not want to be disturbed but still send and receive messages via e-mail.

E-mails are also very useful for sales representatives and other people who are always travelling. As they move from hotel to hotel carrying their laptops with them, they can easily maintain contact with their head office and clients through e-mail.

Also, e-mails can be used to send documents as attached files. This method of sending information is not as secure as some other methods (e.g. by registered post or by file transfer) but is fine for non-sensitive information.

Not everyone has e-mail, and sometimes the information you want to send is not on the computer, so it cannot be sent as an attached file.

▼▼▼▼▼▼▼▼▼
Fax is short for facsimile
▲▲▲▲▲▲▲▲▲

A **fax** can be very useful for sending a handwritten note or diagram to someone – when it would be difficult to explain something over the telephone. Hotels often send maps by fax to their clients.

Fax machines can be used to send documentary information via the telephone network to someone who also has a **fax machine** (or a fax facility on an IT system). To send a fax, both the sender and the receiver must have a fax facility. There are several ways of having a fax facility:

✪ You may have a fax machine attached to a telephone line and the document on paper

✪ You may have a fax facility on an IT system, linked via a modem to a telephone line, and the document as an electronic file

✪ You may have a fax facility on an IT system, linked via an **ISDN** telephone line, and the document as an electronic file

If the sender is working from a fax facility on an IT system, a connection to the telephone network has to be made before the fax can be sent. If the sender is using a fax machine, the document is simply fed into the fax machine (which is already connected to a telephone line), and the number is dialled direct.

Whether the receiver has a fax machine or a fax facility on an IT system, the sender may get the engaged signal and will have to dial again until a telephone connection can be made.

Exercise 1.7

What are the advantages of using a fax rather than a telephone call?
What are the advantages of using a fax rather than an e-mail?

The fax machine can be programmed to send some basic information along with the message being faxed, which then appears on each sheet of the fax received:

✪ Sender's name

✪ Sender's fax number

The fax received usually also has the page number on each page. If you do nothing extra, at least the person receiving the fax knows where it has come from. However, it is polite – and has become standard practice – to include a fax cover sheet as the first sheet of any fax.

The information in a fax may be confidential, so the sender may include a message warning the receiver of the fax. Then, if the fax arrives at the wrong person's fax machine they are asked not to read it but to inform the sender that it has gone astray.

An interesting development in the uses of faxes is the **fax-back** facility. If your clients are likely to have a fax facility (and most do nowadays), by sending a form they can fax back, you save the client the trouble of writing a letter or making a telephone call.

Publicity flyers

Publicity flyers are adverts printed on single sheets of paper. Publicity flyers are like mini-posters. They can be used to advertise a service or an event. You will find plenty of examples in your nearest tourist information office.

Penhaven Country House Hotel

Alan and Maxine Wade produce a lot of publicity material. Some is sent to prospective guests, some is put in hotel rooms and some appears on their products, e.g. home-made fudge and marmalade. See Figure 1.13.

marmalade is available for sale at reception and served at breakfast

home-made fudge is served with coffee after dinner, and can be bought from reception

HOMEMADE
Marmalade
PENHAVEN COUNTRY HOUSE

PENHAVEN COUNTRY HOUSE
FUDGE
HomeMade

PENHAVEN COUNTRY HOUSE

Penhaven hits the write note

notepads are placed beside the telephone in the guest bedrooms

Figure 1.13 *Publicity material produced by Penhaven Country House Hotel*
Courtesy of Penhaven Country House Hotel

OCC Online Cruising Club

OCC's publicity flyer includes a photograph of ***Overload***, the yacht that members sail on (Figure 1.14). Notice that the OCC logo also appears.

Exercise 1.8

Why do lots of publicity flyers appear on a single sheet of A5-size paper?

★ What other sizes of paper might be used?
★ Look out for flyers that have a different size or style
★ Look out for publicity flyers that involve folding a sheet of A4 paper into three

the club name presented in landscape orientation ←

photo of the deck of *Overload* →

Figure 1.14 *OCC brochure*
Photogragh courtesy of Louise Tongue

Activity 1.9

Design a publicity flyer for Gary Granger's gardening service.

★ Make the flyer A5 size, and decide whether you want to use portrait or landscape orientation
★ Decide what information you will need to include on the flyer
★ Decide what fonts to use

Keep a copy of the flyer for your portfolio.

Include some clip art or colour if you think it improves the appearance of the flyer.

Chris Lane

Chris Lane produces a postcard-sized flyer encouraging members to introduce a friend to the club (Figure 1.15).

front

back

Figure 1.15 *Postcard designed by Chris Lane*
Courtesy of Chris Lane Family Leisure Club

Newsletters and magazines

Newsletters may be produced by an organisation to keep staff, clients or suppliers informed about what is happening within the organisation.

OCC Online Cruising Club

The OCC produces six newsletters a year and an annual journal. The newsletters are mailed out to all members to keep them informed of news and forthcoming events. The journal is given to members at the AGM.

Magazines tend to be published to meet the needs of a particular market.

Chris Lane

Chris Lane produces a magazine called *In Touch* for members. This gives details of social events, news about changes at the club and information about members, e.g. how well the tennis team is doing, and who is Junior Member of the Month. The current *In Touch* is displayed at reception and other parts of the club for members to help themselves to a copy.

Often magazines are bought through subscription and mailed out. Sometimes you can buy them in shops. Most magazines are produced monthly, but some may be produced less frequently.

- ✪ Accountancy Magazine is directed at the accountancy profession

- ✪ *PC Magazine* is written for users of PCs

- ✪ The *BBC Good Food Magazine* is written for those keen on cooking. It gives information about TV programmes that feature chefs and includes the recipes that will be used on the programmes

Activity 1.10

Find samples of newsletters produced by groups local to you.

> Your Neighbourhood Watch group may produce a newsletter.

Find out the names of three specialist magazines. For your samples of newsletters and magazines, answer these questions:

- ★ How often are these newsletters/magazines produced?
- ★ Who produces them?
- ★ Are they free? If so, how are they funded, i.e. who pays the printing costs?
- ★ If they are not free, how much do they cost? Is there a subscription payment method?

> Advertisers pay to appear in newsletters and magazines. This can provide enough money to cover printing costs.

Bodylife

The *Bodylife* magazine is published at two-monthly intervals. It is directed at health clubs, leisure centres and professionals in the health and fitness industry, and it includes articles on sales, marketing and management. See Figure 1.16.

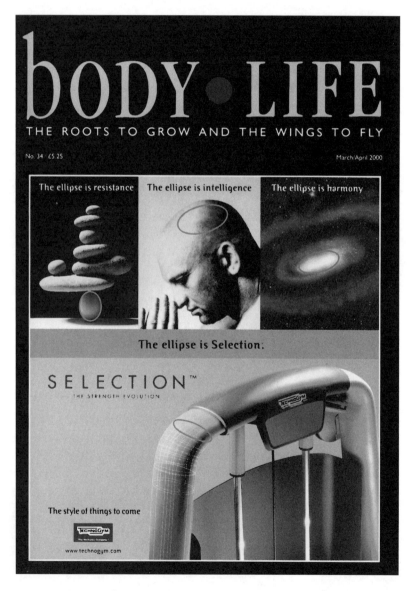

Figure 1.16   Bodylife *magazine is published every two months*
Courtesy of Bodylife

A **banner headline**
fills the width of the
page

The layout of a newsletter is usually in columns – to look like a newspaper. The front page may have a **banner headline** showing the title of the newsletter.

The rest of the newsletter is then divided into columns – the number of columns depends mainly on the width of the page. Columns need not be the same width throughout the newsletter, so each page can have a different layout.

OCC Online Cruising Club

Figure 1.17 shows the front cover and a sample page from the 1999 journal. Notice the style of the report page: banner headline and two-column format.

front cover with scanned photo of *Overload*

a page from the journal – a report of a cruise in 1999

ONLINE '99

The Journal of
The ONLINE Cruising Club

The OCC Eclipse Cruise to Alderney
7-14 August
Jenny Lawson

- MATT LANC
- NIGEL LAWRENCE
- JEAN KING
- LYNDA SAMPLE
- STEVE SAMPLE
- MARGARET WALLIS
- JENNY LAWSON
- BERENICE HOOKER
- LOUISE TONGUE

Figure 1.17 *Extracts from the OCC journal*

Chris Lane

The Chris Lane newsletter has one-, two- and three-column styles. Some pages have a mix of numbers of columns: two columns at the top and three at the bottom. Figure 1.18 shows three sample pages. Notice also the side headings – on the outer side of each page – this helps members to recognise what the news on that page is about.

The same type of heading may appear throughout the magazine, or for more variety, and to create interest, a number of different heading styles may be used.

Exercise 1.9

Look at a newspaper to see what heading styles are used.

★ How many different styles are used on a single page?

★ What effect do these different styles have on readers?

Figure 1.18 *Sample pages from Chris Lane newsletter*
Courtesy of Chris Lane Family Leisure Club

Newsletters may be produced on A4 paper (which may be easier for an organisation to produce in-house) or on 'broad sheets' like a newspaper. The general format for a newsletter is decided, together with which fonts and colours may be used to liven up the material.

The material for a newsletter may be produced by many people. In a newspaper, it will be a team of journalists. The job of the **newsletter editor** is to pull the articles together, following the general design, and lay out the pages in the most attractive way. Once this has been decided for one issue of the newsletter, the same layout may be used in subsequent issues.

Exercise 1.10

Look at one particular page in a newspaper or magazine, but for two issues.

★ Is there much difference between the layouts of these pages?

★ How is this helpful for the reader?

▼▼▼▼▼▼▼▼▼
A **sub-editor** controls what information is printed, and the accuracy of that information. A sub-editor must be very good at **proof-reading**, and this has to be done quickly under the pressure of deadlines
▲▲▲▲▲▲▲▲▲

When an article is received from a writer, a **sub-editor** reads it through and makes any changes that he or she thinks are necessary.

These are the types of check a sub-editor will make:

✪ Correct spelling, punctuation and grammar

✪ Correct spellings, particularly of people's names

✪ Correct facts – dates, places, who someone works for, their job title

✪ Correct tone – reflecting the 'image' of the newsletter or magazine

Sometimes an article has to be cut down to fit available space.

Articles may be produced on word processors, but the editor is more likely to use desktop publishing (DTP) to produce the newsletter. This is because DTP offers more features for page layout. However, for your portfolio work, the DTP features available on most word processors are fine.

In the publishing industry, packages like Quark Xpress, PageMaker and Adobe Acrobat are used instead.

Hawkes Design

Although Peter has Microsoft Word, which he uses for text editing and translating text from his PC, he uses Quark XPress on his Apple Mac computer for page layout and designing of material for his clients. He uses Adobe Illustrator for line graphs, diagrams and charts, and Adobe Photoshop for image manipulation and dealing with scanned images.

Pictures are an important part of any newsletter design. A newsletter with no pictures would be quite dull, and the job of the editor includes making each page attractive enough to catch the reader's attention. The general design of a newsletter will include how much space is given to text and how much to pictures.

Chris Lane

The Chris Lane newsletter includes photos of members. Colour is used for the written text and for many of the headings. See Figure 1.18.

Exercise 1.11

Does your school or college produce a newsletter? If so, who writes the articles?

Does any of your chosen organisations produce a newsletter or magazine? If so, who writes the articles?

Activity 1.11

Working in a group of two or three, agree a general design for a newsletter. This should include at least one graphic and at least one table.

★ Each person in the group first takes the role of journalist and writes at least one article for the newsletter, using a word processor

★ Give one copy (on disk) to everyone else in the group

★ Each person is now to take the role of sub-editor

★ Print out a draft of the articles (in double-line spacing)

★ Check these articles carefully (including your own)

★ Mark up any changes you think are necessary

> It will help everyone if you use the standard proof-reading symbols. See page 413 in the Good Working Practice Guide for details.

★ Each person now takes the role of editor

continued

continued

★ Using the disk copy of each article, make changes suggested by the sub-editor and incorporate all the articles into a single page

★ If you have too much material, make some cuts

★ If you do not have enough, write some more to fill the space

★ Choose headings for the articles and a heading style for each one

★ Choose artwork to include in your page and use colour if you wish

★ Print out your finished page and give copies to the others in your group

★ Compare each other's newsletters

★ Make notes on what was good about your newsletter and what you could do to improve it. Keep a copy of these notes and your newsletter in your portfolio

Agendas and minutes

In some situations, meetings take place and no record is taken. The discussion is 'off the record'. However, there are other situations where it is very important that notice is given that a meeting will take place (an **agenda**), that notes are taken during the meeting, and that a written record is produced (the **minutes**).

Exercise 1.12

Think of two situations where it is important that agendas and minutes are produced.

In many of the activities that you will do during this course, you will work with others as a team. It may be sensible to write agendas for meetings that you need to hold to discuss plans and to review progress. It would also be sensible for one member of the team – the scribe – to write the minutes of the meetings, so everyone has a record of what was agreed.

Agendas

An **agenda** is an internal document that lists details of a planned business meeting:

A **venue** is where something takes place: the meeting place

- ✪ **The title of the meeting** – explaining the purpose of the meeting

- ✪ **The time, date and venue of the meeting** – so those attending know when and where the meeting will be held

- ✪ **A list of topics to be discussed, in order** – a tick list or plan for the meeting to ensure that nothing is forgotten

The list of topics usually starts with some 'standard' items:

- ✪ **Apologies for absence** – from people invited to the meeting who could not attend

- ✪ **Minutes of the last meeting** – a chance for those attending to refresh their memories as to what happened in the last meeting, before moving on to the discussions of the current meeting

- ✪ **Matters arising** – an update on items discussed at the previous meeting which are not on the agenda for this meeting

The minutes of the last meeting should be agreed as being a fair record of the previous meeting, signed by the chairperson and filed by the secretary. Then, at a later date, if there is any dispute, there is a record of what was decided, and proof that this was a true record according to those attending the next meeting.

The main discussion topics of the meeting are then listed. Finally, there are some standard closing items:

✪ **Any other business** – an opportunity for anyone at the meeting to introduce another topic for discussion, although the secretary ought to be warned about this before the meeting, and if time does not allow discussion, this topic may be postponed till the next meeting

✪ **The date and time of the next meeting** – no meeting should close without deciding when and where the next meeting will take place. This allows those present to consult their diaries and agree a mutually convenient date

An agenda is sent to everyone who is invited to attend the meeting. The agenda is usually prepared by a secretary, and if someone cannot attend, apologies should be sent to the secretary before the date of the meeting.

Word-processing packages provide wizards for agendas. Figure 1.19 shows three formats offered in Word 6, plus (bottom right) the first page of a note taker's copy, which has spaces for the notes to be made about discussions that take place, decisions that are made and action items. From this note taker's version, the minutes can be produced very easily.

Exercise 1.13

Find out which wizards are available in your word-processing software.

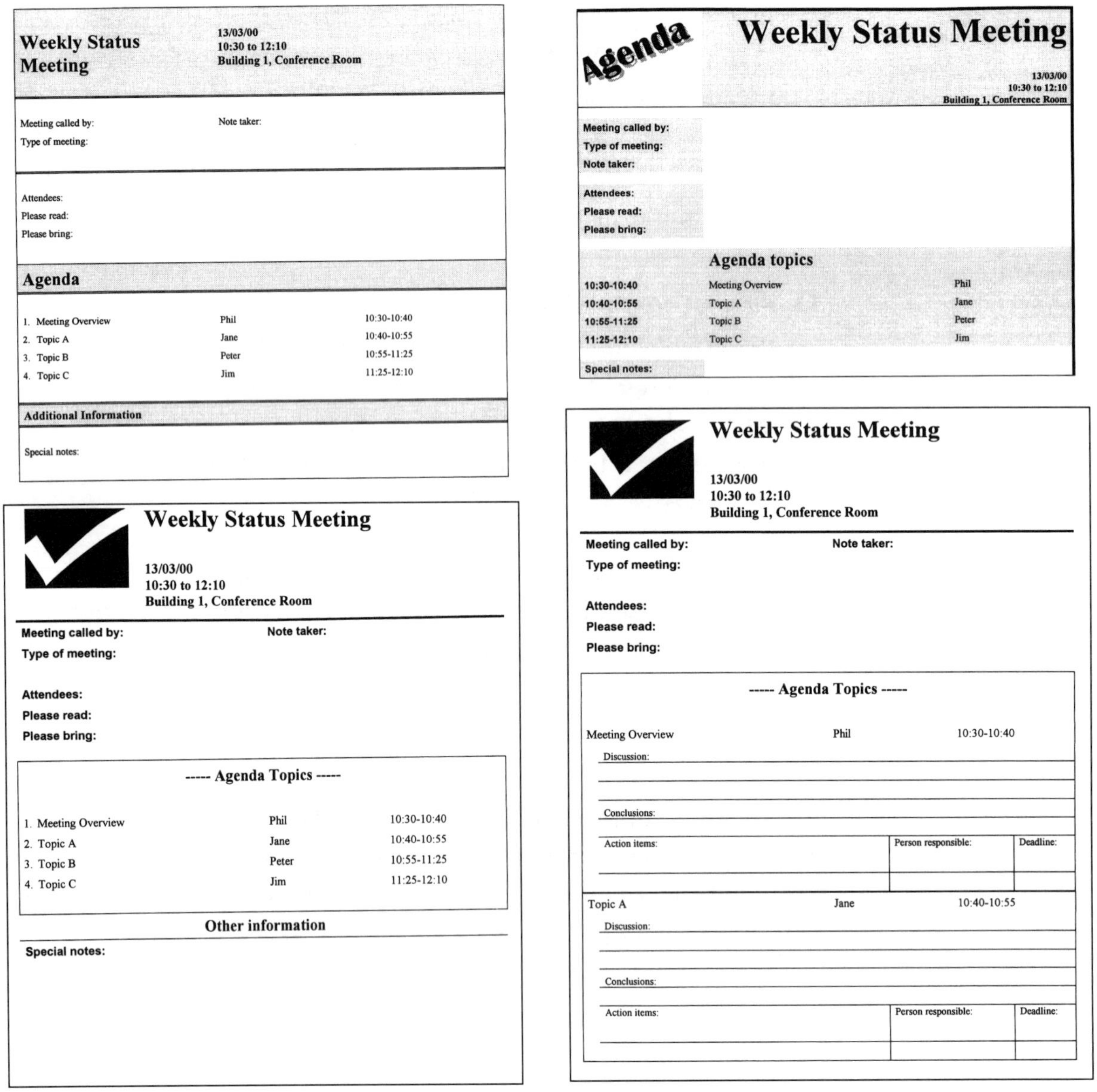

Weekly Status Meeting
13/03/00
10:30 to 12:10
Building 1, Conference Room

Meeting called by: Note taker:
Type of meeting:

Attendees:
Please read:
Please bring:

Agenda

1. Meeting Overview	Phil	10:30-10:40
2. Topic A	Jane	10:40-10:55
3. Topic B	Peter	10:55-11:25
4. Topic C	Jim	11:25-12:10

Additional Information

Special notes:

Agenda **Weekly Status Meeting**
13/03/00
10:30 to 12:10
Building 1, Conference Room

Meeting called by:
Type of meeting:
Note taker:

Attendees:
Please read:
Please bring:

Agenda topics

10:30-10:40	Meeting Overview	Phil
10:40-10:55	Topic A	Jane
10:55-11:25	Topic B	Peter
11:25-12:10	Topic C	Jim

Special notes:

Weekly Status Meeting
13/03/00
10:30 to 12:10
Building 1, Conference Room

Meeting called by: Note taker:
Type of meeting:

Attendees:
Please read:
Please bring:

----- Agenda Topics -----

1. Meeting Overview	Phil	10:30-10:40
2. Topic A	Jane	10:40-10:55
3. Topic B	Peter	10:55-11:25
4. Topic C	Jim	11:25-12:10

Other information

Special notes:

Weekly Status Meeting
13/03/00
10:30 to 12:10
Building 1, Conference Room

Meeting called by: Note taker:
Type of meeting:

Attendees:
Please read:
Please bring:

----- Agenda Topics -----

Meeting Overview Phil 10:30-10:40
Discussion:
Conclusions:
Action items: Person responsible: Deadline:

Topic A Jane 10:40-10:55
Discussion:
Conclusions:
Action items: Person responsible: Deadline:

Figure 1.19 *Agenda templates*

Minutes

So that those present can remember what was discussed at a meeting, what decisions were taken and what actions are planned, the secretary keeps a written record of the main points: the **minutes**. Minutes contain the same headings as the agenda, but with the details filled in. On the right-hand side, there is also an action column to show the initials of the person who has agreed to put that decision into action. Details include:

- ✪ A list of who was present at the meeting and those who sent their apologies

- ✪ For each topic, a summary of the discussion that took place – not a word-for-word record, but the main points made, decisions taken and who is going to act as decided

Minutes should be sent out as soon as possible after the meeting. Those who attended can then be reminded about what action (if any) they need to take, and those who could not attend the meeting can see what decisions were made and what actions are expected.

At the next meeting, those present decide whether what was written was accurate and can ask for amendments to be made to the minutes. These corrections are done by hand and initialled before the minutes are signed as being a 'fair record' of the meeting.

Activity 1.12

You need to prepare an agenda for a meeting, hold the meeting and then prepare the minutes for circulation to those who were invited to attend.

★ Working as a group, decide which topics should appear on the agenda

★ Individually prepare your agendas using word-processing facilities. (The agendas should have the same information, but you may present it differently)

★ Hold the meeting to discuss the points on the agenda

★ Take notes during the meeting

★ After the meeting, write up the minutes

★ Make sure you proof-read your minutes carefully

★ It is important that there are no errors in the minutes

★ Print out a draft of your version of the minutes

As a group again, compare your individual versions of the minutes. You should have a similar format, with headings to match the agenda.

★ Did you have the same content?

★ Did anyone miss anything important?

★ Were any mistakes made?

Make notes on your own version of the minutes to correct any mistakes you made, and to amend the content so that it truly reflects what happened at the meeting. Amend your minutes and print out a final copy. File both copies (your draft and your final copy) in your portfolio.

If you are a member of a group, e.g. a sports team committee that meets regularly to discuss topics of interest to you, you may choose to write up the minutes for the meeting you attend. You will then need to compare your minutes with those prepared by the secretary of your committee.

Styles of writing

Before you start to prepare a document, or the text for a presentation, you must know what it is that you want to communicate. As you start to write (or key in to the keyboard, more likely) you must decide how you will express your message. For this, there are two important things for you to remember:

✪ Your reader

✪ The occasion

Remembering your reader

The age and situation of your reader may be important:

✪ Your reader may be **someone like you**: the same age, doing the same course or in the same type of job

✪ Your reader may be **older than you**. The people you write to in your chosen organisations are likely to be quite a few years older than you. They will have been in work for several years and may have higher qualifications than you

✪ Your reader may be **quite young**, maybe as young as 6 or 8 years old. A child as young as this will be able to read but may not understand many long words

✪ Your reader may be **very old indeed**, e.g. a pensioner you are inviting to a Christmas party. Some very old people have difficulty in reading, and a long letter may be too much for an elderly person to cope with. So it is best to keep your message simple and short. Perhaps you could use a slightly larger point size too

Did You Know?

For complete strangers, it is polite to use formal language. With your friends and people you know quite well, you can be more informal

Your reader may be someone you know very well, know slightly or have never met before.

Compliments slips are often used for informal notes between people who know each other but work for different companies.

The relationship you have with your reader is also important.

✪ Your reader may be someone who works for you, or someone you work for

✪ Your reader may be one of your clients, or one of your suppliers

✪ Your reader may be a prospective client – or a prospective employer – that you want to impress

Your reader will remember you by the way you express yourself: in words, sentences and paragraphs.

✪ Unusual words might impress the reader of a job application, but they might annoy someone needing directions to your house

✪ Long sentences may be more difficult to follow, so try to make your sentences as short as possible

✪ Paragraphs are used to divide your message into separate 'thoughts'. Grouping sentences into paragraphs can help the reader to follow what you have to say

✪ Use correct punctuation and grammar. Failure to do this can mislead your reader

Hawkes Design

Peter Hawkes sends informal notes on a compliments slip. See Figure 1.20.

Figure 1.20 *Informal note from Peter Hawkes*
Courtesy of Peter Hawkes

Remembering the occasion

You remember the occasion by thinking about the style of your writing – not so much the font that you use (although that can be important) but how you put your message together.

✪ Formal occasions need a formal style

✪ Less formal occasions need an informal style

Exercise 1.14

Suppose you were to write two letters: an informal letter to a friend and a formal letter to a prospective employer.

★ Apart from the body of the letters, what else would be different?

★ How would you start the letters?

★ How would you end them?

One way of using the correct style is to use an appropriate standard document.

✪ For short informal notes within an organisation, send a memo or an internal e-mail

✪ For short informal notes to a contact outside your organisation, send an e-mail

✪ For formal messages, send a letter

Standard styles are also used in a number of other standard business documents, such as invoices, orders, delivery notes, agendas, minutes and itineraries.

Tools such as a grammar checker may offer a choice between *strict* (all rules), *business* and *casual*. You may also be able to design your own set of rules to be used by the grammar checker.

Activity 1.13

Look at the documents you have collected from your chosen organisations.

★ Could any of them be expressed better?

★ Choose one section of one document, key it into your word processor and try to reword it in a simpler way.

> Tools such as a **thesaurus** may help you to replace particular words with more appropriate ones. This can help to improve the readability of a document.

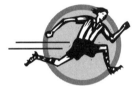

Exercise 1.15

Apart from the many standard documents you have seen already in this chapter, can you think of any other types of standard format or style?

★ Look at information about your school or college timetable. How is this presented?

★ Look at railway and bus timetables. How are these presented?

★ Look at some pages on teletext. Is a standard format or style in use?

★ Look at some pages on the Internet. Is a standard format or style in use?

Accuracy and readability

When starting to write something new, e.g. a letter, it is sometimes difficult to think of exactly what you want to say. However, if you use word-processing software, you can key in your first thoughts, and then you can review and improve them until it says exactly what you want to say. This is called **drafting** and redrafting!

Did You Know?

Using draft view mode saves a lot of memory and allows the processor to concentrate on the editing you are doing rather than having to update the screen all the time

Each new version is called a **draft**. Figure 1.21 shows three drafts of the same letter. The term 'draft' is also used to describe a version, on screen or printed, that does not include any formatting or graphics.

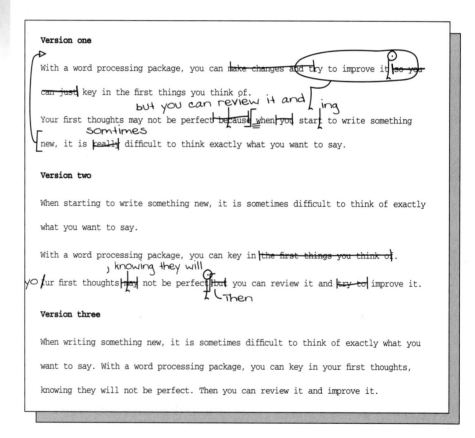

Figure 1.21 *Drafting and redrafting*

Activity
1.14

If you have access to the Word software package, see Tools/Options/View and select 'draft' to see what effect this has on screen.

Most documents have lots of text, some tables and some artwork. When you are drafting, it is the wording of the text that you are trying to finalise.

▼▼▼▼▼▼▼▼▼

Double-line spacing has one extra space line after each line of text

▲▲▲▲▲▲▲▲▲

The standard style for a draft is for the text to appear in **double-line spacing**. This is useful because you may need space to write in corrections (see the first and second drafts shown in Figure 1.21).

The artwork and tables can be replaced by 'flags' showing where they will appear in the final version of the document. It is not necessary to print out the tables and artwork with every draft, because it is only the words you are thinking about changing.

Drafts can provide evidence that you have used a spell-checker, so it may be useful to retain an early draft, annotated with the words that you fixed, while doing a spell check on your document. It is important to label drafts. You will then know which is the most recent, up-to-date version. Each version is checked by proof-reading the draft. There are two types of proof-reading:

✪ **Comparing the two drafts**: the most recent version against the previous one, to make sure all corrections have been made as planned

✪ **Reading through the most recent draft**: to make sure it still makes sense and to look for further improvements

Both methods should be used.

Spell-checkers

Spell-checkers are a form of **validation check**. They help you to correct your spelling and **punctuation**. Spell-checkers work by comparing each word against a list of words kept in a **dictionary**.

The spell-checker scans the text in your document, looking for spaces and punctuation marks. A space or a punctuation mark tells the spell-checker that a 'word' has just finished. The group of characters between two spaces or punctuation marks – the 'word' – is then matched against 'words' in the dictionary. If there is no match, it could mean one of two things:

✪ You miskeyed the word, and it needs to be edited

✪ The dictionary does not have that word in its list, but – if the word is correct – it could be added to the dictionary

Sometimes a spell-checker will suggest that a word is incorrect when you know it is correct. This is often the case with proper names, for example 'GNVQ' and 'Hamid'.

A spell-checker is an excellent tool, but as the lager adverts say: 'It's good, but not that good.' What will spell-checkers miss? If there is a match, it does not guarantee that you did not make a keying error. For example, if you press M instead of N (they are close on the keyboard), you could key in

✪ *worm* instead of *worn*

✪ *mane* instead of *name*

The spell-checker will not catch 'worm' and 'mane', because they are correctly spelled words. So, since spell-checkers are not foolproof, you must use some other checking method to be sure your finished work is perfect – proof-reading.

Exercise 1.16

Spell-checkers accept some names (e.g. Peter) but reject others. Check which of the names of people in your group are accepted by a spell check and which are rejected. Can you explain why this happens?

Using your thesaurus may help.

Proof-reading

A proof-read is a visual check of the content of your document.

✪ Print early drafts in double-line spacing to allow plenty of room for you to correct by hand

✪ In later drafts, include all tables and artwork to allow you to check the layout, including the positioning on the page of any figures and tables

▼ ▼ ▼ ▼ ▼ ▼ ▼ ▼ ▼

Proof-reading is used mainly to check the sense of your text. It can also be used to check that no tables have been split across two pages or that artwork does not overprint text

▲ ▲ ▲ ▲ ▲ ▲ ▲ ▲ ▲

There are two types of **proof-reading**:

✪ Comparing one draft against the next

✪ Reading through a draft

Both methods should be used.

Suppose you had a first draft and had written corrections all over it. Then you (or a friend) edited the text to correct it. Figure 1.22 shows an example of both documents. Your first job would be to proof-read the second draft against the first draft to make sure that all the planned corrections had been implemented.

You should check each correction, one at a time, and tick them off on the first draft as you go. You can then mark the second draft with any corrections that were missed and still need to be done.

```
First draft                          The tag is punched with holes – to record
                                     the item type and other information –
Kimball tags are small pieces of card punched with holes which can be attached to a garment,
        is
and│torn off when the item is sold. The part torn off is then put into a computer system

Some stores use tags with bar codes nowadays. This makes the process more automatic

More expensive items have a security tag which sets of an alarm if you try to leave the

shop without paying│ for the goods ⊙

Second draft

Kimball tags are small pieces of card which can be attached to a garment. The tag is

punched with holes – to record the item type and other information – and is torn off when

the item is sold.

The part torn off is then input into a computer system.

Some stores use tags with bar codes nowadays. This makes the process more automatic.

More expensive items have a security tag which sets of an alarm if you try to leave the

shop without paying for the goods.
```

Figure 1.22 *Drafts of a document: can you find the deliberate mistake?*

Then – most importantly – file the old version away. You may need to keep it for your portfolio. Next, you should read the second draft through at least once more.

✪ Does it still make sense?

✪ Can you improve it?

✪ Can you spot anything the spell-checker missed?

It is quite difficult to spot your own errors. Sometimes it is better to ask a friend to proof-read your work. In return, you can proof-read your friend's work.

You need a partner for this activity.

★ Each of you key in three paragraphs. Do not look at the screen while you touch the keys, and work as fast as you can. This way you are likely to make quite a few mistakes! Save your file and print out two copies of your document in double-line spacing.

★ Swap documents with your partner and spend five minutes or so proof-reading the work to find any errors.

★ Load your partner's document file, make the corrections and resave your partner's file.

★ Print out the second draft and return both drafts to your partner.

★ Check the editing work your partner has done to your own document and mark up any corrections he or she has missed.

★ Read through your own document once more to see if you can spot any more errors.

It may help you to see the errors more clearly if you mark corrections in red.

So that people can work together on documents, it is important to understand and use a standard convention for the proof-reading symbols for omissions and corrections. See the Good Working Practice Guide on page 413 for details.

Checking for accuracy

To make sure the end result is absolutely accurate, you will need to apply accuracy checks to your work.

There are two main types of accuracy check:

✪ **Validation check**: spell-checkers

✪ **Verification check**: proof-reading

Finally, how well you express yourself will depend on your communication skills. Spell-checkers cannot tell you when you use a word wrongly, so you may want to learn when and how to use grammar checkers. **Grammar checkers** rely on a number of rules:

✪ Your sentences must have a subject and a verb that agree

✪ You should write mostly in the active voice rather than the passive voice

✪ When you are writing academic reports, you should avoid writing 'I' (by using the passive voice)

If you break any of these rules, the grammar checker will warn you.

Exercise 1.17

Find out how the grammar checker works on your word processor.

Presentation

It is important to present information clearly. It may annoy or confuse your reader if you present information poorly. A common mistake is to vary the style of headings or layout. You should think of what you want to achieve with your document and what will appeal to your readers.

Having decided on **paper size**, you can decide the structure and layout of your document and what **margins** you will use. Letters have a different layout from memos. Newspapers use several columns. Textbooks like this may have a single column but use the margin for messages.

Figure 1.23 shows a page from this book. Notice that some information appears in the margin. You can then collect together relevant data and present this information in the most appropriate way:

✪ Using graphs and charts, and including pictures, drawings and clip art

✪ Scaling images to fit the available space

Exercise 1.18

★ Make sure you know how to produce graphs and charts
★ Make sure you know how to include clip art in a document

You should be able to design a good page layout:

✪ **Including margins** (top, bottom, left and right) – documents are usually filed, so they need a left margin wide enough for hole punching

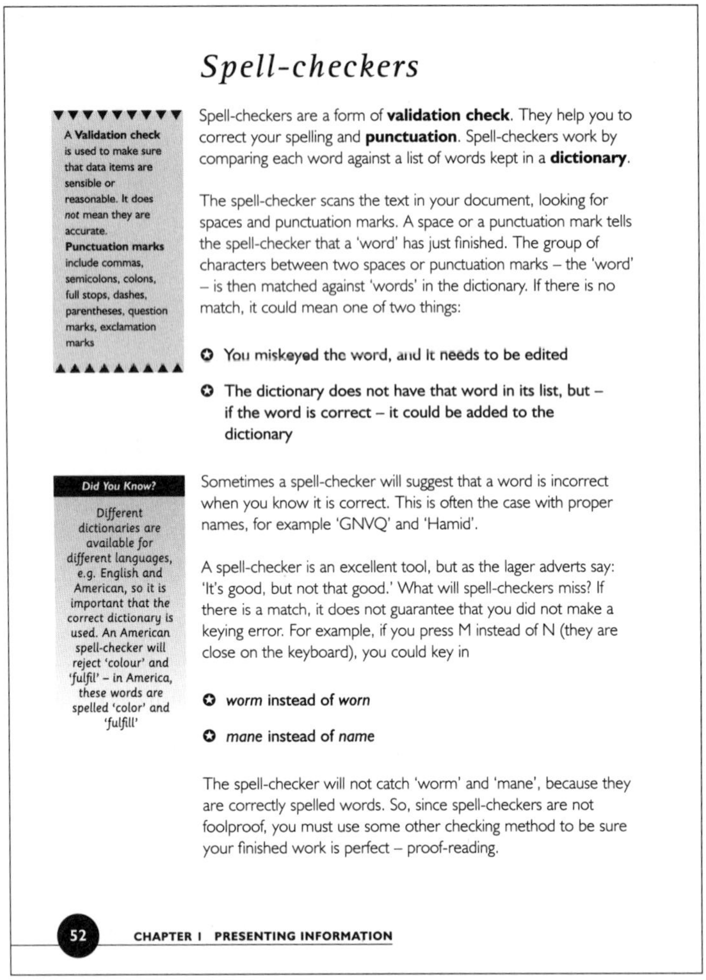
Spell-checkers

A **Validation check** is used to make sure that data items are sensible or reasonable. It does *not* mean they are accurate.
Punctuation marks include commas, semicolons, colons, full stops, dashes, parentheses, question marks, exclamation marks

Spell-checkers are a form of **validation check**. They help you to correct your spelling and **punctuation**. Spell-checkers work by comparing each word against a list of words kept in a **dictionary**.

The spell-checker scans the text in your document, looking for spaces and punctuation marks. A space or a punctuation mark tells the spell-checker that a 'word' has just finished. The group of characters between two spaces or punctuation marks – the 'word' – is then matched against 'words' in the dictionary. If there is no match, it could mean one of two things:

- You miskeyed the word, and it needs to be edited
- The dictionary does not have that word in its list, but – if the word is correct – it could be added to the dictionary

Did You Know?
Different dictionaries are available for different languages, e.g. English and American, so it is important that the correct dictionary is used. An American spell-checker will reject 'colour' and 'fulfil' – in America, these words are spelled 'color' and 'fulfill'

Sometimes a spell-checker will suggest that a word is incorrect when you know it is correct. This is often the case with proper names, for example 'GNVQ' and 'Hamid'.

A spell-checker is an excellent tool, but as the lager adverts say: 'It's good, but not that good.' What will spell-checkers miss? If there is a match, it does not guarantee that you did not make a keying error. For example, if you press M instead of N (they are close on the keyboard), you could key in

- *worm* instead of *worn*
- *mane* instead of *name*

The spell-checker will not catch 'worm' and 'mane', because they are correctly spelled words. So, since spell-checkers are not foolproof, you must use some other checking method to be sure your finished work is perfect – proof-reading.

52 CHAPTER 1 PRESENTING INFORMATION

Figure 1.23 *Sample page from this book*

- Deciding on **line spacing** (single, double, etc.)
- Planning **white space** to good effect. Too little white space may give a cramped impression. Too much white space may make a document much longer than it needs to be
- Setting **tabs** (left, right, decimal, etc.). The benefit of using tabs rather than hard spaces is that you can change tab positions very easily. Depending on the software you are using, you will set up a **ruler** with **tab positions** marked. If you move the tab positions on the ruler, all text controlled by that ruler will move to the new positions
- Using **tables** to present data in columns

White space iincludes the margins, space above and below headings, and around figures and tables

Tab positions are set and then, when the tab key is pressed, the cursor jumps to the next tab position along the ruler

Exercise 1.19

Make sure you know how to use all of these features. If you are not sure about any of them, ask your teacher for help, or use the on-line help facility to find some information.

If you are not sure how to use on-line help, see the Good Working Practice Guide on page 407.

Having produced the 'perfect' text, you need to think about **highlighting** important words or phrases. These will then catch the reader's eye. You can **enhance** your text, tables and graphics:

Words in **bold** stand out more and will be noticed

Italics can be used for headings, but it is better used to stress words

- Using **bold highlighting** for added emphasis. You should use bold only for headings or to highlight important words

- Using **italics** or **underlining** to stress important words or phrases. If a word is important for the sense of what you are saying – and if the reader might miss the importance otherwise – use italics. Examples: in the event of fire, do *not* use the lifts; the cost is £25 *plus* VAT

- Using **bullets** (•, ❑, ⇒, etc.) to make the text easier to follow

Left justification means that the left-hand edge of the text will be straight but the right-hand edge will be ragged

Right justification means that the right-hand edge of the text will be straight but the left-hand edge will be ragged

- Choosing which **justification** to use (left, right, full or centre). Right justification would look strange on normal text, e.g. in a letter, but it can be used when text and graphics are incorporated in the same document. This style may also be used for special effects. To achieve **full justification**, the software adds extra spaces between pairs of words so that the words that do fit into one line fill the line completely. The spaces you key in are called **hard** spaces; the spaces inserted by the software are called **soft** spaces. Full justification is used in newspaper

▼▼▼▼▼▼▼▼

Full justification is used for most business documents. It results in both edges of text being straight

Centred text appears in the centre of each line

▲▲▲▲▲▲▲▲

columns and textbooks. It is sometimes referred to as justification **on**; justification **off** means left-justified only. **Centred text** is often used on menus, programmes or front pages of reports

✪ Deciding which **fonts** to use (**typeface** and **point size**)

For simplicity, it is best to stick to only one or two highlighting techniques, as using too many makes a document look cluttered. Figure 1.24 shows two examples: one shows good highlighting; the other has too much.

You should know how and when to use these techniques in a document. You may need lots of practice, creating many documents, before you can use them correctly.

Using a word processing package

When starting to **write something new**, it is sometimes difficult to think of exactly what you want to say. With a **word processing package**, you can key in your first thoughts, knowing they will not be perfect. Then you can review it and improve it.

The word processing package also offers a **spelling checker**, a **thesaurus** and a **grammar checker**.

The spelling checker highlights **words not found in the dictionary**. The thesaurus suggests **alternative words to use**. The grammar checker highlights sections of text where **you might have made an error**, e.g. using a *singular* noun with a *plural* verb as in 'The *man are* working' or a *plural* noun with a *singular* verb: 'The *men is* working'.

Too much highlighting

Using a word processing package

When starting to write something *new*, it is sometimes difficult to think of exactly what you want to say. With a **word processing package**, you can key in your first thoughts, knowing they will not be perfect. Then you can review it and improve it.

The word processing package also offers a spelling checker, a thesaurus and a grammar checker.

The **spelling checker** highlights words *not* found in the dictionary. The **thesaurus** suggests alternative words to use. The **grammar checker** highlights sections of text where you might have made an error, e.g. using a *singular noun* with a plural verb as in 'The *man are* working' or a *plural noun* with a singular verb: 'The *men is* working'.

Good use of highlighting

Figure 1.24 *Use of highlighting*

Exercise 1.20

★ Make sure you know how to enhance your text

★ Check with your software what bullet point styles are available

★ Make sure that you know the difference between left, right and full justification

Activity 1.16

Produce a document, demonstrating your skills in layout and design. Make notes on your drawing to show what features you have used in presenting this information.

> You might decide to produce this document using desktop publishing (DTP) software.

Your portfolio should now contain many examples of your work in completing this unit. The next three activities complete your work for this unit. (Remember that advice on how to present your portfolio material is given on page 429 in the Portfolio Guide.)

Activity 1.17

Review your portfolio of documents and identify six original documents for different purposes that show your ability to produce documents in a range of writing styles and layouts.

> In selecting the best six documents, use this checklist to decide which to include.

★ Do the six documents present a range of styles and occasions with a variety of forms of information from different sources, making effective use of tables and graphics?

★ Have you written in a style and layout that suits the purpose of each document?

★ Have you chosen appropriate styles and formats for the information presented?

★ Is the purpose of each document clear?

★ Have you shown that you have correctly identified and met the needs of your documents?

★ Have you included examples to show you can combine textual, graphic and tabular information appropriate to your purpose?

★ Do the six documents show that you have used appropriate margins, tabs, bullets and page layout?

★ Have you made good use of the facilities available, including adjustments to line spacing, highlighted text and justification?

★ Have you chosen suitable font styles and sizes for body text, headings and other purposes?

★ Have you achieved an appropriate impact by making imaginative use of document layouts and styles?

continued

continued

★ Do you have early drafts of at least two of your documents, showing how you have changed your work to improve it, and that you have been using good working practices?

★ Do the final versions of your six documents show that you have checked your work and corrected obvious errors?

Activity
1.18

Of the six documents selected for your portfolio, choose two that are similar to documents produced by organisations for similar purposes.

★ For each of these two documents, write notes comparing them with similar examples produced by organisations

★ Explain any differences between your documents and those produced by organisations

★ Suggest improvements for each document

Activity 1.19

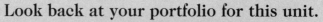

Look back at your portfolio for this unit.

★ Review your work and identify good and less good features

★ Suggest how you might improve it if you were to do it again

★ Relate your work to the standards used by organisations

Ask others for their opinions on your documents.

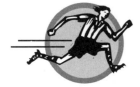

Revision questions

1. Give three examples of standard documents.

2. What information appears on a business card?

3. Explain the difference between landscape and portrait orientation.

4. What does sans serif describe?

5. Give one example of a document used for internal communication and one example used for external communication.

6. What is a fax-back facility?

7. What is an agenda used for?

8. What is recorded in the minutes of a meeting?

9. What is a draft?

10. Give three examples of punctuation marks.

11. What is the purpose of a validation check?

12. Explain how proof-reading should be done.

13. What is white space?

14. What is justification?

15. Explain the effects of left justification, right justification and full justification, giving one example of when each might be used.

Handling Information

- Learn how information is stored

- Find and use relevant information

- Put information into database and spreadsheet structures

- Develop information

- Present information in suitable ways, including reports, tables, charts and graphs

This unit also offers the opportunity to develop good working practices. Details about these, which apply to all units in this course, are on page 407 in the Good Working Practice Guide.

This chapter looks in detail at three topics:

- ✪ Information and information processing

- ✪ Database design

- ✪ Spreadsheet design

In your activities, you will practise handling information and produce a database and a spreadsheet to meet a given requirement.

This chapter uses one case study, a sailing club called the OCC – Online Cruising Club. Background information about this case study, and others used in this book, appears in the Case Studies section, starting on page xvii.

Information and information processing

This first section looks at data and information, finding information, classifying data and information and information processing.

Data and information

At first sight, the two words 'data' and 'information' seem to describe the same thing. In fact, there is a difference, which for this course in ICT you need to understand.

The word 'information' comes from the verb 'to inform' and this is the key to understanding the difference between data and information. Information has meaning – it informs the reader. Data items have no meaning – on their own.

The words in this sentence – taken one at a time – are good examples of data. Each word, on its own, has no meaning. It is only when they are strung together to make a sentence that together the words mean something.

Similarly, numbers mean little until we know what the units are, and what they are counting or measuring. So items of data are put together – in some structure – to make meaningful information.

DATA + STRUCTURE = INFORMATION

OCC Online Cruising Club

Here is some data: the OCC committee has six officers (commodore, vice commodore, secretary, treasurer, sailing secretary and membership secretary). The officers are (alphabetically) Angela, Gerry, Jenny, Linda, Mark and Tom.

Table 2.1 shows how this data can be structured into information, using a table.

OCC Committee 2000	
Commodore	Tom
Vice Commodore	Mark
Secretary	Angela
Treasurer	Gerry
Sailing Secretary	Jenny
Membership Secretary	Linda

Table 2.1 *Example of information*

There are many ways of structuring data: text in a letter, numbers in a table structure or spreadsheet, or names and addresses in database records.

Database design

All organisations collect data – about their employees, their customers and their suppliers. Some organisations also collect information about their competitors.

All organisations are required to obey health and safety regulations. They have to display information to all staff about special measures in place, for example in the case of discovering a fire. These instructions are likely to be stored as a word-processed file.

Some organisations have reason to collect data because of the nature of their business. For example, an estate agency would keep details about the houses it has to sell. It may also keep information on the people who have registered with it as looking for a new home. This type of data may be stored in a database.

Processing of numerical information can be done using spreadsheet software. We look at the practical problems of this in greater detail on page 106. Some organisations use spreadsheets for planning and costing purposes.

Records could be a person's name and address, information about a hotel in a travel database or flights and destinations in an airport.

Exercise 2.1

Here are three examples of record-structured data:

★ A directory entry – name, telephone number, address
★ A patient record – name, diagnosis, date
★ An order – item, quantity, price, total

Think of three more examples of record-structured data.

Record-structured databases are discussed in detail, starting on page 89.

> ▼ ▼ ▼ ▼ ▼ ▼ ▼ ▼ ▼
>
> **Record-structured databases** have rows of information set in a **table**. Each row of the table is called a **record**
>
> ▲ ▲ ▲ ▲ ▲ ▲ ▲ ▲ ▲

You can use a spreadsheet to calculate results such as totals or to produce graphs and charts.

Exercise 2.2

Here are three examples of number-structured data:

★ Income and expenditure

★ Sales forecasting

★ Staff hours, rates of pay and tax

Think of three more examples of number-structured data.

▼▼▼▼▼▼▼▼▼
Spreadsheets record numerical information in **cells**, in **rows** and in **columns**
▲▲▲▲▲▲▲▲▲

Number-structured databases, or **spreadsheets**, are discussed in detail, starting on page 106.

Internet pages, CD-ROM encyclopaedia pages and on-line help pages are examples of **hypertext databases**. These contain separate pages of information with items of text or graphics. The pages are linked, so that pointing at a highlighted item – a **hot link** – results in a jump to a different page and reveals more information. Setting up this type of database is beyond the scope of this chapter, but you will access hypertext databases throughout your course whenever you use the help facility on your computer or explore the Internet.

Activity
2.1

When you are next on-line to the Internet, move the mouse around the screen and see how the cursor changes.

Make a note of the different cursor symbols and the ways in which hot links like e-mail addresses are shown on screen.

You need to be able to understand these types of data structure and hence know what type of software is used to store and process the data – word-processing, spreadsheet or database.

The starting point for any information-processing system is to answer these two questions:

✪ What is its purpose?

✪ What does the user need?

OCC Online Cruising Club

The purpose of keeping a database of members' names and addresses (Figure 2.5 on page 94) is for mailing out newsletters. A speedy and accurate method of producing labels (as in Figure 2.2 on page 82) is needed.

The purpose of the spreadsheet used by the membership secretary (Figure 2.9 on page 106) is to keep a record of members analysed by type, from which the subscription income can be forecast. Accurate calculations are required.

The purpose of the spreadsheet used by the sailing secretary (Figure 2.15 on page 126) is to keep track of bookings and to forecast charter income. It also allows the sailing secretary to concentrate on trips for which not enough crew are booked and which may therefore need to be cancelled.

Finding out what the user needs, and defining the purpose of the ICT system, involves detailed discussions with the user. From this information, a suitable design is produced and the requirements of your system are defined:

- What data items you need to store

- The order in which data items are needed – for access and for printing reports

- The output needed – printed or on screen

- Details of special outputs such as line graphs and charts

- The calculations and formulae and functions that are to be used

- Details of searches or queries that will be needed

Most of these might be gleaned by looking at the information that is currently kept. Having established everything you need to know, you can set up a data structure – a database – ready for data handling.

Data handling is the processing of records in a database. The practical problems of processing databases begin on page 89. Sometimes data items are recorded in a spreadsheet, and this is discussed on page 106.

Finding information

There are many places where you can find out what you want to know. During your GNVQ course, there will be many situations where you will need to do research. When looking for relevant information, you can choose to use sources like these:

- Class notes and textbooks

- Magazines and pamphlets

- Computer databases

- The Internet

- Timetables

- People

Table 2.2 shows these sources of information and other details about them. Copy the table, extending it to include ten sources of information that you use regularly. For each one, complete the other columns.

Source	Type	Order of information	Use
1. GNVQ textbook	Paper-based	In chapters; topics are listed alphabetically in index	To find out subject information
2. A magazine	Paper-based		
3. Computer databases	Electronic		
4. The Internet	Electronic		
5. Timetable			
6. People			

Table 2.2 *Sources of information*

OCC Online Cruising Club

The address information about members is collected on a registration form, which they complete the first time they sail on *Overload*. Members who move house are expected to inform the membership secretary of their change in details. The full list of names and addresses is published each year in the OCC journal, so a special check is needed prior to publication. Other items of information, such as subscription rates, are decided by the committee. The sailing secretary and the membership secretary compile statistics such as the number of members booked to sail on a trip, or the number of members in a particular membership category.

Most sources of information are paper-based or available electronically, e.g. on the Internet. One extremely valuable source of information is people. People have knowledge, experience, beliefs and opinions – any of which might be important to your research. Various methods can be used to obtain information from people, and this is covered in Chapter 5.

When collecting information from people, the information may need to be transferred on to paper at some point. This then becomes the **source document**.

Information handling involves four main techniques:

- ✪ Setting up the information structure – the letter, the spreadsheet, the database or the web page

- ✪ Entering information

- ✪ Accessing the information and interrogation – trying to find the answers to questions

- ✪ Presenting results – as reports, tables, or charts

Setting up an information structure may seem straightforward, but the design of any information-handling system is actually quite complex. So, before tackling this, it makes sense to use information systems that have already been set up, and to learn from them what makes a good system – and what makes a poor system!

Presentation techniques are the subject of Chapter 1, in particular presentation of reports using word-processing software. In this chapter, you will create tables and charts.

This section concentrates on the two remaining topics: entering information and search techniques.

Entering information

▼ ▼ ▼ ▼ ▼ ▼ ▼ ▼ ▼
A **toggle key** is used to turn something on and off, like a light switch. You press it once to turn it on. To turn it off you press it again
▲ ▲ ▲ ▲ ▲ ▲ ▲ ▲ ▲

Most data entry is via the keyboard. The mouse is also used, but mostly to select choices offered on the screen. There are two main 'modes' of data input via the keyboard – **insert** and **overtype** –to control which you **toggle** the **Insert key** on the keyboard.

With word-processing software, data items are usually input in a free format. You just type what you want where you want it. Where you type is mostly controlled by moving the mouse around the screen and repositioning the cursor by a single click.

Exercise 2.4

Apart from using the mouse, how else can you move the cursor around the screen?

With spreadsheet software, data entry is often straight into the cell, so you need to be positioned on the correct cell before you start keying in data. This is called the **active cell**.

Activity 2.2

Look for on-line help on data entry in your spreadsheet software. What tips are given to speed up moving from one cell to another?

Once you are positioned on the correct cell, you can start to key in data. How this is understood by the software is covered in detail on page 111.

With database software, data can be entered straight into the table. Data-entry forms are often displayed on the screen and are designed to make entry as easy and as error-free as possible. It is important that errors are not made during data entry. Methods of trapping errors – **validation** and **verification** – are explained in Chapter 1 (page 56).

If you find errors in your work – and you should check it very carefully – you should correct the errors. This is called **editing**. You may also decide to **delete** data, e.g. if the information is no longer relevant.

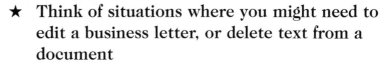

Exercise 2.5

- ★ Think of situations where you might need to edit a business letter, or delete text from a document
- ★ Think of situations where you might need to edit information in a database. When might information be deleted from a database?
- ★ When might data be edited in a spreadsheet. When might data be deleted from a spreadsheet?

Searching techniques

To use an ICT system at all, you must be able to find data already stored in an ICT system. You must know where to look for the information, what instructions (or commands) to use and how to say what it is you want. Accessing information is also covered in Chapter 5 (page 221).

Search and **sort** facilities are available in most software applications: word processing, spreadsheets and databases. These two terms are easily confused, but it is important that you know which to use.

Sorting means rearranging records in a database table into some order, typically numerical or alphabetical.

Activity 2.3

Find out how to use the sort facility on your word-processing software.

★ In what situations is it available?

★ When might you want to use this facility?

How data items are sorted depends on the type of data:

✪ Text is sorted alphabetically

✪ Numbers are sorted numerically

On the contents page, the page numbers appear in numerical order. The index in this book is sorted in alphabetical order by topic.

Data can be sorted in two different orders: **ascending** or **descending**:

In Figure 2.1, both the page numbers and index topics are in ascending order.

✪ **Text** sorted in ascending order (going up) will put Andrew before Zach. Descending order (going down) will put Peter before Paul

✪ **Numbers** sorted in ascending order (going up) have the smallest numbers first. Descending order (going down) has the largest numbers first

Contents

Index

Figure 2.1 *Numerical and alphabetical order*

Exercise 2.6

Think of an example where data might be sorted in descending order.

Think about sports results.

Exercise 2.7

In what order are the labels for the OCC members printed in Figure 2.2?

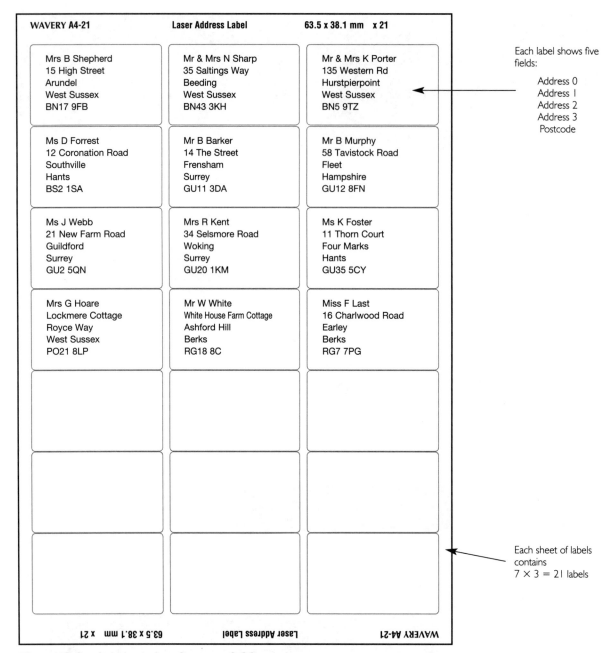

| WAVERY A4-21 | Laser Address Label | 63.5 x 38.1 mm   x 21 |

Mrs B Shepherd 15 High Street Arundel West Sussex BN17 9FB	Mr & Mrs N Sharp 35 Saltings Way Beeding West Sussex BN43 3KH	Mr & Mrs K Porter 135 Western Rd Hurstpierpoint West Sussex BN5 9TZ
Ms D Forrest 12 Coronation Road Southville Hants BS2 1SA	Mr B Barker 14 The Street Frensham Surrey GU11 3DA	Mr B Murphy 58 Tavistock Road Fleet Hampshire GU12 8FN
Ms J Webb 21 New Farm Road Guildford Surrey GU2 5QN	Mrs R Kent 34 Selsmore Road Woking Surrey GU20 1KM	Ms K Foster 11 Thorn Court Four Marks Hants GU35 5CY
Mrs G Hoare Lockmere Cottage Royce Way West Sussex PO21 8LP	Mr W White White House Farm Cottage Ashford Hill Berks RG18 8C	Miss F Last 16 Charlwood Road Earley Berks RG7 7PG

Each label shows five fields:

Address 0
Address 1
Address 2
Address 3
Postcode

Each sheet of labels contains
7 × 3 = 21 labels

Figure 2.2   *Label printout for some OCC members*

For reasons of confidentiality, you cannot be shown actual data from the OCC database, so dummy names and addresses are given in this book instead.

Exercise 2.8

Why is it not possible to publish actual data from the OCC database in this book?

Activity 2.4

Obtain a copy of a bus or train timetable. Into what order are the data items sorted?

Searching is different from sorting. In word-processing software, you can use the **Find function** to search the text for a particular word or phrase that you have included in the text. This facility allows only a simple search, but you can choose to look for whole words only, or words that sound like the one you key in.

Activity 2.5

Explore the Find function in your word-processing software. Write notes on how it works. Find is often used with the Replace function. How does this work? How can it help you to edit your data efficiently and accurately?

You could use on-line help to find out more about this facility.

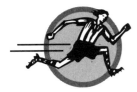

▼ ▼ ▼ ▼ ▼ ▼ ▼ ▼

A **contents list** is arranged in the same order as the pages of the book and tells you on what page each chapter starts

▲ ▲ ▲ ▲ ▲ ▲ ▲ ▲ ▲

Sometimes, to access the information you want, you have to search a large source of information for a small amount of information that is going to be useful to you.

This book has 488 pages. To find out about one particular topic, you could look at every single page until you spotted what you want. This could take ages! If you are already familiar with the book, it might be that referring to the **contents list** will speed up your search. If this is not helpful enough, you might decide to refer to the **index**.

Exercise 2.9

While doing this exercise, time yourself and think about what 'data' you are using to complete the exercise.

★ **In this book, on what page does the Examination Guide start?**

★ **Where is 'double-line spacing' explained in this book?**

▼ ▼ ▼ ▼ ▼ ▼ ▼ ▼

The entries in an **index** are arranged alphabetically, and each entry points to the pages in the book where that topic is mentioned

▲ ▲ ▲ ▲ ▲ ▲ ▲ ▲ ▲

If you are accessing information using a computer, you have to give the computer instructions about what you want to find.

To complete the first part of Exercise 2.9, a computer (or someone who does not know how to find out this type of information) would have to be given these instructions:

✪ Go to the contents page

✪ Start at the top line of text and check each line until you find 'Examination Guide'

✪ Tell me what page number it starts on

Exercise 2.10

Write similar 'instructions' for accessing the index.

If you are searching for information in an ICT system, rather than a paper-based file, having found the correct data file, you will probably want to look at a particular record or group of records.

If a data file relates to all the people employed by a company, then this file is separated into many **records**, each one related to one particular employee. Each record may have details such as name, address and job title. These details are stored in separate **fields** within the record, one field for name, one field for address, and so on.

Each record is the same 'shape' – as shown in Figure 2.3.

To find information about a particular employee, you must know something about him or her that will uniquely identify the record. This is called the **key**. Usually, one data item is used as a **key field**. In the case of the employee file, it will probably be an employee number.

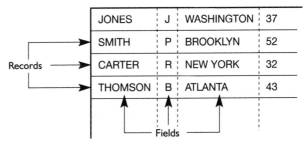

Figure 2.3 *A data file, split into records and fields*

Exercise 2.11

What would you expect the key field to be in a data file held by a bank about each of its customers? Think of three more data files and suggest what information might be kept in each record, and what field might be the key field. For example, think about data held by libraries, electricity companies and schools or colleges.

▼▼▼▼▼▼▼▼▼
Relational operators: = (equals), < (less than), > (greater than), <= (less than or equal to), >= (greater than or equal to)
▲▲▲▲▲▲▲▲▲

A search instruction always includes a **condition**, and the condition always includes a **relational operator**.

These are all examples of simple conditions:

✪ surname = "Lawson"

✪ crewtotal < 10

✪ age > 18

✪ credit <= 100

✪ balance >= 0

▼▼▼▼▼▼▼▼▼
Logical operators: AND, OR and NOT
▲▲▲▲▲▲▲▲▲

Sometimes accessing information is not so simple, because to present it in a meaningful way, the information has a more complex structure. Suppose you want to know the telephone number of Joe Brown. First you look for the Browns. There are lots of them! So you then look for those with a first name of Joe. The surname is the **primary sort field**; the first name is the **secondary sort field**.

More complex conditions can be created by joining together two or more simple conditions using **logical operators**.

These are all examples of complex conditions:

- ✪ surname = "Brown" AND firstname = "Joe"
- ✪ surname = "Lawson" OR surname = "Lawrence"
- ✪ credit <= 100 AND balance >= 0

Once you know which record (or group of records) you want to access, you need to enter a command that will make the software search for that data.

Exactly how you do this will depend on the software you are using. Some use a Find command; others use Select. There may be an icon with a pair of binoculars. Some offer you a blank record and ask you to fill in the data items you want to match.

Activity 2.6

Check how searching (or finding) works on your spreadsheet software.

Most database software will allow you to **search on a match**. This means you can find a record that has a data item that exactly matches a data value you key in. For example, you may match on CUST_NAME = "SMITH" and get a printout of all customers whose surname is Smith. CUST_NAME is the **field title**. The computer will look at every record and, in particular, at the data in the field called CUST_NAME. If the data in the field match, then that record is **selected** for printing.

Activity 2.7

Investigate how to find particular data in your spreadsheet software. Write down an explanation that would help someone who has never used this software before.

You may also want to **search on a range**. For this, you might use a search command including the test PRICE > 100. This might find all records of products that have a sales price greater than £100. You might need to write more complicated instructions, which ask for records **within a range**.

Activity 2.8

Find out what commands you should use to find particular records on your database software.

★ Write down the command you would use to find a matching record
★ Write down the command you would use to find a range of records
★ Use these commands to produce printouts of data extracted from a database file

Database methods

Did You Know?

Simple databases, called *flatfile databases*, comprise a single table. More complex databases, called *relational databases*, comprise several tables, linked by relationship

We often use the term 'database' instead of 'record-structured database'.

In a table, there are two main database components, **records** and **fields**, as shown in Figure 2.3 on page 85.

In this section, you will learn to identify the database components in a given data-handling problem and set up records to store these data.

Records and fields

A database table is divided into many **records**, all the same 'shape'; each record holds the same kind of information but about a different person or thing or event.

- ✪ If a database file keeps information about the employees in a company, for each employee there will be one record. The same information will be kept about each employee

- ✪ If a database file keeps information about the products available for sale in a supermarket, one record will contain the details for a particular stock item. The same information will be kept about each stock item

- ✪ If a database file keeps information about holiday bookings, one record will hold the information about one holiday booked. The same information will be kept about each booking

Exercise 2.12

Think of three different database files – related to people, things and events – and for each one, write down what information may be kept in one record in that file.

There are a number of **fields** in each record of the database file; these contain the data items.

○ In the employee database file, the employee records will have fields for the employee's name, address, telephone number, job title, etc. (Figure 2.4(a))

○ In the product database file, the product records will have fields for product number, product description, price, quantity in stock, etc. (Figure 2.4(b))

○ In the holiday bookings database file, the bookings record will have fields for departure date, destination country, resort, date booked, customer details, etc. (Figure 2.4(c))

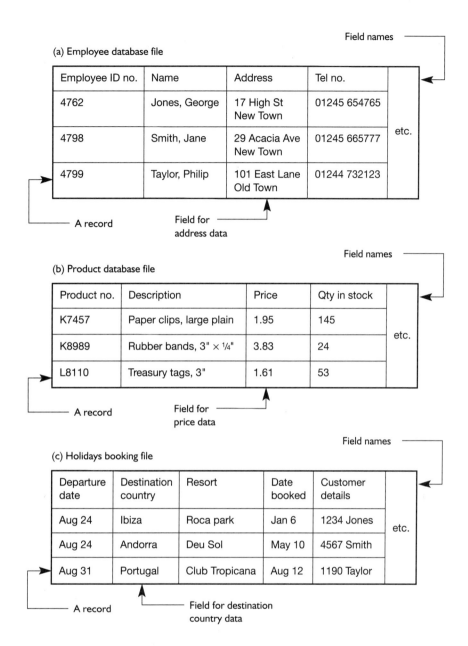

Figure 2.4 *Different types of database files*

OCC Online Cruising Club

In the OCC members' addresses database (Figure 2.5), each record holds the address details for one household. If two people in the same family belong to the OCC club, they appear only once in the database, so they receive only one mailing of each newsletter.

In each record, the fields kept for each household are the people to send the mailing to (addressee), their address (three lines) and a postcode.

In the Sailtrips database, each record holds the information for one sail. The fields are departure date, the number of days sailing, and a title (or description of the sail). See Figure 2.6.

When designing a database file, you need to list all the fields that will appear in each record. For each field, you need a unique **field name**. This name will be used when you interrogate the database file.

For the employee database file, the field names might be: EMP_NAME, EMP_ADDR, EMP_TELNO, EMP_JOBTITLE.

> *It makes sense to choose field titles that are as meaningful as possible.*

Exercise 2.13

For each of the database files from Exercise 2.12, list the fields, using a unique name for each field.

Data types and key fields

Each field has a data type, character, numeric, date, etc., which determines how the data will be stored and displayed or printed. There are three main types of data that you need to know about:

✪ Character (sometimes called text)

✪ Number (integer and decimal)

✪ Date

In the records of a product database file, there are fields for product number, product description, price, quantity in stock, etc. In deciding what data types to use to store or display these data, you need to think about the values they might have. Table 2.3 shows an example.

Field	Possible Values
Product number	Character string – only letters of the alphabet or numbers, no decimal point or other characters
Product description	Text / character string – may include numbers, e.g. 0.5 to describe thickness of string, etc.
Price	Currency – 2 decimal places for pence
Quantity in stock	Number – integer, cannot be less than zero

Table 2.3   *Deciding data types for a database*

OCC Online Cruising Club

In the members' addresses database, all the fields are text fields. See Figure 2.5.

Field names

Each record holds the address information for one member

Addressee	Address 1	Address 2	Address 3	Postcode
Mrs G Hoare	Lockmere Cottage	Royce Way	West Sussex	PO21 8LP
Mr B Murphy	58 Tavistock Road	Fleet	Hampshire	GU12 8FN
Mr & Mrs K Porter	135 Western Rd	Hurstpierpoint	West Sussex	BN5 9TZ
Mrs B Shepherd	15 High Street	Arundel	West Sussex	BN17 9FB
Mr W White	White House Farm Cottage	Ashford Hill	Berks	RG18 8CN
Mrs R Kent	34 Selsmore Road	Woking	Surrey	GU20 1KM
Mr B Barker	14 The Street	Frensham	Surrey	GU11 3DA
Miss F Last	16 Charlwood Road	Earley	Berks	RG7 7PG
Ms D Forrest	12 Coronation Road	Southville	Hants	BS2 1SA
Mr & Mrs N Sharp	35 Saltings Way	Beeding	West Sussex	BN43 3KH
Ms K Foster	11 Thorn Court	Four Marks	Hants	GU35 5CY
Ms J Webb	21 New Farm Road	Guildford	Surrey	GU2 5QN

Figure 2.5 *Database of members' addresses*

Activity 2.9

These are the fields in the database for holiday bookings: departure date, destination country, resort, date booked, customer details. For each field, suggest what values the data might take and create a table (similar to Table 2.3) to record this information.

In any database table, each record needs a unique key to identify it. This is called the **primary key field**.

✪ In the Employee database, the key field is Employee ID no.

✪ In the Product database file, the key field is Product no.

✪ In the holiday bookings file, there appears to be no key field. It would be sensible to add an extra field – booking number – and use that as a key field.

You will need to decide how much data needs to fit into each field, and therefore how long each field needs to be. This is called the **field length**.

Exercise 2.14

For your three databases, decide on a field type and length for each field.

> When deciding on the length of text fields, look at some sample data and see what the longest possible entry could be. Choose a field length at least as long, perhaps a few characters more.

When deciding on numeric fields, you are choosing not how it is stored (which is controlled by the software) but how it is displayed.

✪ How many decimal places will you need to produce the required level of accuracy? For amounts of money, you usually need two places of decimals (for the pence), but on a telephone bill you will notice more decimal places on the itemised list of call charges.

✪ Do you want the pound sign to appear?

✪ Do you want a comma to separate the figures in large amounts? For example, would you prefer to see 123,456 or 123456?

For dates, you also control how they are displayed rather than how the data items are stored.

Activity
2.10

Find out what date formats are available in your database software. Write notes about this.

OCC Online Cruising Club

Another OCC database records details of all sailing trips. Figure 2.6 shows the trips for the sailing season 2000 from this table. In the sail trips database, notice that there is one text field, one numeric field and one date field.

Field names →

Title	Departs	No of days
Basic training weekend	21–Apr–00	2
Open days	28–Apr–00	2
Weekend sail	05–May–00	2
Family weekend sail	12–May–00	2
Weekend sail	19–May–00	2
Royal Escape Race	25–May–00	4
Weekend sail	31–May–00	4
Round the Island Race	08–Jun–00	3
Haslar to Brittany passage	17 Jun–00	7
Brittany cruise	24 Jun–00	14
Brittany & Golfe de Gascogne cruise	08 Jul–00	14
North coast of Spain cruise	22 Jul–00	14
North coast of Spain cruise	05–Aug–00	14
North coast of Spain cruise	19–Aug–00	14
North coast of Spain cruise	02–Sep–00	7
Northern Spain to Haslar passage	09–Sep–00	15
Weekend sail	29–Sep–00	2
Weekend sail	06–Oct–00	2
Regatta	13–Oct–00	2
Basic training weekend	20–Oct–00	2
Weekend sail	27–Oct–00	2
Advanced training weekend	03–Nov–00	2
Weekend sail	10–Nov–00	2
Weekend sail	17–Nov–00	2

Data for one sail is stored in one record →

Text field

Date field used to sort the data

Numeric field

Figure 2.6   *The OCC sail trips table*

Database facilities

Database software allows you to manage the data for a particular situation within a single table.

- ✪ **Queries** are used to extract data from the table to create a new table

- ✪ **Tabular information** can be viewed on screen, edited and printed out

- ✪ **Reports** can summarise data, giving **grouped totals** and presenting the information in whatever order you want

How your database software works will affect how you approach this section. Unlike spreadsheet software, where most software does things in very similar ways, database software can be very different.

▼▼▼▼▼▼▼▼▼

A **cue card** is a reminder note that helps you to operate the software more successfully

▲▲▲▲▲▲▲▲▲

Even upgrading from an older version to a newer version of the same software package can be a bit tricky at first, so it is important that you read the on-line help carefully, before tackling this section. Most packages offer on-line help, e.g. in the form of **cue cards**, and/or they offer demonstrations.

Activity
2.11

Find out the name of the database software that you will be using. Find out what on-line help it offers. Watch any demonstrations that are available.

To create a database, these are the steps you will need to follow:

✪ Set up a table and enter data

✪ Set up a query to extract data from your table

✪ Design a report to present the results of your query

Tables

A table has rows (for records) and columns (for fields).

Activity 2.12

For your database software, find out how to set up a table, how to enter data into your table, how to sort the data on one field and how to print out a table. Set up a database for something of interest to you.

> You could choose something from this list: a CD or other collection; a Christmas card; or friends' telephone numbers.

★ Create a table, making sure you include at least one text field and one numeric field

★ Enter the data for ten records. Use real or imaginary data to test your database design

★ Sort your records on one numeric field and print out the data

★ Sort the data items by one text field and print them out

Queries

A query is simply a question that you want to have answered by your database.

Here are some examples of queries:

- ✪ How many CDs do I have in my collection that feature Tom Jones?

- ✪ How many Christmas cards do I need to buy?

- ✪ Which of my friends are on e-mail?

Exercise 2.15

Write a list of queries that could be answered by the data in the OCC Sailtrips database.
What limits the questions you can expect to have answered?

How you ask the query depends on the software. Microsoft software uses QBE (query by example). Other software may use a particular query language – they usually end in the letters QL, e.g. SQL (structured query language).

Activity 2.13

Find out how to set up a query using your own database software. Watch a demonstration if this is available to you.

> Share this information with others in your class. Check how other database software works. It may be important in your first job that you can work on a different database from the one you usually use. So take this opportunity to learn as much as you can about the many different databases on the market.

For your database, set up a query. Here are some example queries.

★ **CD collection database:** Can your database design give an answer to this query: How many CDs do you have by the Beatles?

★ **Christmas card list:** You are planning to send your Christmas cards before the second-class postage deadline. Can your database estimate the cost of your postage bill? Could your database take into account cards that you may hand deliver? If not, could you add a field to record this extra information?

★ **Friends' telephone list:** In April 2000, some telephone numbers changed. If a similar change happened again, could your database provide a list of all numbers that would have to be changed?

Reports

Reports are used to view your data – either on screen or on paper.

Each report has a general structure:

- ✪ **Report header** – appears on first page only

- ✪ **Page header** – appears at the top of every page

- ✪ **Report detail** – appears within a page and is repeated for each record in the table on which the report is based

- ✪ **Page footer** – appears at the bottom of every page

- ✪ **Report footer** – appears at the very end of the report, only once

When designing your report, you need to decide what information you would like to appear on each page, or only at the start, or only at the end. These fields should then be positioned in the report structure to make the output match what you want. Note that you may choose to have an empty section – you do not need to have something printed at the foot of every page. If this is the case, this section is left blank in your design.

> In Microsoft Access, everything that appears on a report – whether it is a label/heading, a total or other calculation, or a field – is called a **control**. In a single report you may have as many as 20 controls, and each one needs to be placed in the design of the report, in the appropriate report section. This can take a while to do, so the software also provides a wizard to speed up the process.

One of the strengths of a database is the facility to sort the data into an order that is helpful to the user. When designing a report, the order in which the report detail section appears is very important and, usually, is easily controlled.

Grouping of report details should also be possible, but this changes the structure of a report. The new structure includes a group header and a group footer:

- ✪ Report header

- ✪ Page header

- ✪ **Group header** – appears **ahead** of those report details belonging to this group

- ✪ Report detail

- ✪ **Group footer** – appears **after** those report details belonging to this group

- ✪ Page footer

- ✪ Report footer

OCC Online Cruising Club

From the Sailtrip table, a list of sailing trips in departure date order is sorted on departure field. See Figure 2.7. Note that there is no page footer on this report because it runs to only a single page, so page numbering is not necessary. The date already appears in the report header.

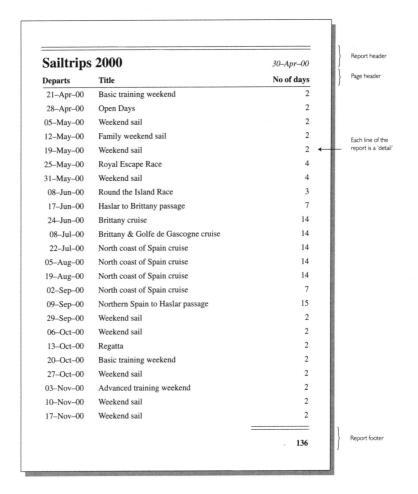

Sailtrips 2000		30–Apr–00
Departs	**Title**	**No of days**
21–Apr–00	Basic training weekend	2
28–Apr–00	Open Days	2
05–May–00	Weekend sail	2
12–May–00	Family weekend sail	2
19–May–00	Weekend sail	2
25–May–00	Royal Escape Race	4
31–May–00	Weekend sail	4
08–Jun–00	Round the Island Race	3
17–Jun–00	Haslar to Brittany passage	7
24–Jun–00	Brittany cruise	14
08–Jul–00	Brittany & Golfe de Gascogne cruise	14
22–Jul–00	North coast of Spain cruise	14
05–Aug–00	North coast of Spain cruise	14
19–Aug–00	North coast of Spain cruise	14
02–Sep–00	North coast of Spain cruise	7
09–Sep–00	Northern Spain to Haslar passage	15
29–Sep–00	Weekend sail	2
06–Oct–00	Weekend sail	2
13–Oct–00	Regatta	2
20–Oct–00	Basic training weekend	2
27–Oct–00	Weekend sail	2
03–Nov–00	Advanced training weekend	2
10–Nov–00	Weekend sail	2
17–Nov–00	Weekend sail	2
		136

Report header

Page header

Each line of the report is a 'detail'

Report footer

Figure 2.7 *OCC sailing trips in departure date order*

The group header and footer – with the report details relating to that group – appear as many times as there are groups, and this depends on what you decide is a group.

When designing grouped reports, it is usual to place data that apply to the whole group in the group header (or group footer). The group footer usually contains any totals.

OCC Online Cruising Club

From the Sailtrip table, a list of sailing trips in departure date order is sorted on the departure field but is now grouped by the number of days sailing. See Figure 2.8. Note that there is no group header on this report. Also, as in Figure 2.7, there is no page footer.

Sailtrips 2000, by length of sail		30–Apr–00		Report header
Departs	**Title**	**No of days**		Page header
21–Apr–00	Basic training weekend	2		
28–Apr–00	Open Days	2		
05–May–00	Weekend sail	2		
12–May–00	Family weekend sail	2		
19–May–00	Weekend sail	2		
29–Sep–00	Weekend sail	2		
06–Oct–00	Weekend sail	2		
13–Oct–00	Regatta	2		Group
20–Oct–00	Basic training weekend	2		NB no group
27–Oct–00	Weekend sail	2		header is used
03–Nov–00	Advanced training weekend	2		
10–Nov–00	Weekend sail	2		
17–Nov–00	Weekend sail	2		
			26	
08–Jun–00	Round the Island Race	3		
			3	
25–May–00	Royal Escape Race	4		Report details
31–May–00	Weekend sail	4		for one group
			8	Group footer
17–Jun–00	Haslar to Brittany passage	7		
02–Sep–00	North coast of Spain cruise	7		
			14	
24–Jun–00	Brittany cruise	14		
08–Jul–00	Brittany & Golfe de Gascogne cruise	14		
22–Jul–00	North coast of Spain cruise	14		
05–Aug–00	North coast of Spain cruise	14		
19–Aug–00	North coast of Spain cruise	14		
			70	
09–Sep–00	Northern Spain to Haslar passage	15		
			15	
			136	Report footer

Figure 2.8 *OCC sailing trips grouped by number of days sailing*

Activity 2.16

If you have not already produced a database, do so now. Include a description of the database and annotate your printed output to demonstrate its operation and show its purpose.

★ Describe clearly the purpose of the database, the information to be processed and the processing required

★ Create a table structure using suitable field names, field lengths, data types and primary keys

★ Use database facilities to enter data, sort the records, search for particular data and produce different types of printed report

★ Annotate your printed reports so that it is clear why and how all printed items are produced

Remember to check the accuracy of your data and keep backup copies of all files.

Spreadsheet design

Spreadsheets are used to store and analyse numerical information so that you can solve numerical processing problems.

OCC Online Cruising Club

Linda, the membership secretary, keeps track of how many members belong to the OCC. According to their membership type (full, associate, cadet, etc.), members pay a different annual subscription. To be able to budget properly, Gerry (the treasurer) needs to know how much he can expect to receive in subscriptions in total. Figure 2.9 shows this information.

	A	B	C	D	E
1	Subscription income – forecast				30-Apr-00
2					
3	**Membership**	**Code**	**Number**	**Subs**	**Income from subs**
4	full members	F	126	£70	£8,820
5	life members	LM	3	£0	£0
6	associate members	A	44	£5	£220
7	cadets under 25	C	17	£35	£595
8	outport members	O	14	£35	£490
9	non-sailing members	N	3	£35	£105
10	Total membership		207		£10,230
11	Average per member:				£49

Figure 2.9 *OCC's expected subscription income*

In this section you will explore spreadsheet methods used to store and make sense of information:

✪ Presentation techniques, e.g. using borders and shading

✪ Using formulae and functions, and calculating results (such as totals)

✪ Creating line graphs and charts from numerical data, and identifying patterns in graphs or charts

The components of a numerical processing problem include items, dates, totals and calculations.

✪ **Items** are the things about which calculations are necessary, e.g. holidays, room bookings, costs and examination results

✪ **Dates** are important in most numerical processing problems: e.g. when a holiday is booked and when it is to start; when an examination is due to take place and when the results will be available

✪ **Totals** are often needed: the total sales for a week; the total number of people booked for a holiday flight; the total number of students entered for an examination; and so on

✪ **Calculations** are often needed. In invoicing, VAT (value-added tax) at 17.5% has to be calculated

Numerical processing problems are often solved using spreadsheet software. These components of the numerical processing problem have to be placed in the spreadsheet structure to model the problem and find a solution.

Exactly how you use spreadsheet software depends on whether you are using a **DOS-based** system or a **Windows-based** system.

Find out how to load your spreadsheet software, how to retrieve a spreadsheet file, and how to print it out. Write notes on how to do this.

Layout of a spreadsheet

The spreadsheet is laid out in **rows** and **columns** as shown in Figure 2.10. Notice that the columns are labelled A, B, C, ... and that the rows are numbered 1, 2, 3, ...

Cells are labelled by their column and row number. In Figure 2.10, column E is shaded, and so is row 3. The cell at the intersection of row 3 and column E is called E3 – the letter first and then the number. E3 is an example of a **cell reference**.

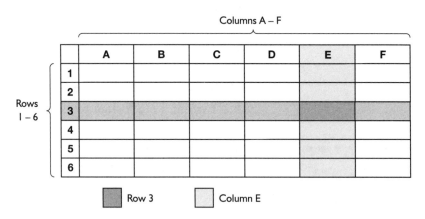

Figure 2.10 *Spreadsheet layout*

Exercise 2.16

Look at Figure 2.9 and identify what is displayed in these cells: A1, B5, C10, D9, E1, E9, E10 and E11.

When designing a spreadsheet, you decide how many rows and columns you will need. To begin with, all columns will have the same width – called the **default width** – which will be set by your spreadsheet software.

Activity 2.18

Find out what the default width of columns is on your spreadsheet software. What happens if you enter data items that are wider than the column width?

Try keying in the alphabet into cell A1. How is this displayed? Key HELLO into cell A2. What effect does this have?

Now try keying 12345678901234567890 into cell B1. What effect does this have?

If the column is not wide enough to display your data, you will have to increase the **column width**. You may also want to reduce the width of some columns, either to save paper or to improve the overall look of the spreadsheet. Notice that the columns B, C and D of the spreadsheet in Figure 2.9 are narrower than columns A and E.

Activity 2.19

Find out how to change the width of columns using your spreadsheet software. Can you also control the row height?
Write notes that would help someone who has never used your spreadsheet software before.

What you see on the screen sometimes does not match what is printed out. With some spreadsheet software, you think all your data can be seen, i.e. your column width is wide enough on the screen, but when you make a printout, some data items are lost or **truncated**. This is a design fault in the software, but it is up to you, the user, to check this carefully.

Activity 2.20

Experiment with different column widths – say six, seven, eight, nine and ten characters – and fill these columns with data items of varying lengths. See if the data items displayed are always printed in full.

Each cell of a spreadsheet can hold only one of four different types of data:

- **Numeric** – for numbers, including **currency** and **dates**

- **Character** – for messages, text, labels, and so on

- **Formula** – calculations based on other data in the spreadsheet

- **Blank** – contains nothing

OCC Online Cruising Club

In Figure 2.9 there are examples of all four:

★ Numeric items are entered into cells C4–C9 and B4–B9

★ Text is entered into cells in row 3 and column A

★ Formulae are entered in column E and rows 10 and 11

★ Row 2 is blank. Cells B1, C1 and D1 are also blank

The first character you key tells the software what type of data you are entering and helps it to decide how to display it:

✪ If you start with a digit, the software assumes you are entering a number

✪ If you start with a letter of the alphabet, the software assumes you are entering some text

Activity 2.21

Starting with a blank spreadsheet, type your name in cell A1 and press Return. How does the software display this text?
In cell B1, enter a number (e.g. your age) and press Return. How does the software display this number?

Figure 2.11 shows that the software automatically displays numbers right-aligned and text left-aligned. If the automatic (default) display does not suit you, you can control how the items in a spreadsheet are displayed; see page 115.

All text cells left aligned and all numeric cells right aligned

	A	B	C	D	E	F
1		Jan	Feb	Mar	April	TOTAL
2	Black	42	56	71	30	199
3	Blue	45	60	80	28	213
4	Green	12	15	20	9	56
5	Yellow	24	32	38	21	115
6		123	163	209	88	583

Figure 2.11   *Different alignment within a spreadsheet*

Activity 2.22

Enter this in a blank cell: =4+5. Then press Return. What happens?

The third option for the contents of a cell – a formula – is what makes spreadsheet software so useful.

✪ Formulae can be used to calculate sums, adding numbers in one row or column

✪ Formulae can be used for more complicated calculations, using the usual maths symbols

✪ The value displayed in each cell is automatically updated. So if you change any of the numbers that form part of a calculation, the spreadsheet recalculates all formulae for you

Explore how your spreadsheet software reacts to what you enter in a cell.

★ What happens if you enter something starting with a plus sign (+) or an equals (=) sign?

★ What happens if you enter something starting with an apostrophe (')?

★ What happens if your data includes a forward slash (/) or a dash (–)?

★ What happens if you type a zero, a space and then some digits, including one forward slash, e.g. '0 1/5'?

Check the entries in Table 2.4 'work' the same on your spreadsheet software. Then copy and complete Table 2.4 to show how your spreadsheet software reacts to what you enter.

What was entered	How it was displayed	How the software interprets the data
+27/3	9 (right aligned)	Worked out 27 divided by 3; treated it as a formula
27/3	27-Mar	Thought it was a date
27-3		
+27-3		
=27/3		
.75		
0 3/4		
'27/3		

Table 2.4 *Data entry to a spreadsheet*

Exercise 2.17

What is the difference between an empty (blank) cell and one that contains a space?

It is important to include **titles** on your spreadsheet. Otherwise, it may not be clear what the spreadsheet does, or when it was produced. There are several types of title in a spreadsheet:

- ✪ The **main title** appears at the very top and should include a description of the spreadsheet

- ✪ At the top of each column you should have a **column title** to label the data in that column

- ✪ At the start of every row you should have a **row title** to label the data in that row

You may also include a message on the final row of the spreadsheet, e.g. explaining any codes that you have used. Some rows may be left blank for spacing purposes; these do not need row titles. Some rows may have lines of dashes to create the effect of ruling off before a total; these do not need titles either. Any row (or column) that has a **total** calculated from other rows (or columns) should be labelled carefully (Figure 2.12).

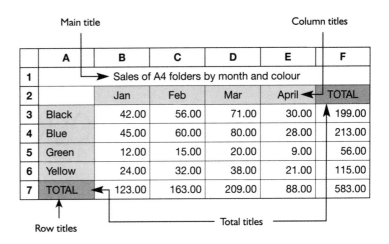

	A		B	C	D	E		F
1			Sales of A4 folders by month and colour					
2			Jan	Feb	Mar	April		TOTAL
3	Black		42.00	56.00	71.00	30.00		199.00
4	Blue		45.00	60.00	80.00	28.00		213.00
5	Green		12.00	15.00	20.00	9.00		56.00
6	Yellow		24.00	32.00	38.00	21.00		115.00
7	TOTAL		123.00	163.00	209.00	88.00		583.00

Figure 2.12 *Titles on a spreadsheet: row and column titles get light shading, total titles get darker shading*

Exercise 2.18

Looking at Figure 2.9, identify which cells contain the main title, the row titles and the column titles.

If the data in each cell were presented just as you keyed it in, the end result could be unattractive and, possibly, difficult to read. **Cell formats** control the presentation of information in a cell. Cell formatting is used to improve the overall look of the spreadsheet, and your aim should be to make it easier for a reader to understand. Here are some examples of what can be done to improve the presentation of data in a spreadsheet:

✪ Controlling the position of text or labels, e.g. right-align text to match numeric data in a column, centre headings

✪ Displaying numbers in currency format, e.g. with a pound sign preceding them

✪ Deciding on the number of decimal places to be shown, e.g. most currency is shown with two decimal places

- Choosing between different date formats, e.g. 'dd-mm-yy' (12-06-99) or 'dd mmm yyyy' (12 Jun 1999); or showing time in the 24-hour format

OCC Online Cruising Club

In Figure 2.9 the money amounts are shown with a £ sign. The subscriptions are in whole pounds, so no decimal places are used. The average per member is not actually £49 – this result has been rounded to the nearest pound by formatting the cell as 'currency with no decimal places'.

It is especially important that information 'lines up' within the columns of a spreadsheet. This is called **justification** or **alignment**.

- For **text data**, left-alignment is normal for row titles and most data items. You might choose to centre the text (and its column heading) if you prefer

- For **numeric data** that involves only whole numbers (integers), it is usual to right-align the data. Then the units are all in a line, the tens are all in a line, and so on. If the numbers have a decimal point (e.g. with a column of currency data), it would be normal to align on the decimal point

Figure 2.13 shows three examples of layout choice: all data cells centred; numeric data aligned on a decimal tab; and numeric data with two decimal places.

All data cells centred

	A	B	C	D	E	F
1	Sales of A4 folders by month and colour					
2		Jan	Feb	Mar	April	TOTAL
3	Black	42	56	71	30	199
4	Blue	45	60	80	28	213
5	Green	12	15	20	9	56
6	Yellow	24	32	38	21	115
7	TOTAL	123	163	209	88	583

Numeric data right-aligned on a decimal tab

	A	B	C	D	E	F
1	Sales of A4 folders by month and colour					
2		Jan	Feb	Mar	April	TOTAL
3	Black	42	56	71	30	199
4	Blue	45	60	80	28	213
5	Green	12	15	20	9	56
6	Yellow	24	32	38	21	115
7	TOTAL	123	163	209	88	583

Showing decimal places

	A	B	C	D	E	F
1	Sales of A4 folders by month and colour					
2		Jan	Feb	Mar	April	TOTAL
3	Black	42.00	56.00	71.00	30.00	199.00
4	Blue	45.00	60.00	80.00	28.00	213.00
5	Green	12.00	15.00	20.00	9.00	56.00
6	Yellow	24.00	32.00	38.00	21.00	115.00
7	TOTAL	123.00	163.00	209.00	88.00	583.00

Figure 2.13 *Examples of data alignment within a spreadsheet*

OCC Online Cruising Club

In Figure 2.9 the entries in the left-hand column are left-aligned. The column headings (Number, Subs and Income from subs) are right-aligned. The numeric items are automatically right-aligned.

Activity 2.24

Find out how to control the alignment of a single cell of the spreadsheet. Find out how to control the alignment of a block of cells. Write notes on how to do this.

You might also decide to incorporate **colour** and/or **shading** in your spreadsheet. Figure 2.12 includes shading for the row and column titles with darker shading for the TOTAL titles.

Activity 2.25

Find out what display formats are offered with your spreadsheet software.
Enter some data into a spreadsheet and choose some display options to show what you can do. Print out your spreadsheet, and make notes on how you achieved the effects shown.

When setting up a spreadsheet to hold information, it helps to identify the different components of a numerical processing problem and to try to match their data types to those available on a spreadsheet.

- ✪ The **item**, i.e. the thing we are interested in, will have a name or a description that can be stored as a string of characters. Examples could be holiday destinations such as Spain, Portugal or France. It could be examinations such as GNVQ ICT, GNVQ Leisure and Tourism or GNVQ Science. These items will usually be placed as **row titles** or **column titles** in a text field

- ✪ **Numeric data** relating to the items will be stored as a numeric data type. This will be all the numbers involved in the problem, e.g. the number of students entered for GNVQ ICT, the number entered for GNVQ Leisure and Tourism, and so on. It is important that these items are entered with 100 per cent accuracy. All calculations will be based on this data, so if anything is incorrect, the results will be incorrect too

✪ **Dates** may be used to label rows or columns, or be part of the data used in a calculation. This may happen, for example, if the fine on a library book depends on the numbers of days it is overdue. Dates that are simply row or column labels can be entered as text. Dates used for calculations are actually stored as numbers in the spreadsheet

✪ **Formulae** are used to make the calculations required to solve a problem. This could be a simple **total**, e.g. the cost of a list of items (calculated using a column sum), or a more complicated **calculation**, e.g. the cost of a quantity of goods (calculated as quantity $\times$ price), or the VAT due on an item (calculated as $0.175 \times$ price)

Calculations are the most important part of a spreadsheet, so we now look at them in some detail.

Calculations

Calculations can be done automatically by the spreadsheet software, so writing the formulae to perform the calculations is an important part of solving the numerical processing problem. All calculations that can be done on a calculator can also be done using spreadsheet software. This includes the usual four arithmetic operations:

✪ Addition

✪ Subtraction

✪ Multiplication

✪ Division

Activity 2.26

Find out how to add two data items in a spreadsheet.

> Look in the on-line help for 'addition'.

Find out how to subtract one data item from another.

What symbols do you use for multiplication and division?

How do you make sure the result appears in a particular cell?

To help you to write formulae, the spreadsheet software offers lots of built-in **functions**.

Activity 2.27

Find out what functions are available with your spreadsheet software.

One special function allows you to **sum** a row or column of numeric data items. You must tell the software where to start adding, where to stop and where to put the result. Exactly how this is done will depend on your software.

Activity 2.28

★ Copy the data shown in Figure 2.14

★ In cell B4 enter this formula:
+SUM(B1..B3)

★ What happens?

★ In cell B4, enter this formula instead:
+SUM(B1,B3)

★ What happens?

▼ ▼ ▼ ▼ ▼ ▼ ▼ ▼ ▼

The **SUM function** displays the result of adding the contents of cells. Two dots are used to identify a **range of cells**. B1..B3 means B1, B2 and B3

▲ ▲ ▲ ▲ ▲ ▲ ▲ ▲ ▲

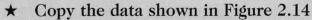

OCC Online Cruising Club

In the spreadsheet shown in Figure 2.9, formulae have been used to calculate the total number of members (207 displayed in cell C10), the income from subs for each category of membership (£0, £8,820, and so on in column E), the total expected subscription income (£10,230 in cell E10) and the average subscription income per member (£49 in cell E11).

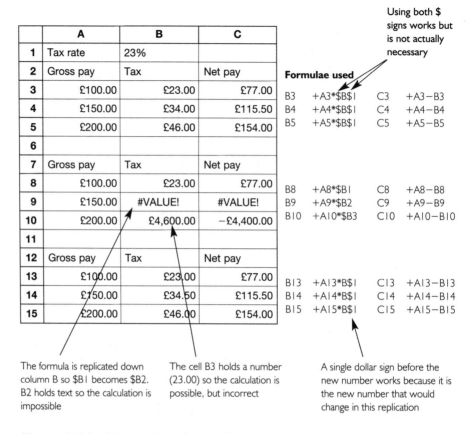

	A	B	C
1	Tax rate	23%	
2	Gross pay	Tax	Net pay
3	£100.00	£23.00	£77.00
4	£150.00	£34.00	£115.50
5	£200.00	£46.00	£154.00
6			
7	Gross pay	Tax	Net pay
8	£100.00	£23.00	£77.00
9	£150.00	#VALUE!	#VALUE!
10	£200.00	£4,600.00	−£4,400.00
11			
12	Gross pay	Tax	Net pay
13	£100.00	£23.00	£77.00
14	£150.00	£34.50	£115.50
15	£200.00	£46.00	£154.00

Using both $ signs works but is not actually necessary

Formulae used

B3	+A3*B1	C3	+A3−B3
B4	+A4*B1	C4	+A4−B4
B5	+A5*B1	C5	+A5−B5

B8	+A8*$B1	C8	+A8−B8
B9	+A9*$B2	C9	+A9−B9
B10	+A10*$B3	C10	+A10−B10

B13	+A13*B$1	C13	+A13−B13
B14	+A14*B$1	C14	+A14−B14
B15	+A15*B$1	C15	+A15−B15

The formula is replicated down column B so $B1 becomes $B2. B2 holds text so the calculation is impossible

The cell B3 holds a number (23.00) so the calculation is possible, but incorrect

A single dollar sign before the new number works because it is the new number that would change in this replication

Figure 2.14 *Using a formula to add the contents of cells*

Activity 2.29

Find out how to add all the numeric data items in a single row of a spreadsheet. Write notes to explain this process to someone who does not know how to use your spreadsheet software.
What happens if you try to add up items that are not numeric?

The **IF function** allows you to control what appears in a particular cell depending on a condition. The **AVERAGE function** adds the contents of a range of cells and then divides by the number of cells, producing the average for those cells.

Activity 2.30

Access some spreadsheets and look at the formulae they use. Look in particular at the IF and AVERAGE functions. Work out which cells are linked to other cells by formulae.

When you write a formula, you will refer to other cells using the **cell reference**. If you want to copy a formula, you have two options:

✪ **Relative cell referencing** results in the copy of the formula being correct 'relative' to its new position.

✪ **Absolute cell referencing** results in an exact copy of the formula, with no change being made to take its new position into account.

In Figure 2.12 the formula in cell B7 is +SUM(B3..B6). It adds the other numbers in column B. This formula was replicated across row 7. Table 2.5 shows the contents of the other cells in row 7. Notice that when copying across a row, the column numbers are changed automatically.

Replication: copying the contents of one cell to a range of other cells

Use **replication** to copy formulae wherever possible. If you enter the formula only once, you have only one chance of making a mistake. If you enter it many times, you are quite likely to introduce an error.

Cell reference	Contents	Displayed value
A7	TOTAL	TOTAL
B7	+SUM(B3..B6)	123.00
C7	+SUM(C3..C6)	163.00
D7	+SUM(D3..D6)	209.00
E7	+SUM(E3..E6)	88.00
F7	+SUM(F3..F6)	583.00

Table 2.5 *Formulae in row 7 of the spreadsheet shown in Figure 2.12*

Activity 2.31

Copy the data for the OCC subscription forecast into a spreadsheet.

Use the same alignment as shown in Figure 2.9 and use formulae to calculate the income from subs and the totals. Use today's date rather than 30-Apr-00.

Calculate the average – what is the actual average? Display this average with two decimal places (instead of none as shown in Figure 2.9).

OCC Online Cruising Club

The sailing secretary wants to design a spreadsheet to keep track of the number of bookings made to date, and to calculate the expected income from charter fees.

In total, 24 sailing trips are planned for the 2000 season, as shown in Figure 2.15. Notice that each sail lasts for two, three, four, seven, fourteen or fifteen days. The charter fee is £26 per day. A maximum of ten people can sail together, but if there are fewer than five, the trip may have to be cancelled.

Activity 2.32

Using the data from Figure 2.15, create a spreadsheet with at least 28 rows and at least eight columns to solve the OCC's numerical processing problem.

Adjust column widths to suit the data and choose appropriate display options. Include a main title, column headings and row headings as shown in Figure 2.15.

Use formulae to calculate the total number of sailing days, berth days, the total expected charter based on the number of bookings to date, and the maximum charter income if all ten berths are taken on every sail.

Use the IF function to display a warning message for trips that may have to be cancelled.

Print out your spreadsheet. Write notes on how you solved this numerical processing problem and the calculations used in the spreadsheet.

Trip	Trip details	Departs	Days	Booked	Berth days	£ Due	Cancel?
1	Basic training weekend	21–Apr–00	2	8	16	£416	
2	Open Days	28–Apr–00	2	8	16	£416	
3	Weekend Sail	05–May–00	2	5	10	£260	
4	Family weekend sail	12–May–00	2	10	20	£520	
5	Weekend sail	19–May–00	2	10	20	£520	
6	Royal Escape Race	25–May–00	4	10	40	£1,040	
7	Weekend sail	31–May–00	4	9	36	£936	
8	Round the Island Race	08–Jun–00	3	7	21	£546	
9	Haslar to Brittany passage	17–Jun–00	7	5	35	£910	
10	Brittany cruise	24–Jun–00	14	9	126	£3,276	
11	Brittany & Golfe de Gascogne cruise	08–Jul–00	14	7	98	£2,548	
12	North coast of Spain cruise	22–Jul–00	14	10	140	£3,640	
13	North coast of Spain cruise	05–Aug–00	14	10	140	£3,640	
14	North coast of Spain cruise	19–Aug–00	14	7	98	£2,548	
15	North coast of Spain cruise	02–Sep–00	7	10	70	£1,820	
16	Northern Spain to Haslar passage	09–Sep–00	15	6	90	£2,340	
17	Weekend sail	29–Sep–00	2	7	14	£364	
18	Weekend sail	06–Oct–00	2	2	4	£104	cancel?
19	Regatta	13–Oct–00	2	7	14	£364	
20	Basic training weekend	20–Oct–00	2	1	2	£52	cancel?
21	Weekend sail	27–Oct–00	2	3	6	£156	cancel?
22	Advanced training weekend	03–Nov–00	2	5	10	£260	
23	Weekend sail	10–Nov–00	2	3	6	£156	cancel?
24	Weekend sail	17–Nov–00	2	1	2	£52	cancel?
	Number of sailing days		136			£26,884	
	Number of berth days			160			
	Maximum income from sailing berths					£35,360	

Figure 2.15 *OCC's sailing programme and bookings*

Spreadsheet facilities

Once a spreadsheet has been set up, many facilities are on offer:

✪ You can **interrogate** the spreadsheet to find information, print selected parts of the spreadsheet or the whole worksheet

- ✪ You can create **charts** and **graphs** automatically to present the data in a more user-friendly way

- ✪ You can use trial-and-improvement techniques to carry out a **what if? query** and hence to solve a particular prediction problem

Interrogating a spreadsheet

In Activity 2.5 on page 83, you explored the **Find function** in word-processing software. The Find function works differently in a spreadsheet: you can search by rows or columns, and look in cells, notes or within formulae.

Activity 2.33

Explore the Find function in your spreadsheet software. Write notes on how it differs from the Find function in your word-processing software. Explore the **Filter function** in your spreadsheet software.

A **printout** of a spreadsheet usually shows the values for each cell, rather than the formulae that were used to calculate these values.

Document your spreadsheet by showing the formulae used.

Find out how to control how much of a spreadsheet is printed, and how to control **pagination**. Find out if your spreadsheet software allows you to print out the formulae used in each cell.

Charts and graphs

When you present numerical information in the form of line graphs or charts they should be made easy to understand. Spreadsheet software provides many facilities to title and label graphical information appropriately and clearly:

✪ Main titles on charts

✪ Axis titles and axis scale labels

✪ Legend titles

✪ Data or series labels

✪ Colours and patterns

OCC Online Cruising Club

Figure 2.16 shows two pie charts created from the OCC membership spreadsheet. The first pie chart shows the breakdown of members by type. The majority of members are full members.

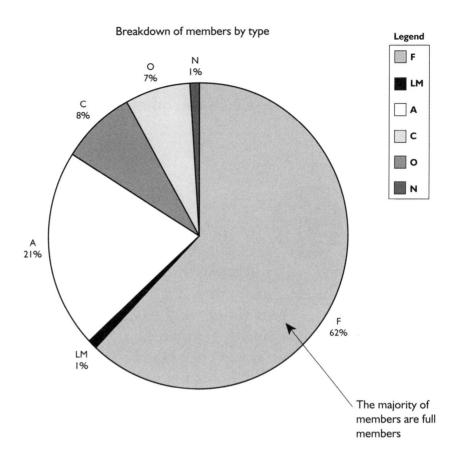

Breakdown of members by type

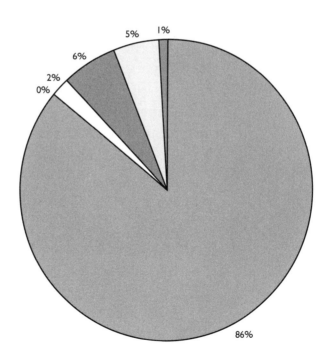

Figure 2.16 *OCC membership by type: pie chart*

Exercise 2.19

What does the other pie chart show?

Activity 2.35

Using your on-line help facility, watch the demonstration of how to create a bar chart. Make notes if you think you will not be able to remember what to do.

Using the spreadsheet you created in Activity 2.31, produce a bar chart to show the number of berths booked on each trip to date.

> Make sure you include a main title and titles for both axes.

Why would it *not* be appropriate to produce a bar chart for the expected charter income for each trip? If you are not sure, produce this chart and see how informative it is.

What other charts might be useful for this particular spreadsheet?

A **break-even point** is where there is no profit and no loss – you have broken even. The point may be a point in time, or a certain number of items that need to be sold to break even

Exploring trends and predicting results

One purpose of a spreadsheet is to explore trends and to predict results. You can calculate **break-even points** and carry out 'what if?' queries using spreadsheet software.

To carry out a **what if? query**, you must loop through a number of steps:

1. Set up the data in a spreadsheet. Your spreadsheet is then a **model** of the real-life situation

2. Identify what particular cell (or cells) hold the data that you are trying to maximise or minimise or meet some criteria

3. Identify what options you have, i.e. what cells hold data that you can change

4. Try a new value. It does not really matter what value you try

5. See what happens. Did your new value make the situation better? Or worse? Are you heading in the right direction even? Maybe you need to go further in the same direction, or maybe you went too far

Repeat steps 4 and 5 until you are close enough to your solution to want to stop. For some problems, you have to find the exact solution; for others you just need to be close.

OCC Online Cruising Club

Each year, Gerry has to balance the money collected from members with that spent on the upkeep of *Overload*, the club's yacht. If Gerry knows that an extra £500 may be needed next year for mooring fees, he might suggest to Linda that she try to recruit more members. Another option is to increase the membership fees. If Gerry changes the data in columns C or D of the spreadsheet shown in Figure 2.9, this affects the amount shown in column E, especially the total subscriptions. From this, using trial and improvement, Gerry could work out how many more members are needed and/or by how much to increase the annual subscription.

A 'what if?' query is very like trial and improvement, which you may remember from your maths classes. It helps if you keep a note of all your trials. Figure 2.17 shows a spreadsheet used to calculate the square root of 3, and the trials that were used to reach the 'answer'.

	A	B	C	D	E	F	G
1	Calculating the square root of			3			
2						Root is between	
3				Square it	Too big or too small?	0	3
4	First guess		1.5	2.25	too small	1.5	3
5	Next guess		2.25	5.0625	too big	1.5	2.25
6	Next guess		1.875	3.515625	too big	1.5	1.875
7	Next guess		1.6875	2.847656	too small	1.6875	1.875
8	Next guess		1.78125	3.172852	too big	1.6875	1.78125
9	Next guess		1.734375	3.008057	too big	1.6875	1.734375
10	Next guess		1.710938	2.927307	too small	1.710938	1.734375
11	Next guess		1.722656	2.967545	too small	1.722656	1.734375
12	Next guess		1.728516	2.987766	too small	1.728516	1.734375
13	Next guess		1.731445	2.997903	too small	1.731445	1.734375
14	Next guess		1.73291	3.002978	too big	1.731445	1.73291
15	Next guess		1.732178	3.00044	too big	1.731445	1.732178
16	Next guess		1.731812	2.999171	too small	1.731812	1.732178
17	Next guess		1.731995	2.999805	too small	1.731995	1.732178
18	Next guess		1.732086	3.000123	too big	1.731995	1.732086
19	Next guess		1.73204	2.999964	too small	1.73204	1.732086
20	Next guess		1.732063	3.000043	too big	1.73204	1.732063
21	Next guess		1.732052	3.000004	too big	1.73204	1.732052
22	Next guess		1.732046	2.999984	too small	1.732046	1.732052
23	Next guess		1.732049	2.999994	too small	1.732049	1.732052
24	Next guess		1.73205	2.999999	too small	1.73205	1.732052
25	Next guess		1.732051	3.000001	too big	1.73205	1.732051
26	Next guess		1.732051	3	too small	1.732051	1.732051
27	Next guess		1.732051	3.000001	too big	1.732051	1.732051

Annotations (pointing to rows):
- $\sqrt{3} = 1$ to the nearest whole number → 7
- $\sqrt{3} = 1.7$ (correct to 1 d.p.) → 9
- $\sqrt{3} = 1.73$ (correct to 3 d.p.) → 14
- $\sqrt{3} = 1.732$ (correct to 3 d.p.) → 19
- $\sqrt{3} = 1.7320$ (correct to 4 d.p.) → 19
- $\sqrt{3} = 1.73205$ (correct to 5 d.p.) → 25
- $\sqrt{3} = 1.732051$ (correct to 6 d.p.) → 27

Figure 2.17 *Trial and improvement: continue until you have the accuracy you want*

Activity 2.36

The formulae used in the spreadsheet shown in Figure 2.17 are listed in Table 2.6. The formulae in cells C5, D4, E4, F4 and G4 need to be replicated, for as many rows as you want to make guesses.

Enter the data but amend it to calculate the square root of 3, or 8. How many guesses does it take to get an answer correct to six decimal places?

Try to amend the spreadsheet so that it will work out the square root of any number placed in a particular cell, e.g. D1.

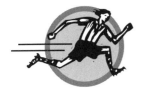

Cell reference	Formula
D4	C4 ≥ C4
E4	=IF(D4 > 5, "too big", "too small"
F4	=IF(D4<5,C4,F3)
G4	=IF(D4 > 5,C4,G3)
C5	+(F4+G4)/2

Table 2.6 *Formulae used in the spreadsheet shown in Figure 2.17*

OCC Online Cruising Club

As the year progresses more bookings are received, but some people also cancel their bookings. The total bookings as at 1 June are shown in Table 2.7.

Trip number	Berths booked	Trip number	Berths booked	Trip number	Berths booked
1	9	9	8	17	8
2	10	10	10	18	4
3	4	11	9	19	7
4	10	12	10	20	6
5	10	13	10	21	4
6	10	14	7	22	4
7	10	15	10	23	8
8	8	16	8	24	2

Table 2.7 *Up-to-date sail trip bookings*

Refer to the spreadsheet that you designed for Activity 2.31 on page 124.

★ Update the spreadsheet so that the bookings to date are correct

★ **What if** you assume that trips for which five or fewer bookings are made will not sail? What effect does this have on expected charter income?

Ideally, on average, each trip that sails should have a minimum of eight bookings.

★ Amend your spreadsheet to work out 80 per cent occupancy for each trip, and calculate the total charter income if this were to be achieved

★ Identify which trips should be advertised most strongly, so that trips might not be cancelled

★ Perform a 'what if?' query to find out how many extra berths must be booked to achieve 80 per cent occupancy

Activity 2.38

Choose one spreadsheet that you have already created or create another to put in your portfolio.

★ Include a description of the spreadsheet and annotated printed output demonstrating its operation and showing how it meets user needs

★ Describe clearly the purpose of the spreadsheet, the information to be processed and the processing required

★ Create and use suitable spreadsheet row heights, column widths, cell formats and formulae

★ Use spreadsheet facilities to enter data, sort, search, investigate what happens to the output result when input values are changed, and produce different types of chart or line graph

★ Annotate your printed reports so that it is clear why and how all printed items are produced

Remember to check the accuracy of your data and to keep backup copies of all files.

Revision questions

1. What is the difference between data and information?

2. Name three different sources of information.

3. Explain the difference between the insert and overtype modes of data entry.

4. What is a toggle key?

5. What is the difference between searching and sorting?

6. Explain how entries are ordered in an index.

7. Give two examples of ascending order and two examples of descending order.

8. Give two examples of a relational operator and two examples of a logical operator.

9. Which logical operator can be used to narrow down a search?

10. Explain the difference between a table, a record and a field.

11. Explain what is meant by a primary key field.

12. Which data structure is presented in cells, in rows and columns?

13. Which cell is the active cell?

14. What is the difference between a pie chart and a bar chart?

15. Explain how to perform a 'what if?' query.

Hardware and Software

3

- Choose hardware and software for an ICT system

- Configure the software for an ICT system

- Create templates and macros

This chapter looks in detail at hardware and software and then focuses on macros.

You should try to identify some local organisations that may give you information about the hardware and software they use.

Several case studies and examples are used to introduce and illustrate the ideas of this chapter. Background information about these organisations is given in the Case Studies section of this book, starting on page xvii.

This unit is assessed only through an external assessment. You will have to undertake some tasks before the test and take this work into the external assessment with you. The grade on that assessment will be your grade for the unit. Information about how to prepare for the external test is given in the Examination Guide on page 447.

Hardware

These are the five main **hardware components** of an ICT system (Figure 3.1):

- ✪ Input devices

- ✪ Output devices

- ✪ Main processing unit

- ✪ Memory devices

- ✪ Storage devices

Cables and connectors hold everything together.

Activity 3.1

Make a copy of Figure 3.1 and label it with the items of equipment in your own ICT system.

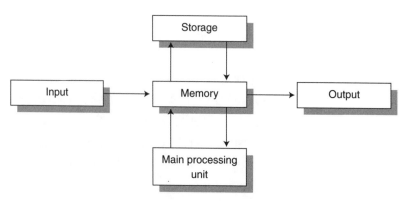

Figure 3.1 *Main components of an ICT system*

Input devices

Input devices allow data to be entered for the first time into an ICT system. This is called **primary input**.

Exercise 3.1

This section looks at different types of input device: keyboard, mouse and scanner.
Can you think of any other input devices? If so, make notes on their features and purpose.

Keyboard

A **keyboard** (Figure 3.2) is the most common input device for ICT systems. Keyboards have lots of keys, but these are not necessarily the same for all computers; nor is the arrangement of keys the same. Most keyboards have three parts:

✪ The main part is most likely to be arranged as on a traditional typewriter, i.e. a **QWERTY keyboard**

✪ Another section may have a block of keys for the digits 0–9. It may also have keys for add, subtract, multiply and divide, and an Enter key. This part is called the **numeric keypad**

✪ There may also be **special keys**, e.g. Enter (or Return), Escape (Esc), Control (Ctrl) and some function keys labelled F1 to F12. What these keys do depends on the software being used rather than the hardware

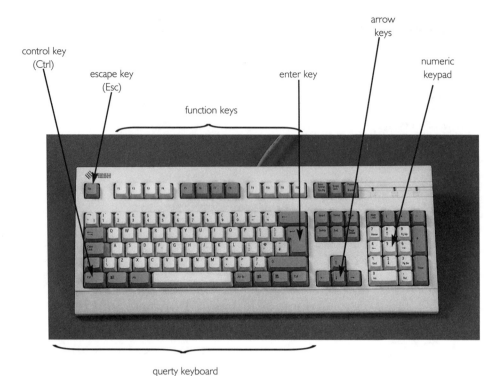

control key
(Ctrl)

escape key
(Esc)

function keys

enter key

arrow
keys

numeric
keypad

querty keyboard

Figure 3.2 *Typical keyboard layout*

Activity
3.2

Find out what features your word-processing
software provides for users who cannot use
the standard QWERTY keyboard.
Find out what function key operations are
available with your spreadsheet software. Do these
keys have the same function in your database
software?

Some keyboards are specially adapted. Some primary schools
introduce children to a **concept keyboard** first, because when
very young, children have difficulty in pressing only one key of a
'normal' size accurately. Instead, overlays are used with special
software, and these may represent different colours, or different
shapes for the child to choose from.

Chris Lane

The bar staff use a concept keyboard to record purchases, e.g. an orange juice and a packet of nuts. The prices are automatic, so the bar staff do not need to remember the prices of any items.

Exercise 3.2

In what other situations are concept keyboards used? Find out about other ways in which keyboards have been adapted to meet the needs of some users.

Mouse

A **mouse** is a pointing device (Figure 3.3), usually connected to the computer by a thin cable. Moving the mouse across a flat surface (a **mouse mat**) causes a cursor, or pointer, on the display screen to move to a new insertion point. A mouse has one or more finger-operated switches, called (mouse) **buttons**.

Pressing a mouse button is called **clicking**, because this usually produces a 'click' sound.

- ✪ If you **left click** the mouse in a new position on the screen, this position becomes your **insertion point**, and you can start keying

- ✪ If you **left click** when the pointer controlled by the

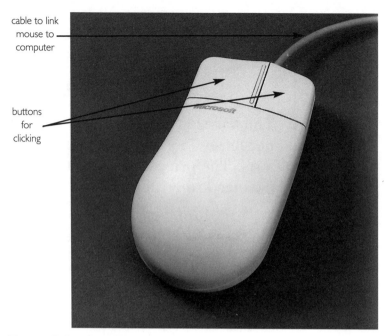

Figure 3.3 *Typical mouse*

mouse is on an icon, or a screen button, then the operation represented by that icon (or button) may be **selected**

✪ A **right click** may result in a menu of options, relevant to your position on the screen, being displayed. This can save time

Exercise 3.3

Modern designs of mouse include a third control – a roller positioned between the two main buttons. Find out what extra features this type of mouse offers the user.

Some software expects the mouse button to be pressed twice in quick succession. This is called **double clicking**.

Activity 3.3

Notice how the cursor design changes as you move it around the screen in three separate software applications, such as word processing, spreadsheets and databases. Find out what happens when you left click, right click or double click – for each cursor design.

Did You Know?

A **trackerball** is a ball, set into a cup, that can be made to roll in any direction by using a finger or the palm of a hand, depending on the size of the ball. Trackerballs are now sometimes mounted on laptop computers, being easier to use in this position than a mouse

Dragging – moving the mouse while holding down a button – is used to move an area of a screen display from one location to another. Before such movement can take place, the text to be moved has to be highlighted or the graphic marked, e.g. by its boundaries. Moving things around in this way is called **drag-and-drop editing**. This may also be used to copy part of a screen display.

Mouse operations, such as clicking, dragging or combining these with the use of keys on the keyboard, provide a wide range of possible options at any moment. Actions such as pressing or releasing the mouse buttons are called **mouse events**.

Activity 3.4

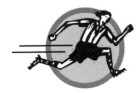

Using the mouse is not the only way to move around the screen. The arrow keys can also be used. Table 3.1 shows some shortcuts keys to use instead of the mouse. Find out what other keys can be used to move quickly through a document:

★ to the beginning or end of a line
★ to the beginning or end of the document

To move	Press this key
One character to the right	Right arrow
One word to the right	Ctrl + right arrow
Down one line	Down arrow
Down one screen	Page down
Down one page	Alt + Ctrl + page down

Table 3.1 *Shortcuts for moving around a document*

Scanner

A **scanner** is an input device that allows you to transfer data, e.g. from a sheet of paper, straight to the computer. It looks and works very much like a photocopier. It shines a light across the paper and measures the reflected light. These light levels are turned into a bitmap file and can then be processed using graphics software.

Hawkes Design

Peter has a scanner with a transparency adaptor. It scans prints up to A4 size. It also scans slides and transparencies.

Sailing Breaks

John Hore has a combined scanner, copier and ink-jet printer. John works from home, and he chose an all-in-one device to reduce the space used on his desk.

Output devices

Data display is the purpose of most output devices – the screen and printer in particular. Display of data is an important part of data entry; it shows the operator what has been keyed in, so it can be checked against the original input document. This is called **screen verification**.

Display is also necessary for **interaction** between the operator and the ICT system. **Menus** are displayed, and the operator makes a choice; **messages** are displayed if the operator does something strange, or if the equipment does not perform as expected.

Output devices present the data that has been processed in the computer as information for the user.

Exercise 3.4

This section looks at VDUs, printers and speakers. Can you think of any other output devices? If so, make notes on their features and purpose.

Visual output is presented on a screen.

Printed output – called **hard copy** – is often a main product of an ICT system: invoices, payslips, management reports, letters to clients, and so on. It is produced on a **printer** or a **plotter**. Hard copies of data are **portable**. They can be taken away from the computer area or passed on to someone else. This may be more suitable than giving them a copy of the data on disk.

When **interrogating** a database, the number of matches may be one or two, and you could copy this information from the screen, or just remember it. If the query resulted in 200 matches, it would make more sense to have a printout of the records.

Aural output is presented using a loudspeaker, e.g. an alarm bell ringing in a security system.

VDU

VDU stands for **visual display unit**. A VDU is sometimes called a **screen** or **monitor**. The screen displays information in a similar way to a TV except that it cannot receive TV signals. Instead, signals are sent from the computer for display on the screen. The **size** of screen is the diagonal length of the screen (Figure 3.4). The VDU **control panel** allows you to adjust the brightness and contrast of the display.

control buttons and wheels allow you to adjust the display

dimension of screen (e.g. 14")

on/off switch

swivel base allows positioning of screen to suit user

Figure 3.4 *Typical monitor or display*

Activity 3.5

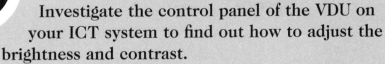

Investigate the control panel of the VDU on your ICT system to find out how to adjust the brightness and contrast.
What other controls are available? Check you know what they do, and the setting that best suits your system.

Exercise 3.5

Why were screen savers invented? What is their purpose?
What is a screen filter? What is its purpose?

Monitors can be **monochrome**, displaying one colour, e.g. white, green or orange, on a dark (usually black) background. **Colour monitors** display in many different colours according to the type of screen and computer being used.

Hawkes Design

Peter Hawkes uses two 21-inch colour monitors. This size of screen allows him to view two A4 pages at actual size at the same time – essential for his work.

Activity 3.6

What screen sizes are available for a stand-alone PC? What are the advantages and disadvantages of the various sizes?
Find out how much the larger screens cost to buy compared with smaller screens.

Printers

Printers are used to produce hard copies of data as a permanent record. The type of printer used, e.g. ink-jet or laser, depends on the quality of output required, the speed of printing needed and the cost.

Ink-jet printers (Figure 3.5) 'squirt' small bubbles of ink at the page, so these are sometimes called **bubble-jet printers**. The paper must be of good quality, otherwise the printing may 'bleed', giving a poor result. Colour printing offers good opportunities to produce excellent artwork and designs. Ink-jet printers are inexpensive to buy, but the print cartridges can prove expensive.

▼▼▼▼▼▼▼▼▼

Consumables are the things you use with an ICT system that are consumed by the system and need replacing. Examples include paper, ink cartridges and floppy disks

▲▲▲▲▲▲▲▲▲

Laser printers (Figure 3.6) work on the same principle as a photocopier. A laser beam 'draws' the shape on to an electrostatically charged light-sensitive drum. This drum rotates over a source of **toner** – powdered ink – which sticks to the parts of the drum that have been affected by the laser beam. The drum then rotates over a sheet of paper, and the toner sticks to the paper as it passes. Laser printers offer good **resolution** but are expensive to buy and to run. Toner cartridges need replacing frequently, and running costs can be high.

Exercise 3.6

Find out what 'resolution' means.

instructions

paper

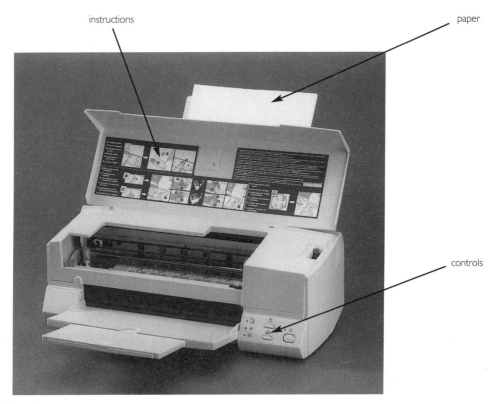

controls

Figure 3.5 *Ink-jet printer*

paper fed
in here

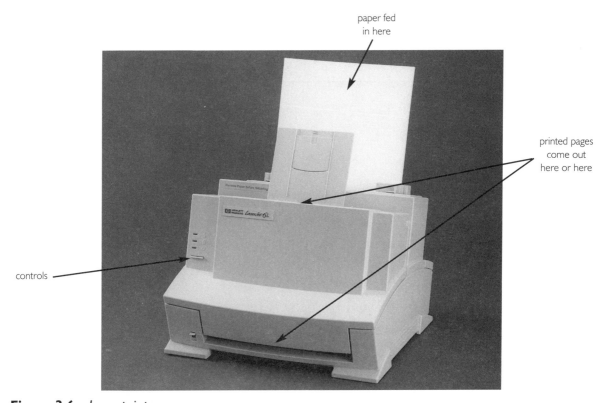

printed pages
come out
here or here

controls

Figure 3.6 *Laser printer*

Hawkes Design

Peter has a B&W (greyscale) laser printer which prints onto A4 and A3 edge-to-edge, i.e. with no white border. Peter also has a colour ink-jet printer, which prints up to super A3 size, i.e. A3 plus the crop marks, which he uses to position the pages correctly when they go to a professional printer for publication.

Sailing Breaks

John Hore has a laser printer, which he uses for high-quality printing of his course notes for the shore-based RYA course that he teaches.

Activity 3.7

For each of four different printers, investigate what features are offered, and at what price. Find out how much the consumables, such as ink cartridges, cost. Include laser printers as well as ink-jet printers, and present your findings as a table or a chart.

Activity 3.8

For each printer that is available to you, check that you understand how to load paper correctly.

Find out what to do if the ink runs out. Check that you know how to replace consumables correctly. Find out what to do if there is a paper jam. What can you do to avoid paper jams?

Loudspeaker

Nowadays, PCs are multimedia systems, and you can listen to a music CD played through the loudspeakers while working on a PC. For the loudspeaker to produce music (or any other sounds), a **sound card** is needed in the computer. Sound can also be used as output in a number of other situations.

Activity 3.9

Find out what opportunities you have to hear sounds on your ICT system. Make notes.

Input/output devices – memory and storage devices

Some devices are used for input *and* output. These are called storage devices. Storage devices are an essential part of an IT system. There are two main types: internal and external devices.

- ✪ **Internal devices** – within the computer itself – are called **memory** devices

- ✪ **External devices** – connected to the computer by cables from the I/O ports – are called **storage** devices

Memory is where data items are held. These items are made up of files – either program files or data files.

Memory is measured in **bits** (binary digits). One bit can hold 0 or 1. Bits are grouped into bytes (8 bits = 1 byte). A **byte** has enough bits to represent numbers from 1 to 256, and these are used to represent characters.

Exercise 3.7

How many bytes are there in a kilobyte?
How many bytes are there in a megabyte? In a gigabyte? In a terabyte?

Did You Know?

Kb is short for kilobyte. Mb is short for megabyte. Gb is short for gigabyte. Tb is short for terabyte

Computer memory serves two purposes:

- ✪ To hold programs or data that the processor needs immediately – in the **immediate access store (IAS)**

- ✪ To hold data that may be needed at some time – in the **backing store**, e.g. on a tape drive or a zip disk

Did You Know?

Immediate access memory is usually about 1000 times as fast as the backing store

IAS memory must be able to be read (and be written to) very quickly, but backup memory can have much slower reading and writing times.

Note that memory is different from storage:

- ✪ In memory, data is immediately available. This is the **primary** memory, but it may also be called main memory, or the store

✪ From storage, data has to be retrieved, e.g. from a floppy disk or the hard disk drive. This is called **secondary** storage but is more usually called the backing store

Did You Know?

For files to be **portable**, they are usually stored on a floppy disk or CD. The file can then be output from one ICT system and input to another

The **backing store** provides long-term storage on disk or tape and, when you **back up** your data files, you do so to a backing store. It is a permanent store on a device attached to the IT system, e.g. the hard disk, a zip drive or a rewritable CD.

The backing store allows you to access data files that are much larger than the capacity of your computer memory. It also allows data and programs to be **portable**, i.e. they can be moved from one computer to another.

Exercise 3.8

What is the memory capacity of your ICT system? What device is used to back up files on your ICT system? What alternative devices could be used? What are the advantages and disadvantages of your backup system compared with an alternative system?

Memory is either **volatile** or **non-volatile**. Temporary (RAM) and permanent (ROM) stores exist within the computer housing itself. The difference between them is the type of storage used:

✪ **Volatile** memory holds data only while power is supplied and is therefore a **temporary** store

✪ **Non-volatile** memory keeps its contents even when the system is switched off. This **permanent memory** cannot be erased or altered by the user

All auxiliary stores (e.g. CDs, disks and tapes) are non-volatile and provide a permanent storage for data and programs. Some internal storage – the **read-only memory (ROM)** – is also permanent. It holds that part of the operating system needed on startup.

Some internal storage is temporary – the **random-access memory (RAM)**. It holds data that may change during the running of your programs.

All the storage locations in IAS memory can be acessed directly, and the access time for all locations is the same, i.e. they are accessed equally quickly. This is described as random-access memory (RAM). Data stored on a tape can only be reached by going through the tape, in sequence, until the right place is found; this is called **serial access**. Storage on a disk is in concentric rings and is a collection of small sequential lengths of storage. Since disk storage can be so quickly accessed, it is called **direct (random) access** storage.

When first introduced, CD-ROMs were (as the name suggests) read-only. Nowadays, recordable and rewritable CDs are available. **Write-once, read-many (WORM)** devices use a laser system to etch data on to a blank disc; the recorded data can then be read as often as needed but cannot be rewritten.

Exercise 3.9

DVDs are a recent invention. Find out all you can about them.

Activity 3.10

For an ICT system that you use, compare the different types of storage for:

★ Storage capacity
★ Read capability
★ Write capability
★ Cost

Disk

A **magnetic disk**, usually made of plastic, is coated with a layer of magnetic material on which data can be stored. Disks may have data stored on one side only (single-sided) or on both sides (double-sided). The disk may be rigid (a hard disk) or flexible (a floppy disk).

To use disk storage, you need two things:

✪ The **device** – the hardware machine to write to or read from the disk – which is called the **drive**

✪ The **medium** – the disk on which you write (or read from)

Peter Hawkes

Peter has an external CD drive and an external hard disk drive – for writing to 650 Mb CDs (for archive purposes). He has a zip drive for writing to 100 Mb zip disks – for backup and file transfer to clients. He also has a Syquest drive, but that is now obsolescent. For small files, Peter uses floppy disks.

A **disk drive** is the device or unit made up of the mechanism that rotates the disks between the read/write heads and the mechanism that controls these heads. Most disk drives have one set of read/write heads for each surface, which have to be moved to the required track. A disk unit with one set of heads for each disk track is called a **fixed-head disk unit**. This arrangement gives much faster access to data on the disk(s), but at increased cost.

A **hard disk drive** uses rigid magnetic disk(s) enclosed in a sealed container. It has the advantage of allowing high recording density, because the recording heads can be very close to the magnetic material on the disk.

floppy disk drive

hard disk drive (within processor)

Figure 3.7 *Floppy drive and hard drive*

A **CD-ROM drive** (sometimes called a CD-ROM player) is very similar to an audio compact disc player and is used to read CD-ROMs. A CD-ROM jukebox is a CD-ROM drive with a mechanism to change the current disc for another selected disc automatically.

Floppy disk drives use flexible disks, which can be removed from their drives by the user, unlike hard disks, which are permanently mounted in the computer.

A **floppy disk** (sometimes called a diskette) is protected by an outer covering that prevents the magnetic coating being damaged and keeps out dirt. Floppy disks are made to agreed standard designs and so can be used on any drive for the same-size disk. The commonest size is 3.5 inches.

Main processing unit

The main processing unit is the central part of every ICT system. All other items are referred to as **peripherals** – things on the side.

The main processing unit contains the decision-making part of the ICT system (Figure 3.8).

- ✪ Central processing unit (CPU)

- ✪ Memory (RAM and ROM)

- ✪ Ports (input and output connectors)

- ✪ Motherboard

The **CPU** controls every piece of hardware attached to it and all software running in it. The ability of a CPU is measured in terms of its speed of processing: the faster the processor, the more powerful the IT system. The amount of memory (RAM and ROM – see page 154) is also important. Generally speaking, more

front view of PC
with VDU

rear view of main
processing unit

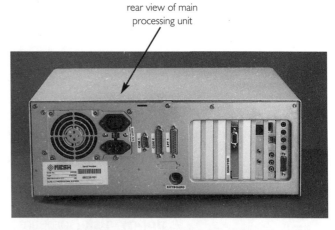

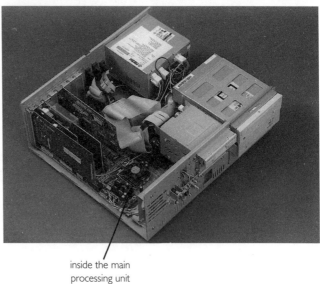

inside the main
processing unit

Figure 3.8   *Front, rear and inside views of a typical PC*

powerful machines are more expensive, although as time passes, newer machines are far more powerful than their predecessors yet the prices do not rise at the same rate.

There are a number of **ports** at the back of a computer (Figure 3.9). These connection points or sockets allow the internal circuits of a computer to be connected to peripheral devices, e.g. a printer.

The output ports allow **control signals** to be sent from the computer, and different kinds of port allow signals (continuous or pulsed) along two different types of cable. **Serial** cables can take only one bit of information at a time; **parallel** cable looks like a ribbon and can take several bits of information at the same time. Parallel connections allow faster transfer of information.

A **printer port** is the connection point for a printer. In the computer, an interface provides the electronic link between the processor and the printer. When the computer prints, a **software utility** called a **printer driver** changes the font and layout codes used in the computer into a form that the printer understands. Although several different printers may use the same port, each one may require a different printer driver.

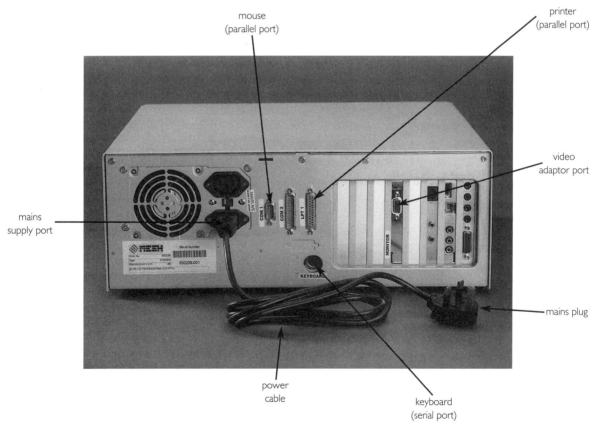

Figure 3.9 *Ports in the back of a typical PC*

Exercise 3.10

Make a list of the printers that are connected to the systems you use (at school, home and work).

★ Which ones are serial printers?
★ Which are parallel printers?
★ What printer drivers are available?

Cables and connectors

▼▼▼▼▼▼▼▼▼

Twisted-pair (TP) cable is a pair of insulated copper wires twisted together and surrounded by a copper braid and external insulation

▲▲▲▲▲▲▲▲▲

Wire is a standard form of cable used to provide the connections in a network:

✪ **Copper cables** tend to be used in local area networks (LANs), since they are readily available and have suitable electrical characteristics

✪ **Coaxial cable** is the same kind of cable that is used for connecting a TV aerial to a TV set. It has two conductors: one wire down the centre of the cable, which may be a single strand, insulated from a second wire, which is made up of many strands braided around the insulation for the inner wire

▼▼▼▼▼▼▼▼▼

Fibre-optic cable (or optical fibre) – a very fine glass strand – transmits data using light beams

▲▲▲▲▲▲▲▲▲

Exercise 3.11

What is an unshielded **twisted-pair (UTP)**? What are the benefits of **fibre-optic cable**?

Sailing Breaks

John Hore's BT Home Highway connection gives him two high-speed data connections for the Internet plus two analogue lines, one for voice and the other for fax.

Activity 3.11

Look carefully at the rear of an ICT system to see exactly how each peripheral has been attached to the main processing unit.

★ Make a note of how these peripherals are attached: mouse, keyboard, VDU and printer

★ Look carefully at the cable that connects each peripheral to the PC

★ Make a note of which peripherals have their own power supply cables

★ Look at the connectors. See whether they push into place, screw into place, or clip into place

At some point during your course, your teacher will ask you to show that you can connect an ICT system. When you do, make sure that you follow safety procedures. See the Good Working Practice Guide on page 417 for more details about this.

Software

The software – the elements of the system that are not hardware – is what makes the IT system do what you, the user, want it to do.

There are two main types of software:

- ✪ Operating systems

- ✪ Applications software

Sailing Breaks

John Hore uses a Windows ICT system: Windows 98 with MS Office – Word for writing and Excel for accounting. He also has Publisher 98, which is used to design brochures and his website. To scan in graphics, John has Corel Photo House 2, and for scanning OCR documents he uses OmniPage Pro 10.

Hawkes Design

Peter has two Apple Macintosh computers – as used by most graphic designers. The latest model is the G4, but Peter has the G3 (1999) and a PowerMac 8500/180 from 1996. Table 3.2 shows the software Peter Hawkes has on his system.

Type of software	Software installed on Peter Hawkes' system
Operating systems	Mac OS8.5
Applications software	Quark XPress – for page layout and design, typography
	Adobe Illustrator – for line graphs, diagrams and charts
	Adope Photoshop – for image manipulation, dealing with scanned images
	Microsoft Word – for text editing, translating text from PCs
	Xerox Textbridge – for OCR
	Adobe Streamline – for translating bitmap images to vector graphics
	Binuscan Photoperfect – for automatic colour balancing of scanned images
	Adobe Acrobat – for creating PDF files for transfer to various computer systems

Table 3.2 *Software on Peter Hawkes' system*

Exercise 3.12

For an ICT system that you use, produce a similar table listing all software available.

Operating system

Each ICT system is controlled by its operating system: a program resident in the computer (usually, at least in part, in ROM) built from lots of small programs, each of which controls some part of the hardware. Together, these programs allow the operator to use the computer. Operating systems are very complex, even those that control a simple stand-alone computer.

There are two main types of operating system: **command-driven** operating systems and operating systems with a **graphical user interface (GUI)**.

With a command-driven operating system, all communication with the user – the man–machine interface, or **human–computer interface (HCI)** – is done by the user keying in commands via the keyboard.

▼▼▼▼▼▼▼▼▼
WIMP stands for window, icon, mouse, pointer
▲▲▲▲▲▲▲▲▲

With a GUI, the user is presented with a screen on which icons appear, and communication will include the keyboard for text input, but a mouse is used most of the time, especially for selecting options. This is called a **WIMP environment**.

Sailing Breaks

John Hore works in a WIMP environment.

Find out which type of operating system is used on your computer. Use your computer system and another that has the other type of operating system.

★ For a command-driven operating system, list some commands that are used and explain their effect

★ For a system with a GUI, copy some of the icons that are presented on the screen and explain what happens when you select them

Which type of operating system do you prefer to use? Why? Discuss this with others in your group.

Table 3.3 lists the main functions of an operating system.

Function	Purpose
Startup	Checking that all the peripherals are working and properly connected
Security	Logging-on procedures, controlling user access, checking passwords
Communication	Receiving commands from the user (e.g. from the keyboard), displaying messages to the user (e.g. on the screen)
Control of peripherals	Sending data to a printer and communicating with the printer so that all data is printed, even though the printer prints slower than the computer sends the data to it
Control of memory	Keeping track of what is held on a disk by updating the disk directory
Error control	Checking data on entry and displaying messages if anything is not okay, e.g. a letter keyed into a numeric field

Table 3.3 *The main functions of an operating system*

Make a list of operating systems for stand-alone ICT systems that are currently on the market.

Default values are the values assumed by the manufacturer when you buy an ICT system

The **configuration** of an ICT system is the combination of hardware and software used in the system

Customising an operating system means making decisions about how you want it to present information

Configuring/customising an operating system

When an operating system is installed, a number of settings are preset at **default values**, and one of these is the **configuration**.

If the system assumes a standard keyboard, standard mouse, etc., and the user wants to use a special mouse or a higher-resolution screen, telling the operating system is called **configuring** the system. Some more modern operating systems do this automatically. Other default values relate to how the interface between the user and the machine will operate, e.g. the background colour on the screen, or security options, e.g. passwords.

All operating systems also allow the user to **customise** settings, i.e. to set up new default settings that will apply every time the system is powered up:

- ✪ Set up security passwords

- ✪ Include anti-virus checks

- ✪ Create directory structures (folders)

- ✪ Change the desktop appearance

- ✪ Provide icons or menus to start software

- ✪ Select the language to be used

- ✪ Set or select keyboard properties

- ✪ Select suitable printer drivers

If you have your own ICT system at home, setting up **security passwords** may be one of the first things you decide to do.

It makes a lot of sense to include **anti-virus checks** on an ICT system. Sometimes viruses are date-dependent, i.e. they have no effect until a certain date, and then they activate, filling your screen with daft messages or images, for example. Viruses can infect your ICT system if you allow them to be introduced. They transfer from machine to machine via disk files, so if you accept a floppy disk from someone else, that disk may be infected.

Anti-virus software is produced to prevent virus infection. It scans files and warns you if a virus is found. It can then try to 'clean' the disk. New viruses are being invented all the time, so the virus-protection industry is thriving.

Exercise 3.14

Find out what anti-virus software is used on your school or college system.

If you like, you can change the screen prompts or **desktop appearance**.

You may decide that it is useful to have a clock and today's date visible on your screen at all times.

Explore the options available to you to change the desktop appearance on your ICT system. Make notes on the options and list the current default values.

Keyboard settings such as the reaction time can be controlled, usually using the Control Panel utility.

Exercise 3.15

Find out the current default value for the keyboard reaction time on your ICT system.

Activity 3.14

Find out what other things you can change using the Control Panel.
Change the mouse settings so that the right and left buttons are interchanged. Use the mouse like this, then change the settings back to how they were originally.

Quite soon after using an ICT system for the first time, the number of files increases to the point where, unless you set up **directory structures (folders)**, you will have great difficulty in finding anything at all. The structure is like a tree – except that it is upside down. At the top is the **root directory**. Beneath this, the first level of files or **subdirectories** leads on to further subdirectories.

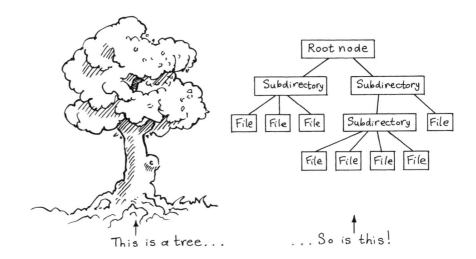

This is a tree...   ... So is this!

Activity 3.15

Find out what directories already exist on your ICT system. Find out how to create a new directory (folder).

When installing new applications software in a WIMP environment, the software often provides icons or menus automatically to start the software and open specific files. This then allows you, the user, just to click on the icon to start the software.

Exercise 3.16

Identify icons that start software applications automatically.

Activity 3.16

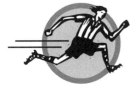

Find out how many different ways you could start an application *without* using the icons provided.

> Your on-line help may offer several ways of starting software.

As noted on page 160, all printers can be connected to the printer port on an ICT system, but you have to select an appropriate printer driver so that the codes sent by the computer are understood correctly by the printer.

Activity 3.17

In Exercise 3.13 you discovered which printer drivers are available on your ICT system.

★ Choose a one-page document (or one page from a longer document) that includes more than one font

★ Change the printer driver to one for a completely different make of printer and see what effect this has on printing a document

★ Change the printer driver to one for a different model but the same make of printer

> Changing to an 'older' or 'newer' driver than your actual printer may produce interesting effects.

Activity 3.18

With a particular user in mind, describe basic specifications for input and output devices, the main processing unit, software and configuration requirements to meet your user's needs by identifying their purpose and properties.

For a different user, provide detailed definitions of input and output devices and accurate descriptions of the main processing unit, software and configuration requirements to meet this second user's needs, including their purpose and properties.

> Choose your two users to be as different as possible. Choose people whose jobs and hence their day-to-day use of ICT is very different, even if they are in a similar industry: someone on the move all day like a reporter, and someone based in an office or at home, e.g. an author.

Applications software

Once the computer has an operating system, you can load applications software to do a particular task, such as word processing or payroll. There are various types of application software to meet user needs:

- ✪ Document (word) processing and desktop publishing (DTP)

- ✪ Databases, spreadsheets and graphics

- ✪ Utilities, such as anti-virus checkers

Hawkes Design

Peter Hawkes has several applications packages.
See Table 3.2 on page 165.

Many of these applications are considered elsewhere in this
course:

✪ Unit 1 includes presentation of information using word
processing

✪ Unit 2 introduces spreadsheets and databases

✪ Unit 6 looks at graphics and DTP

✪ Unit 7 concentrates on multimedia systems

So you will have lots of opportunities to use applications software
during your course.

You must learn how to match applications software to users'
processing needs. For this, you need to recognise the main
features of the applications. *All* applications share these features:

✪ Programs are grouped to form a **package** or suite of
programs that together perform a particular function,
e.g. invoicing or database management

✪ A manufacturer of software will tend to use the same
operating methods for all its software, which makes it
easier for a user to learn new packages – the emphasis is
on **user-friendly** software

✪ Most software packages are **menu-driven**: you might
select using arrow keys and pressing Enter or by
pressing the initial letter of your choice (P for print, S for

save, and so on) or by moving the mouse pointer to your choice and clicking on it

✪ DOS-based software is likely to use **functions keys** or **multiple keystrokes** to make special things happen

✪ Windows-based software will involve using the **mouse** to click, or double click, **icons**

✪ If you get stuck, you can use **on-screen help**; press the Help key and find out what to do next

Table 3.4 list the applications and gives brief details of their particular features.

Application	Features
Document (word) processing	Processes text; features include 'find and replace', spell check and grammar check; styles allow consistent presentation; choice of fonts (typefaces and point sizes)
Desktop publishing (DTP)	Integrates text and images to create paged layouts
Databases	Record-structured data; sorting of records based on key fields; searching of records to match criteria; selection of fields to present in a report
Spreadsheets	Number-structured database; rows and columns of cells; cells contain text, number, a formula or blank; formulae allow automatic calculations; 'what if?' queries
Graphics	Creation of images; editing; bitmap and vector graphics
Utilities such as virus checkers	Stand-alone applications that can be enabled to run while you work

Table 3.4 *Applications software features*

Customising applications software

In the same way that operating systems can be customised, so too can applications software. Users often know little about their applications software. To enable a given user to make immediate and effective use of the software, they must be able to customise it to meet their needs:

- ✪ Setting spelling and grammar checks

- ✪ Setting/modifying default templates and creating simple macros

- ✪ Setting suitable printer drivers

- ✪ Setting toolbar display

- ✪ Setting options for file locations

When applications software is first installed the manufacturer's default setting will apply. So, for example, the **default language** may be English (USA). If you want to use the spelling and grammar checks, you need to ensure that this is changed to the language you are actually using – probably English (UK) – otherwise the spell-checker will not trap all the errors you would like it to, and it may flag words that you think are correctly spelled.

Activity 3.19

★ Key these two sentences into a blank document (mistakes included):

The colour of an organisation's logo are grey. It was modelled using graphic software.

★ Make sure the language is set to English (UK).

★ Perform a spell check and note any words that are flagged as incorrect (but do not change them).

★ Change the language from English (UK) to English (USA) and do another spell check. Compare the results with the previous spell check.

★ Which words were rejected by both spell checks?

★ Which were accepted in one language but not in the other?

★ Were all errors flagged?

★ Does the grammar checker (for either language) find the grammatical error?

Setting/modifying default templates is covered in Chapter 1, and **creating simple macros** is covered elsewhere in this chapter (page 179).

Printer drivers are discussed on page 161 and explored in Exercise 3.13 and Activity 3.17.

Display parameters control the choices you make about what appears on your screen. These include the enlargement (zoom control), show/hide paragraph marks, toolbars, scroll bars, etc.

★ Compare the display options available on at least two applications.

★ How do you switch on/off the show/hide option? What is the benefit of having this on?

★ Change the enlargement from 100% to 50%. What is the benefit of this option?

★ Explore the Options menu to discover what default options are current.

It will speed up processing, e.g. editing text, if you customise applications software by setting up key-operated commands and macros. **Macros** are discussed on page 179, and the method for setting up key-operated commands is dealt with at the same time because they are similar.

When applications software is installed, a **default file location** (directory or folder) setting often specifies where all documents created by that application are to be filed. It may suit you to save your files in a different location. If so, changing this default setting will save you having to respecify the desired location every time you save a file.

★ Explore one software application to find out what default settings exist.

★ Check another application to see if the same settings are in operation.

★ Find out how to change the default setting for saving files.

When the operating system and applications software are configured to suit user needs, you should test that they work. A typical test might include:

- ✪ Powering up

- ✪ Using the operating system

- ✪ Accessing the applications software

- ✪ Using the macros and templates you have created

- ✪ Entering and saving information

- ✪ Retrieving and printing information

Activity 3.22

With a particular user in mind, configure the operating system and applications software appropriately to meet the user's needs. Fully test your system, producing actual screen prints. Annotate your screen prints accurately and clearly to show how you configured the operating system and applications software.

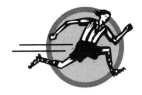

▼▼▼▼▼▼▼▼▼

A **macro** is a sequence of instructions that is defined by a single element, called the **identifier**. When you **call** a macro, the sequence of instructions is used. Macros save time and can reduce errors

▲▲▲▲▲▲▲▲▲▲

Macro programs

Programs that are used to automate actions in applications software are called **macros**.

Macros can be produced by simply recording the keys that a user presses or using a routine or 'wizard' that guides the user through a sequence of operations and records the result. Macros can be used in a number of situations, but essentially a macro is used to **replace multiple keystrokes**.

Activity 3.23

Using your word-processing software, look in your on-line help for 'macro'. Read the material supplied and then go through any demonstration that is provided.
Check that you understand how to create a macro by recording a macro to display highlighted text in red (instead of the default colour, black). Call the macro REDTEXT.

You could create macros for any other sequences of keystrokes that you find you have to do over and over again. This will save you time.

The code created is shown in Figure 3.10.

```
Sub MAIN

FormatFont .Points = "9", .Underline = 0, .Color = 6,
.Strikethrough = 0, .Superscript = 0, .Subscript = 0, .Hidden = 0,
.SmallCaps = 0, .AllCaps = 0, .Spacing = "0 pt", .Position = "0 pt",
.Kerning = 0, .KerningMin = "", .Tab = "0", .Font = "Arial", .Bold
= 0, .Italic = 0

End Sub
```

Figure 3.10 *Macro code for displaying highlighted text in red: REDTEXT*

Activity 3.24

Assign the macro REDTEXT to a toolbar button.

If you are using Word 6, choose Tools/Customise/Toolbars and select the Macro Box. Then drag the cursor to wherever you would like the button to appear in your toolbars. You will then see the Custom window, and choosing Edit will allow you to draw a suitable picture for the button.

If you are using a more recent version of Word, choose Tools/Customise/Commands and select Macro Box. You can then drag the button to wherever you want it. It appears with text 'Normal.New.Macros.Box', but you can edit this (choose default style and draw a picture instead) and this reduces the size of the button.

If you are using another word-processing application, ask your teacher to explain anything you do not understand about generating macros on your system.

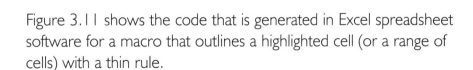

Activity 3.25

Now look at some other applications software, e.g. spreadsheet software. You should find that the software includes many 'supplied macros'. Look at the code for these macros.

Figure 3.11 shows the code that is generated in Excel spreadsheet software for a macro that outlines a highlighted cell (or a range of cells) with a thin rule.

```
" outline Macro

' Macro recorded 01/05/00 by First Class

'Sub outline()

    Selection.Borders(xlLeft).LineStyle = xlNone

    Selection.Borders(xlRight).LineStyle = xlNone

    Selection.Borders(xlTop).LineStyle = xlNone

    Selection.Borders(xlBottom).LineStyle = xlNone

    Selection.BorderAround Weight:=xlThin,
    ColorIndex:=xlAutomatic

End Sub
```

parameter
value for
border rule
weight

Figure 3.11 *A macro created within Excel to outline a cell (or range of cells) with a thin rule*

Activity 3.26

Figure 3.12 shows a similar Excel macro that outlines the cell with a heavy rule. Notice that the only difference between these two macros (apart from the macro name) is the BorderAround Weight. This **parameter** is either ×1Thin or ×1Thick.

```
' heavy Macro

' Macro recorded 01/05/00 by First Class

Sub heavy()

    Selection.Borders(xlLeft).LineStyle = xlNone

    Selection.Borders(xlRight).LineStyle = xlNone

    Selection.Borders(xlTop).LineStyle = xlNone

    Selection.Borders(xlBottom).LineStyle = xlNone

    Selection.BorderAround Weight:=xlThick,    ←— parameter changed to 'thick'
    ColorIndex:=xlAutomatic

End Sub
```

Figure 3.12 *A macro created within Excel to outline a cell (or range of cells) with a heavy rule*

Create a macro in your spreadsheet software to change the format of a cell. You could change the format to currency, or change the font colour. Look at the code it produces. Change a parameter, and see what effect it has.

Most software applications offer macro support, and once you have mastered the sequence of recording macros, you can use them in a variety of situations:

- To insert text or graphics

- To open or import files

- To modify page layout or text format

Activity 3.27

Choose one of the situations listed above and, with a particular user in mind, create a macro to meet the needs of your user. Produce screen prints and printouts to show how your macro works. Annotate your printouts accurately and clearly to show the purpose of your macro and how it works. Decide how you could amend your macro code to produce a new macro. Annotate copies of the code before and after editing to prove that you have edited the macro code to modify the macro. Explain how your macro improves the efficiency and effectiveness of the user and the quality of the output.

Templates

Templates are used to avoid repeating the same work every time you create a document. A letter template might include this information:

- The page layout (e.g. margins)

- The company logo

- Today's date

- Part of any reference, e.g. Our ref: ICT/GNVQ

✪ The opening salutation, e.g. Dear

✪ The closing remarks, e.g. Yours

✪ A graphic image of a closing signature

Exercise 3.17

What information might be presented in a memo template?

Exercise 3.18

Find out what wizards are available in your word-processing software when you decide to create a new document.

Chris Lane Kidsports

Kidsports offers a party service. Two templates are used by the party administrator:

★ A party costing, which confirms the price that will be charged

★ An invoice, which is calculated on the actual number of guests

Both are shown in Figure 3.13.

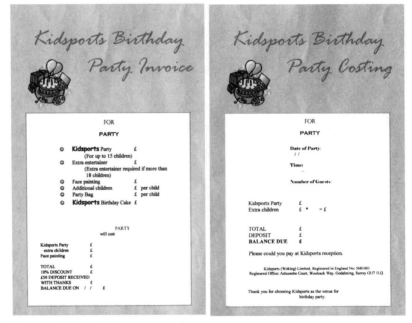

Figure 3.13 *Kidsports templates*
Courtesy of Chris Lane Family Leisure Club

Exercise 3.19

Why does the Kidsports company information appear on the invoice template?
What information needs to be entered on each document *after* the template has been created?

Activity 3.28

Look at a standard document, e.g. an invoice. Decide which information could be part of a template. Decide what information must be added after the template has been created.

Activity 3.29

In Chapter 1 you designed a memo and a publicity flyer for Gary Granger's gardening service.
Set up a template for an estimate and an invoice for Gary Granger. Put only the template information into these document and save them as templates. Print out both templates.
Annotate your templates so that it is clear what information is to be inserted when producing an estimate or an invoice.

Using a template is a bit like printing on headed notepaper. All the standard information is in place before you start.

Exercise 3.20

Find out how to 'attach a template' to a new document that you are creating.

Activity 3.30

Produce a sample estimate from your estimate template and print it out.
Produce a sample invoice from your invoice template and print it out.

> Your samples might refer to Mr Parsons, who appears in Activity 1.7 in Chapter 1.

The benefit of doing this is that, if things change – like the telephone number changes in April 2000 – it is easy to correct the template. No pre-printed stationery has to be discarded, and the change can be instantaneous – no waiting for the printer to supply all new stationery.

If all previous documents of this type have been created from the template, their style is amended too the next time they are opened. So documents that are still in production can have their style amended – just as soon as the style is decided.

Gary Granger's details have changed slightly. His telephone code is now 01355.

Amend his estimate and invoice templates so that the telephone number is correct.

Print out the sample estimate and invoice to show that the number changes automatically on these documents.

Templates can be created for any of the standard documents you studied in Chapter 1.

Choose one standard document and, with a particular user in mind, create a template to meet the needs of your user.

Produce printouts to show what your template contains. Annotate your printouts accurately and clearly to show the purpose of your template.

Decide how you could amend your template to produce a new template. Annotate printouts of the template before and after editing to prove that you have edited the template to modify it.

Explain how your template improves the efficiency and effectiveness of the user and the quality of the output.

If you produce a template for a sales order form, you could amend it to produce a delivery note.

Revision questions

1. Name two input devices that can be used to transfer photos to a computer.

2. Explain the difference between memory and storage.

3. Name two storage devices and two types of memory.

4. Name two output devices that produce hard copy.

5. What is the main difference between an operating system and applications software?

6. List four purposes of an operating system.

7. Name four examples of applications software and for each write down its main purpose.

8. What is meant by the term 'default setting'?

9. Explain the difference between a spell-checker and a grammar checker.

10. What is a virus?

11. What can be done to avoid virus infection?

12. Explain what a macro is.

13. Give examples of macros that you have used or created.

14. Explain what a template is.

15. Give examples of templates that you have used or created.

Design Project

- Identify an ICT project that you would like to carry out

- Describe the work you want to do in some detail

- Plan your work for a project

- Use software to produce your ideas

- Record what you did and review your work

This unit also offers the opportunity to follow standard ways of working. Details about these, which apply to all units in this course, are given on page 410 in the Good Working Practice Guide.

The skills that you learn in this unit will help you in other units, especially the optional units. This unit enables you to work on an ICT activity in which you are interested. You can also build on other work that you have completed during the course.

✪ You may decide to extend and complete a more complex database than the one you may have developed in Unit 2

✪ You could produce a variety of different templates with a common style or some more complex macros than the one you produced for Unit 3

You do need to get approval from your teacher, and you may be restricted by the resources available to you, but, in theory, your project be could be anything from digital photography to setting up a user's diary and e-mail database. It could also be a project formed by creating a number of minor products, such as setting up a series of templates or a number of macros to meet a specific need.

Your success in this unit depends on your making a useful product, and one that works! You will use software to design and create the product to meet specified user needs. Alternatively, you may decide to create a number of small products.

As a guide, your teacher will expect you to spend about 50 hours on the project. This includes the time you spent deciding what to do, completing all the work and documenting your work.

Activity 4.1

It would make sense to keep a log from Day 1, so that you can see how much time you have already spent, how much you probably have left to do, and whether this can be achieved before your deadline. Decide how you are going to record your log – on paper or using software such as a spreadsheet – and set it up.

If you decide to use a spreadsheet, you will need regular access to the computer to update it, but then you may be able to program it to calculate the time you have spent so far on the project. See Figure 4.1.

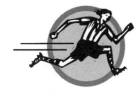

Log sheet					
Date	Time on	Time off	Time spent	Time so far	What I did
01/05/00	09:40	10:45	01:05	01:05	set up my log sheet
	10:45	11:00	00:15	01:20	

Figure 4.1   *Spreadsheet log sheet design*

This chapter looks in detail at six topics:

✪ Identifying a suitable design project

✪ Describing the design

✪ Planning the work

- ✪ Carrying out the work

- ✪ Checking that it works

- ✪ Reviewing your work

This chapter uses two case studies: George Honour and Martin Burley.

Background information about these case studies is given in the Case Studies section of this book, starting on page xvii.

Identifying a suitable design project

Many people who use computers do not really understand them. So they need help, sometimes even to do simple things. You need to identify a suitable project – one that will help someone to make better use of his or her computer.

Exercise 4.1

List some of the problems people that you know have using their computer. What could you do to help these people to overcome their problems?

Brainstorming is a method of generating ideas

In this chapter, in many of the activities, you will need to **brainstorm** ideas. Brainstorming is a method of free expression and can be great fun as well as very useful. Brainstorming is used when you have to create new ideas and works best in groups. One person's idea may not be brilliant, and it may not be the answer to the problem, but it can trigger a better idea from someone else in the group. In this way, brainstorming stimulates the production of ideas.

For any brainstorming session, you may be more successful if, before you start, you follow a few rules:

✪ Have a clear idea of what your problem is

✪ Agree who is in your group and appoint someone as leader. This person will make sure that other rules are followed

✪ Appoint someone else as scribe. This person will write down ideas as they are suggested. A flipchart is excellent for this, but a large piece of paper will be fine

The group size should be somewhere between four and eight. Fewer people means that you'll have too many chiefs (the leader and the scribe) and not enough Indians to generate ideas. With more than eight people, it may become difficult for anyone to get a word in!

When everyone is ready, remind yourself of the brainstorming 'rules':

✪ Each member is asked for an idea in turn

✪ Each member can offer only one idea per turn – if they have no idea to offer they say 'pass'

✪ All ideas are accepted – even if at first they seem really silly – and written down. A flipchart is useful for this, because everyone can see it, and only one person has to take notes

- While ideas are being generated, questions are asked only if an idea is not clear

- No criticism, discussion, interruptions, comments or judgements are allowed during this early stage

- Ideas are not evaluated during the brainstorming session at all – that is left until later

- An informal atmosphere, even with good-natured laughter, helps to create the right environment for new ideas

- Exaggeration may be a useful tactic. It adds humour and can also provoke new ideas

With **brainwriting**, each person writes an idea on a card (or in an e-mail) and then passes it on to the next person in the group. Then each person considers the idea on the card (or e-mail) they have just received, thinks about it, adds their own ideas to the card (or e-mail) and sends it on to the next person. By the time everyone in the group has seen all the ideas, hopefully some excellent ideas will have been developed. With **braindrawing**, each person does a drawing rather than a written description. This can be particularly useful when trying to design something like a new logo.

Whichever method of brainstorming you use, when all ideas have been exhausted – or time runs out – the whole group should spend some time reviewing all the ideas. It can be a good idea to delay this review till the next day, giving everyone time to think through all the ideas and to 'sleep on them' before having to reach any conclusions.

Activity 4.2

In groups of four to eight people, compare the notes you have made and spend time brainstorming your ideas. Follow the 'rules' of brainstorming:

Let your mind run free. Jot down ideas as anyone suggests them – do not discard any ideas. Try hard not to reject any ideas. A poor idea can often lead someone to think of a really good alternative idea. When you have spent five to ten minutes on this, stop. Each person then needs a copy of the ideas generated. On your own, compare the list of ideas with the one shown in Figure 4.2. Think about what you'd like to do and then produce a 'final' list of project ideas.

Remember to record the time spent on this brainstorming session in your log.

You may want to work on a project that provides a number of more simple facilities for a user. There are many facilities that novice users would find useful. At the same time, you will want to do something that interests you. Figure 4.3 shows a list of project topics that might appeal to you and that you might decide to do.

Exercise 4.2

Make a list of some of the things that you have done so far on this course, that you would like to do some more – or things that you have not had time to do that you would like to explore.

- setting up easy ways for users to access software they use often

- configuring a scheduler or calendar to take actions or prompt a user on a set date-time

- creating short cuts (icons or files) to let users access an information service quickly

- setting the options in software to suit user needs

- creating file folder structures to let users store and retrieve their work easily

- creating files of commonly used text or graphics for use as required

- setting toolbars in software to let users access a facility easily

- creating macros in software to let users work more efficiently

- creating templates to let users work more efficiently

- writing simple instructions to tell users how to use your product

Figure 4.2 *The results of a ten-minute brainstorming session*

It is important that you choose something that interests you and suits your abilities. Your project should be one that you will be able to cope with and will not need a lot of teacher assistance.

Exercise 4.3

Keeping one or two of your project topics in mind, start to think about a novice user that you would like to help. Has anyone mentioned that they are having problems recently? Does their problem match something you'd be interested in doing for them?

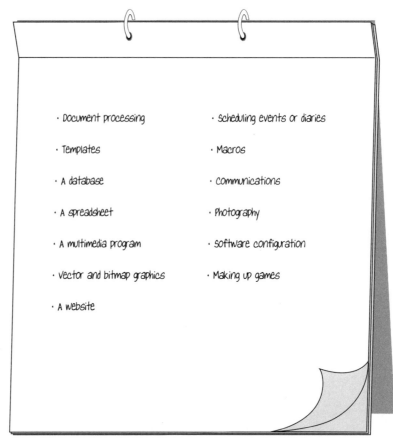

- Document processing
- Templates
- A database
- A spreadsheet
- A multimedia program
- Vector and bitmap graphics
- A website
- Scheduling events or diaries
- Macros
- Communications
- Photography
- Software configuration
- Making up games

Figure 4.3 *Project topics*

George Honour

George Honour is a butcher. He has been a butcher for many years and until recently has felt he had no need for a computer in the day-to-day running of his shop. His son now has a computer and wants to use it to make life easier for George, especially at Christmas.

Each Christmas, regular customers place orders and expect to collect them on Christmas Eve. Keeping track of all the special orders takes more and more time, and they wonder if using a database would be helpful.

If you enjoy designing databases, this type of project might suit you. Do you know anyone who has never used a computer before, or someone who has just bought one?

Martin Burley

Martin Burley is a keen gardener. He grows as many as 30 different varieties of fuchsia at his home in Manchester. His fuchsias are so good that he takes them to shows. He also sells the plants that he grows.

Martin is brilliant at gardening but knows little about computers. However, he'd like to have some literature to give to people who visit his stand at the shows and is planning to buy a computer so that he can produce the literature himself.

If you enjoy designing leaflets, producing Martin's literature might suit you. Do you know someone who is good at what they do and wants to advertise their talents but does not have the skills to design leaflets?

Draw up a shortlist of two or three people you know who might need your help in using a computer system. Make notes on what you think their particular problems are and what you might do to help them.

Arrange to meet these people and, for each one, find out what they think they need in the way of help. Can you make it easier for them to use the computer?

When you have found out what users need, decide if you really can help them. Also decide if what they need matches your needs for a design project. Will their project allow you to demonstrate your ICT skills?

For each user, list as many project ideas as you can. From this, narrow down your list of ideas to what you think is possible and worthwhile.

You may decide that you need another brainstorming session before you can finally decide on some suitable projects. If so, arrange to meet others who may also want to bounce ideas off you. You might consider the list of ideas shown in Figure 4.4.

It will be important for your teacher that each student's project is different, even if the difference is only in the data used. If your project is similar to someone else's, it can be impossible for the teacher to determine which student produces the ideas, who simply copies them and who works relatively independently. So try to think of something different from others in your group.

- creating a series of templates for letters and memos for a small business, including a standardised logo designed by you
- Producing a multimedia program with several pages to teach someone how to use software
- A website explaining . .
- creating some layout templates and macros to help a user to use word-processing software to publish a newsletter
- Designing a database to keep sports club membership records, including pictures of each member
- Designing a spreadsheet for a business to record payment details and to produce a cash flow forecast
- Designing a database for a collection such as stamps, videos or CDs, with details including pictures of each item

Figure 4.4 *Some more brainstorming ideas*

Activity 4.4

Arrange to meet your teacher, present your project ideas to your teacher and discuss all your ideas.

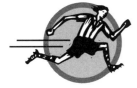

Your teacher will help you to decide what you want to do.

Having decided on a suitable project, you should contact that user to make sure he or she is willing to spend time with you during the development of your project. The next step is to describe the design.

Describing the design

It is important that what you plan to do matches what your particular user needs. One way to do this is to write a brief report describing the user's needs – as you understand them – and what you plan to produce.

You can then show your report to the user and ask for confirmation that you have understood the needs correctly. If your user is very new to ICT, you must make sure your report is written using terms that will be understood. Your report should include all essential information so that the user – and your teacher – can see exactly what you plan to do:

- ✪ The purpose of the project

- ✪ The user requirements

- ✪ The resources you need to do the work

- ✪ A list of the facilities you intend to provide

- ✪ Details of any templates or macros

- ✪ Details of file folder structures or software settings

- ✪ A brief plan for the work showing your planned timescales

Set up a word-processing file with the headings listed on page 204. Refer to notes you made when visiting your user and complete as many sections as you can. Arrange to meet your user and discuss what you plan to do.

> Where you don't have enough information, put questions that you will need to ask the user. Later, when you find out the answer, you can amend the document.

It is quite likely that you will need to have more than one meeting with your user before you fully understand what he or she needs and before you can decide exactly what your project will involve.

George Honour

George writes Christmas orders in a big book. For each order, he writes the customer's name and telephone number. He then writes a list of everything they want, e.g. turkey, sausage meat, bacon, ham and cheese. Beside each item, he writes the quantity. The entries in this book are completed whenever a customer places an order, so they are not in alphabetical order. This can be a problem if someone wants to change their order. Just before Christmas, George has to place an order with his supplier. To do this, he goes through the book and calculates how many turkeys he

continued

continued

needs to order, and so on. It is easy to make a mistake at this stage.

George copies the information from the book on to a bill for each customer – this takes a long time. Then, the day before Christmas Eve, all the orders are prepared. Items need to be weighed and the price written on to the customer's bill. Each individual item for each order is put in a separate bag and labelled with the customer's name. All labels are handwritten, and this also takes time. When the customer arrives to collect the order, the bill is located and the customer pays. Meanwhile, the separate items are collected and put into carrier bags. George's staff try to be systematic, but this is difficult when for each individual customer they need to collect perhaps seven different items. All this takes time.

George needs a system that takes less time and also avoids possible errors. It would also be helpful to customers if they could see what they ordered last year. George needs a form to be designed so that collecting information from customers, and collating that information to create an order for his supplier, is easier to do. Customers' Christmas orders can then be filed in a ring binder according to the customer surname, which makes them easy to locate.

George also needs a database so that all customer orders can be entered and the labels printed out automatically, one per item per customer. The same database could also print bills, ready for actual weights and prices to be entered.

Compare the notes you have about your user with those written about George Honour's Christmas order system. Do you know enough about your user's current way of working to be able to decide what needs to be done, and how you might help your user?

★ Does your user need any forms to be designed?
★ If your user needs a database, what information has to be stored?
★ What printouts are needed?

You may think that fully computerising things for your user is the ideal solution, but this may not be the case.

George Honour

George does not have the computer in his shop and cannot risk anything going wrong. So the initial solution to his problem is partly paper-based. When he has confidence in the computer system, more parts of the process could be computerised. For example, the computer could be used to calculate the bills.

The design stage is expected to take about a quarter of the time you spend on your project. It is important that your design is good. Producing something from a poor design will never result in a successful project.

Exercise 4.5

Look at your log.

★ How much time have you spent on this project so far?

★ If the whole project is going to take 50 hours, have you already spent a quarter of that time on the design?

★ If the design has taken more than 12.5 hours, how long might the rest of the project take? Will you have enough time before your deadline?

It will help if you work with others in discussing your ideas in the early stages. When you decide exactly what you will do, then you can work on your own. However, it would still be a good idea to hold regular meetings with your friends and others in your group to discuss what progress each of you has made and how you might improve what you are doing. It makes sense to take notes at each of these meetings so that any new ideas are not forgotten and you have a record of your own input.

Also, don't forget that your teacher must agree to your project.

Activity 4.6

You have to present a description of your project to your teacher, and he or she is quite likely to ask you to explain your ideas in more detail.

Make sure you have written down everything you can, so that your project design is clear. This should include a description of the main purpose of the project, what the user needs and the resources to be used.

Prepare to talk about what you intend to do. Try to anticipate what questions your teacher will ask and write down what you will say in answering these questions.

> Your teacher will need to know exactly what resources you expect to use, especially if resources are to be shared.

Planning the work

Once you are given the go-ahead by your teacher, you will need to plan the work in more detail. You will need to sketch out, in note or drawing form, all the details of the project. Use this list as a guide:

- ✪ A list of information that you will need (for example, data, general information, sources)

- ✪ People who will help you in the planning (for example, users, colleagues, tutors)

- ✪ Details of directory or folder structures

- ✪ Details of templates, file structures and macros

- ✪ Details of any text or graphics files to be used

- ✪ Sketches of screen layouts for the user (for example, menus, icons, toolbars)

- ✪ Details of the types of output needed (for example, reports or documents)

- ✪ Draft contents of user instructions or a help system

- ✪ Ideas for checking the work that you produce

- ✪ A detailed time chart to show how long each item will take to produce

All the things on the list may not be right for your project. Decide which ones match your project. Set up a file with the items on the list as section headings.

You might also start to prepare a contents list for your portfolio. You need not worry about page numbers, but at least you can begin to decide what you will be including as evidence.

As you work on your project, file everything so that you can find things easily, and nothing gets lost. You can also leave yourself notes stuck on to pages where you still have some work to do, or questions you need to find answers for.

Gradually, your file will grow until it is complete.

One of the problems you might face during this project is getting everything done on time. Your plans should describe each element of the project, the resources needed and the time that you expect the work to take.

Exercise 4.6

You need to take into account any deadlines your user may have as well. Check if your user needs your project completed by a particular time. Are they going on holiday soon? Will they be available when you need to talk to them?

Martin Burley

For Martin, growing fuchsias follows an annual pattern. Each year, plants are grown, they are shown at flower shows, and then they are sold. It is important that his literature is ready in time for the shows. If he is to include photos of his plants, these cannot be taken until the plants are in bloom. Also, he does not decide the layout of his stand at a show until a short while beforehand. This leaves him with very little time in which to produce a plan of which plants are on display. Immediately before a show, Martin is also very busy getting his plants ready.

There are lots of management tools that are used to plan the timing of a project, and that can help you to see if time is running out, or if the deadline is approaching with too much still to do. All of them involve listing all the different stages in a project, noting which things must happen first, which things depend on other things being completed and how long everything is expected to take.

One particularly useful planning tool is a **Gantt chart**. This displays planned and actual progress against a horizontal timescale. As well as showing when each task is due to begin and end, it shows the links between tasks, and from this the 'critical' path of a project. Figure 4.5 shows a simplified Gantt chart for your design project, set up on a spreadsheet.

Use one column per week

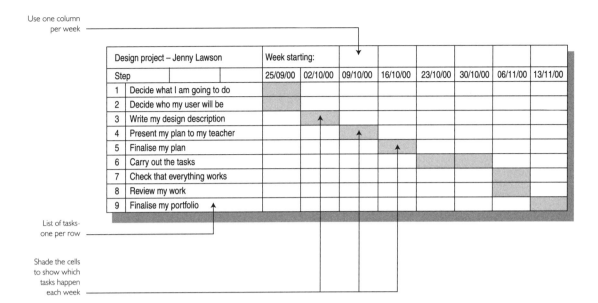

Design project – Jenny Lawson			Week starting:							
Step			25/09/00	02/10/00	09/10/00	16/10/00	23/10/00	30/10/00	06/11/00	13/11/00
1	Decide what I am going to do									
2	Decide who my user will be									
3	Write my design description									
4	Present my plan to my teacher									
5	Finalise my plan									
6	Carry out the tasks									
7	Check that everything works									
8	Review my work									
9	Finalise my portfolio									

List of tasks- one per row

Shade the cells to show which tasks happen each week

Figure 4.5 *Gantt chart*

Activity
4.8

Set up a Gantt chart for your design project, using a spreadsheet.

★ In the first column, write all the tasks you think you will be doing. You could use the list in Figure 4.5 as a guide, but you will need to expand each step to include the tasks you are actually going to do.

★ Along row B, put dates from now until the deadline of your project.

> You may be able to fill in the series of dates automatically, rather than keying them all in.

★ In the body of the spreadsheet, use colour or shading to show when you will be working on any particular task.

In allocating time for each task, it is usually easier to work from the deadline backwards, allowing yourself as much time as you think each stage might take. If you then find that you seem to have too much to do in the time available, you may need to rethink your project design. Are you taking on too much? Or do you need to allocate more time to the project?

You should check your progress against the Gantt chart regularly, e.g. each week. If you are slipping behind schedule, the sooner you know, the more time you'll have to catch up. If you realise that there are extra tasks to do, you could insert an extra row for each new task and allocate some time for it.

Some things may take longer than you planned, or maybe you are ill for a week and cannot work on your project at all. If so, you could insert an extra column and redate the columns from there. The spreadsheet would then show your expected completion date. You may then need to think again about how to make up lost time, or you may need to renegotiate your deadline with your teacher.

The important thing is to be in control of the timing of your design project. A last-minute rush may mean that the quality of your project suffers. Leaving things to the last minute also means that you may be putting yourself under more stress than need be.

Carrying out the work

Once you have made your work plans, you can actually start working. To create your product – whatever it is – you will use software and other resources.

Look at your design description and check that you have listed any software that you will be using. Make sure that all the resources you need are available to you and, if you need to, book these resources.

Then plan the times when you will be working at a computer, when you will be making visits, etc. Make sure that the people you want to see will be available and book appointments if necessary. If you have not done so already, build these tasks and visits into your Gantt chart.

Check that your final deadline is still achievable and then set to work on the first task on your list.

Your production activity will include many tasks, and you need to ensure that you allow time for all of them. For example, you may need to collect sample data from your user and input this information to demonstrate that your product works as hoped.

You will also need to check the accuracy of your work, and that your product works correctly, before preparing evidence to put in your portfolio. Where sensible, you will include technical information of your design work and produce user instructions, so that your user can make best use of the product.

Each project will involve a different list of actions. What somebody else includes may not be right for your project, and vice versa. Your project may involve activities that no one else is tackling.

Activity 4.10

Meet a few others who are also designing a project. Compare your list of tasks with theirs. Have you missed anything off your list that you now realise you must include? Can you see things that others have missed out. Help them to see how to improve their project design. In turn, you should find that they can help you.
Review your Gantt chart to make sure that everything that needs to be included has been. Make adjustments if necessary.

Now you really must start doing the tasks on your list and ticking them off as you complete each one. Review your progress at least once a week, either on your own or in a small group. It can be frightening how quickly time passes, and unless you make a point of working on your project every week, you may well miss your deadline altogether.

Checking that it works

When you have finished your product, before you show it to your user, you need to check that it works. It makes sense to assume that 'what can go wrong, will go wrong'. Remember that your user may not be as good at using computers as you. To make things as easy as possible, your product should be **robust** and therefore **idiot-proof**.

Activity 4.11

Check how your product 'behaves' if operated incorrectly.

★ What happens if you use icons, menus or toolbars incorrectly?
★ What happens if you press the wrong keys or press several keys at once?
★ Have you included enough user information to help the user to step through your product without getting lost?

Also check that all the items you created work as you intended.

★ Is it easy to use the macros, files or file structures you have created?
★ Have you provided all the items as promised in your project description?
★ Does all the output from your product meet user needs?

Once you are satisfied that your product works, you might be tempted to present it to your user straight away. However, it makes more sense to try it out on a friend on your course first. Because you have been working closely on the project, you may not notice if something is wrong. Someone who understands how the system should work and yet is unfamiliar with it – having a fresh set of eyes – may spot something you have missed.

Activity 4.12

Separately, both of you, test the other's product to see if you can find anything wrong at all. Pretend that you are very new to computers and see if the product does what the user is expecting. Write down everything that you think could be improved, then get together and discuss each other's suggestions.

On your own again, decide how you are going to improve your product. Make these improvements and then present the finished product to your user.

> Your portfolio must include proof that you can check the accuracy of your work, and that you have corrected obvious errors. So include evidence of previous drafts of documents, annotated with the corrections made.

Reviewing your work

Having presented your product to your user, you may feel that your work is done and you can now relax. However, you may learn a lot from looking back over what you have done, seeing what worked well and what worked less well in your project. You may also still have to prepare the material to go into your portfolio.

First, think about how well you planned the project:

✪ **Did the timing work out as hoped? If not, why not?**

✪ **Did you run out of time? If so, why?**

✪ **How would you improve the product if you were given more time?**

You may feel that you were hampered by the resources available to you.

✪ **Were you able to use the resources you wanted, when you needed them?**

✪ **How would you improve the product if you were given more and better resources?**

However, do not fall into the trap of blaming the resources. Remember that a poor worker blames his/her tools. Perhaps if you had planned things better, the outcome would have been better. The real measure of the success of your project is what the user thinks of your product:

✪ **How did the user react when first trying out the product? Was he or she happy with what you had produced? If not, why not?**

- ✪ Did your user run into difficulty due to your not supplying enough user help? If so, what could you have done to help them more?

- ✪ Did your product meets the needs of your user? If not, in what ways could you improve your product so that he or she would be happy to use it?

Reviewing how well the work went and what you learned in completing your project will help you to do better next time.

Activity 4.13

Write a review of your work, including a commentary on the quality of the product and ways in which it could be improved.

If you felt that things went really badly, put those thoughts behind you. There is no point in dwelling on them. However, promise yourself that your next project will be a success. Take control of the planning and timing and prevent things going wrong. Then you can look forward to a successful project.

Using Information Resources

5

- Identify and work with different sources of information

- Understand how different sources store information

- Search for information on a subject

- Assess information and draw conclusions

Information is everywhere, and nowadays one of the most accessible sources of information is the Internet. Having the right information at the right time is useful. Having too much information – called **information overload** – or information that is out of date or inaccurate in any way, is not useful.

How and where to find information, and how to make use of it, is the theme of this chapter. You will search for information on a topic of your choice, carrying out searches for the information using a variety of information sources, including paper-based and ICT-based sources. The information you find will be recorded and collected into a pack, together with notes describing the content of the pack.

All this will be presented in your portfolio. See the Portfolio Guide on page 429 for more information on how to present material in your portfolio.

Until now, the majority of information has been stored in printed form. This includes books, newspapers and other documents. Nowadays, much information is available electronically, on the Internet. While you may feel that you will never need to refer to paper-based information, it will help you to make the best use of electronic information if you first understand how to access and use paper-based information. Then you can compare this with electronic sources and see the good and bad points of both forms.

This chapter looks in detail at seven topics.

- ✪ Investigating a subject

- ✪ Paper-based sources of information

- ✪ ICT-based sources of information

- ✪ Finding ICT-based information

- ✪ Using other sources of information

- ✪ Information in organisations

- ✪ Collecting information on a subject

This chapter refers to two case studies: George Honour and the Chris Lane Leisure Club. Background information on these case studies is given in the Case Studies section on pages xx to xxiii.

This chapter complements the work in Chapter 1, which focuses on presenting information, and builds on Chapter 2, so information given in both these chapters will be useful to you, especially where they cover the detailed use of effective techniques for finding, analysing and using information.

Investigating a subject

Information sources help you to find out about a subject. They add to your existing knowledge and may provide answers to particular questions.

Deciding what subject to investigate for this unit may be the hardest decision you have to make. During this course, you will have had to investigate many things, and you may decide that one of these should be the subject of your investigation for this unit. Your teachers may also help you to identify subjects that you should investigate for your other courses.

Exercise 5.1

Make a list of your other courses and, for each one, think of a few situations where you have had to investigate a topic.

Activity 5.1

In a group of five to eight, have a brainstorming session to generate ideas for topics. Keep a note for yourself of all the ideas that were suggested.

The 'rules' of brainstorming are given in Chapter 4, page 196.

When you have settled on a subject, you need an action plan. In the same way as you planned your project for Unit 4, you should plan this investigation. These are some of the tasks you should allow for in your plan:

✪ Decide what information you need

✪ Identify key words that may help you to search for information

✪ Identify possible paper-based and electronic sources of information

✪ Identify people who might be able to help you

✪ Match your questions to the type of source

✪ Use the information you collect to answer questions on a subject

✪ Present your findings as an information pack

You will have to find information from at least three paper-based sources of information, local and remote ICT-based sources and at least one other source, and combine these to produce new information.

> You might collect weather statistics for a seasonal product (like ice cream) and sales data for that product. From these two sources of information, you may be able to show a correlation between the two. Alternatively, you might collect accident statistics for pedestrians and compare these statistics with data on daylight hours.

You need to think about the nature of the information that you expect to be available from each different type of information source and to decide how long you might need to spend searching each different type of information source. If you are accessing information in your local library, you will need to plan a visit. If you are planning to use remote ICT-based resources, you may need to book time on a computer. You also need to allow sufficient time to analyse, organise and present the information as assessment evidence for the unit.

Your teacher will give you a deadline – and it will be important that you complete all your work on time. So allow more time than you think you'll need. Then if the unexpected happens, you'll still have time to complete your information pack before the final deadline. If not, you will need to discuss your schedule again with your teacher to renegotiate the deadline and request an extension. Be warned: missing a deadline may affect your grade for this unit.

Activity 5.2

Set up your action plan. You may not have a firm idea yet on exactly what topic you will investigate, but at least you will know what needs to be done and what time you have to complete the tasks.

Use a spreadsheet and/or Gantt chart if you think this will be useful for you (see Chapter 4, page 213, for details of how to do this.)

Because you need to use at least three paper-based sources, local and remote ICT-based sources and at least one other source, you need to choose your subject carefully. It needs to be sufficiently broad that useful information is likely to exist in a number of different types of source.

A choice of subject such as breeding a particular type of pedigree animal would offer a wide range of possible information sources that are likely to hold relevant information. Electronic databases on the Internet could be searched to locate breed clubs and breeders in different countries; books may have been written about the breed; magazines may exist; and individual owners and vets will have information. Information about the history of the breed, the names of champion animals (in shows) and their descriptions would all be valuable. This topic also lends itself to drawing conclusions: it might be possible to estimate a figure for the total number of animals in the world of the chosen pedigree.

Exercise 5.2

Think again about the various topics that interest you. Are they broad enough to provide you with lots of different sources of information?

Paper-based sources of information

Paper-based sources of information have been available for a long time. Do you know anything about the history of paper and printing?

Activity 5.3

Working in a small group, investigate the history of paper-based information and find the answers to these questions:

★ Before paper was invented, how were facts recorded in writing?
★ What language was used for the earliest writings?
★ What material was paper first made from?
★ How did the knowledge of producing paper spread throughout the world?
★ When was the first paper mill established in England?
★ When was the printing press invented? Who invented it?

Present your findings to the rest of the people in your class. Compare notes on where you found the information. Did everyone find the same information? Did anyone find contradictory information? If so, check your sources again.

Nowadays, books are in danger of being replaced by electronic sources of information. This section concentrates on paper-based sources though, so that you are familiar with how to get information from them. Skills you will use for paper-based sources will also apply to electronic sources:

✪ Accessing information from reference documents

✪ Locating information in a source document

✪ Searching catalogues

✪ Interpreting information

Accessing information from reference materials

Dictionaries, encyclopaedias, directories, thesauri, card indexes, newspapers and magazines are all reference materials.

Dictionaries

Dictionaries list words in alphabetical order and for each word give a definition of its meaning, other forms of the word, and where it comes from. Dictionaries often have other useful information such as foreign phrases, abbreviations and symbols. Dictionaries are available in lots of different languages: English, American English, French, German, and so on.

Dictionaries are also available for particular subject areas, although sometimes these are called **glossaries**.

Activity 5.4

Check what dictionaries are available in your local library. Do they have a dictionary of quotations? A dictionary of . . . ?
Use a dictionary to look up these words:

dictionary, encyclopaedia, directory, thesaurus, card index, newspaper, magazine.

What other information is provided in your dictionary?
Use the BCS glossary to look up these terms:

backup file, Ceefax, Internet, information.

> Sometimes glossaries are not presented in alphabetical order, so you need to refer to the index to find an entry.

Encyclopaedias

Encyclopaedias offer more than a dictionary. Instead of just defining words, they explain them. For this reason, an encyclopaedia may be presented as lots of books in a series. It is also unusual for individuals to buy a complete set of encyclopaedias, because they cost such a lot and can soon become out of date. In libraries, encyclopaedias are kept in the reference section, so they can be looked at but not borrowed and taken away.

Activity 5.5

Find out what encyclopaedias are available in your school or college library. Check the publication date.

Find information in an encyclopaedia about these topics:

digital cameras, Charles Babbage, the human genome project.

Directories

Directories hold information to help you to contact people and organisations. A **telephone directory** holds the name, address and telephone number of nearly everyone in a particular area.

Did You Know?

Some people prefer not to have their telephone numbers included in a directory. Their numbers are called **ex-directory**

Entries in a directory are shown in alphabetical order of surname. Because people move house and change telephone numbers so frequently, telephone directories are published every year but can still be out of date after a very short time.

It helps businesses if their contact details are presented under categories, so that someone wanting a particular product or service can find them listed with other similar traders. For this reason, telephone directories sometimes have a business section. Special **trade directories** are also published, such as *Yellow Pages* and *Thomson Directory*. In these, businesses might also choose to pay for a larger entry, including an advertisement. Then, when you turn to the category, their entries are noticed ahead of others.

Activity 5.6

In a small group, investigate directories available to you:

★ Use a telephone directory to check the telephone numbers of everyone in your group. Is anyone ex-directory?

★ Use a business directory to find contact details for a plumber, a carpenter, a furniture repairer, a car hire company, a hotel and a doctor.

What other useful information is given in directories?

Thesauri

A **thesaurus** is similar to a dictionary. It lists lots of words, but they are grouped into words that are similar in meaning (**synonyms**). The index lists all the words (like a dictionary) and gives reference numbers where the word can be found according to its general meaning.

> In the index of a thesaurus, 'sort' shows two general meanings: sort as a noun (e.g. a particular sort of day) and sort as a verb (to sort into categories). Both entries offer a reference number. If you look up these references, sort (noun) is grouped with lots of other words: *order*, *type*, *variety*, *kind*. Sort (verb) is linked with *sieve*, *bolt*, *sift*, *van*, *winnow*.

A thesaurus is useful for finding a different word to use, especially if you find that you have used the same word too often in a piece of written work.

Activity 5.7

For each of these twenty words, list as many words as you can that mean the same thing:

action, appeal, band, bear, bend, bill, board, body, burst, cut, dance, draw, drive, dry, good, great, love, nice, slow, very.

Then use a thesaurus to find alternative words for the words. Compare your list with the words given in the thesaurus.

If you find words you don't know, look them up in a dictionary.

Card indexes

Card indexes are a useful way of keeping information. Each card relates to one thing: a person, a car, an event, or a topic that you have to revise for an examination. Depending on the situation, the cards may be arranged either alphabetically (e.g. by topic title) or numerically (e.g. in date order). Card indexes are often stored in a box, or in drawers. Sometimes they can be held on a circular stand that allows you to see the contents of one card, for example while making a telephone call.

Card indexes are useful because you can write in additional information as things change and keep notes that are important to you. There is flexibility in how you present information on the card.

Many people use a card index for their telephone list. Adding an extra person's details is easy – just add another card.

Chris Lane

In the gym, a large filing cabinet holds the record cards for every member of the club who uses the gym regularly for a workout. Each card holds brief details of the programme that has been planned and shows the date of every session attended. The ladies' cards are stored separately from the men's, but both sets are arranged alphabetically on surname.

When members arrive at the gym, they find their card and can then refer to their programme while doing their workout. When they finish, they put the cards in a tray. The gym staff initial the cards and refile them, ready for the next visit.

Occasionally, the gym staff look through the cards to see who has not visited the gym recently. These cards are pulled out, and the members telephoned to check that everything is okay.

Libraries sometimes still use card indexes for their books. One card index is arranged in order of author – one card per book title. Another card index – with identical information – may be arranged in order of subject. Having two card indexes allows you to look things up according to how much you know. For the librarian, though, this means changes have to be recorded twice, once in each card index.

Visit your local library. If it still uses card indexes, look up some details, e.g. books available for a GNVQ course. Make a note of what information is written on each card, and how these cards are arranged.

If the library now has a computerised system, ask the librarian how the card index system used to work, and how the new system improves on it. Ask if he or she is completely happy with the computerised system. Is there anything that could be improved?

Newspapers and magazines

Newspapers and magazines provide the most up-to-date news and as such are an invaluable source of information. Past copies of newspapers are kept and can also be very interesting to read.

Newspapers are produced daily, often with a special version on Saturdays and Sundays. Daily **newspapers** contain mostly news, some advertisements and details of what's on television today. Weekend papers tend to have lots of sections and have articles on topics of interest, like films and exhibitions, interviews with celebrities and reviews of fashion, books and music. Some weekend papers have so many sections that it could take all day to read them!

Activity 5.9

There are two types of newspaper: broadsheet and tabloid. Compare the two types.

★ What layout do they use?
★ Who buys them?
★ How much do they cost?
★ What is their circulation?
★ Which are the most popular newspapers?
★ What information do they include every day? What are their regular features?
★ Which newspapers contain the most useful information?
★ Can you believe everything you read in the newspapers? Find an example of a news item that is reported differently in two different newspapers. How do you account for this?

Magazines are produced less frequently. Many **magazines** are produced weekly. Others are produced monthly. Magazines usually focus on a particular market (such as people of a particular age) and a particular topic (things that interest people, e.g. a hobby such as embroidery, or a sport such as golf).

Activity 5.10

Working in a small group, list magazines that provide useful information for someone interested in using a PC.

★ How often are these magazines produced?
★ What do they contain?
★ What proportion of the magazine is filled with advertisements?
★ How much do they cost?

Compare the magazines and recommend the one you think is best value for money and provides the most useful information.

Locating information in a source document

Most reference materials have contents lists, glossaries and indexes to help you to locate information. You will need to develop a list of key words and sub-topics, which will be used to guide the search for information.

For each of these tasks, you could work on your own or with a friend or two. Make notes on how you found the information and any problems that arose.

★ Choose one instruction manual (e.g. for a mobile phone or a video recorder) and make a copy of any diagram that is included to show the main parts of the equipment. In how many languages is the manual provided?

★ Search a CD, e.g. an encyclopaedia like *Encarta*, and find all you can on a single topic. Then explore further by referring to related articles.

★ Compare the way timetable information is supplied at a bus stop and at a railway station.

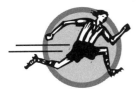

Searching catalogues

Libraries hold a lot of books and need to keep track of them. People who use libraries need to be able to locate books on a particular topic, so librarians catalogue the books. The main catalogue is based on the author of a book. So long as you know who wrote a book, you should be able to find out whether a library has a copy.

Often, though, you are interested in finding books on a particular topic, and you don't know – and really don't mind – who wrote the books.

In 1876, Melvil Dewey invented the **Dewey decimal system** of classifying books. Under this system, all knowledge is divided into ten main classes, and each is given a 100-number span. The first class is 000–099, and these numbers are used for encyclopaedias, newspapers and magazines. Each main class is then subdivided into ten subclasses. So, the 800–899 class is for literature, but the 810s are for American literature, and 811 is for American poetry. More numbers then appear after a decimal point to give even more detail, e.g. a particular place, or period in history.

More recently, the **Library of Congress classification** has offered a system that divides all knowledge into 21 classes, and each class is given a single letter. Within these classes, there is a further breakdown and letters are again assigned, e.g. N represents fine arts but NA refers to architecture, NB to sculpture, and so on. Numbers and more letters are then used to subdivide these classes further.

Activity 5.12

Visit your local library or school library to see what system is used.
Check that you understand how the Dewey decimal system works so that when you are researching your activity you can identify books that may be useful to your investigation.
Find out more about the Library of Congress classification system. Check what information appears at the start of this book (on page iv). Technical journals often include keywords and JEL codes for each article. Find out what these mean.

Interpreting information

Some information is displayed in lists, tables and graphs. To make use of this information, you need to be able to interpret it. Information is often presented in a **list** if you need just a heading or brief notes about each item. Sometimes the list is numbered, perhaps because the number of things in the list is important to remember, or numbering them helps you to remember them.

Your project plan (Chapter 4) should list the tasks you have to do.

Tables are used to present two-dimensional data. Tables have **rows** and **columns** – and these are usually labelled. A **cell** in a table relates to the heading for that row and that column.

Bus and rail times are usually presented in a table. Each column represents one bus or train journey. The rows represent the places stopped at on the route. Each cell shows the time the bus or train should arrive at a particular destination.

Graphs provide a way of showing the relationship between two things. The **axes** are two straight lines drawn at right angles to each other. The horizontal axis (usually called the **x axis**) can be used to represent time or some other independent variable – something that cannot be controlled! The vertical axis (usually called the **y axis**) is then used for the variable that you are actually interested in – the dependent variable. We then say that y depends on x.

The x axis may show the years since you were born. The y axis could show your height in centimetres measured on your birthday each year. This graph would probably rise steadily, with rapid growth in your teens. When you reach adulthood, the graph may start to move downwards. Older people tend to shrink!

ICT-based sources of information

To access ICT-based sources of information, first you need a computer with a telephone link, or access via your television or mobile phone to the Internet. Depending on your route to information, you will need some equipment and software to access different sources:

- Input devices (keyboard, keypad)

- Output devices (screen, printer)

- Storage devices/media (disks, CD-ROMs)

- Software (communications CD-ROM driver, web browsers, search engines)

- A method of access (TV, computer, mobile phone)

Exercise 5.3

Make a note of how you have accessed electronic information in the past. What alternative methods are open to you? Compare your methods with those of others in your group. Make sure you are aware of all possible sources of electronic information.

How you can access the information, once at your source, will depend on how the data items are stored.

Some data may be stored in a record-structured database (see page 89) using tables, records and fields. Other data may be stored as pages. **Viewdata** simply presents one page after another, although you do select the number of the next page you want to see. **Hypertext** – as used on web pages – allows you to move from page to page using **hot links**.

Directories

All data items are stored in data files or databases, and these are stored in directories. Directories are like filing cabinets. You might keep all correspondence files on customers with names starting with the letters A to D in one drawer, the ones for customers E to K in another drawer, and so on.

Each directory can also be split into **subdirectories**; and the subdirectories can be split still further, as shown in Figure 5.1. There may be a limit to the number of files in any one directory; also, each name has to be unique within that directory.

It makes sense to decide where to store your data files before you have too many in one directory. This makes the process of backing up more manageable too. If your directory is well organised, arranging for just one subdirectory to be copied to a backup device is relatively simple. If all your files are in one directory, backup could take a very long time, and you may be saving copies of files that do not need to be backed up.

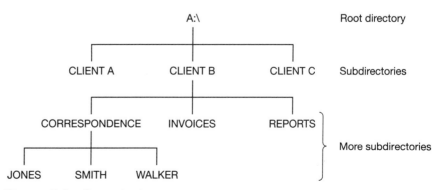

Figure 5.1 *Example directory structure*

In ICT systems, data files created in one application have a special name ending (called a **file extension**), which allows the application software to recognise the file next time you want to access it. For example, this chapter has been written using word-processing software that uses the DOC file extension.

File extensions are important. If you want to transfer data from one software application to another, the formats of the data files must be compatible. Knowing the file extension will allow you to check whether this type of file can be **imported**.

Each data file also has a **file name** chosen by you.

▼▼▼▼▼▼▼▼▼

Importing files
(rather than just retrieving them) involves a translation process. The same process (but in reverse) happens when you **export** data files for use in another software application

▲▲▲▲▲▲▲▲▲

> It is important to choose names that are meaningful. Then, next time you see the name on the directory list, you will remember what data are in that file.

The **path name** of a file is the combination of these:

✪ **The drive letter (the disk drive on which you have stored the data)**

✪ **The directory name**

✪ **Any subdirectory names**

✪ **The file name**

✪ **The file extension**

You need to know all these – or at least recognise them from a list offered by your software – before you can locate a data file! This unit is stored on a floppy disk. Its path name is

A:\GNVQ\FOUNDATION\UNIT5.DOC.

The backward slashes (\) separate the different parts of the path name.

Activity 5.13

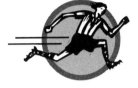

Display the directories of information held in word-processor, spreadsheet and database files.

What extensions do these files have? List all the file extensions used by the software on your ICT system.

Produce a printout of the data files in one of your directories.

Teletext

Teletext is a system that uses part of the broadcast TV picture, otherwise unseen to the viewer, to supply a variety of information, such as news items, weather forecasts, travel information, and so on.

All TV channels in the UK offer this service; the BBC version is known as **Ceefax**. The commercial version was originally known as **Oracle** until Teletext was adopted as a brand name.

Viewers with a specially equipped TV set can replace the TV picture by text pages simply by pressing buttons on a remote-control handset.

Each page of information is numbered, and all pages are transmitted in numerical sequence. A particular choice of page is made by entering the page number. There is a slight delay (until that page is next transmitted) before it appears on the screen.

The viewer cannot talk back to the provider of the pages of information, since this is only a one-way information service. Also, the waiting time limits the number of pages that can realistically be provided.

However, some pages are linked; Speedtext – using coloured buttons – allows viewers to pass from one page to another more rapidly.

Activity 5.14

Use teletext to find out some information, timing how long it takes for this information to appear on the screen:

★ The winning numbers in last week's National Lottery
★ The weather forecast for tomorrow
★ What's on television – Channel 4 – between 4 pm and 6 pm this afternoon
★ The results of a sports fixture that took place last Saturday
★ The latest news headlines

The Internet

The Internet and the **World Wide Web** now offer an almost unlimited amount of information. Like the teletext system, 'pages' of textual and graphical information are displayed either on a TV screen or on the screen of a PC. Unlike teletext, the Internet can use regular telephone lines, rather than a broadcast TV signal, to transmit information. This makes it possible for the user to interact with the system, for instance by requesting searches of valuable information, supplying information for other users to access, and ordering goods and services by credit card. Only those pages requested are transmitted, so (unlike teletext) very large amounts of data are accessible, with no penalty to other users of the system.

Internet browsers

An Internet browser is the software that allows you to navigate your way around the Internet, looking at the pages you want to see. It allows you to jump from page to page using hot links, or to move back through pages you have just looked at.

Exercise 5.4

Find out the name of the Internet browser available to you.

Search engines

Search engines are essential tools for finding information on the Internet. The search engine is software that allows you to specify key words; it then searches the web for sites that include these key words and presents the results of the search as a list. You can then select whichever site seems suitable, and this site is downloaded to your computer.

Exercise 5.5

Lots of search engines are available. Make a list of some that you have used. Compare this list with others in your class. Are any particular search engines better than the rest? If so, why?

Finding ICT-based information

One of the most easily available sources of ICT-based information is the on-line help supplied with applications software.

Exercise 5.6

You should have used on-line help many times by now. Look back through activities that you have done for examples of situations where you relied on on-line help for information.

Several activities in Chapter 2 suggest using on-line help. See Activities 2.2, 2.5, 2.11, 2.26 and 2.35.

Activity 5.15

Explain how questions can be asked, and the different ways in which you can access information in an on-line help database. Write notes on how using on-line help has helped you to make better use of applications software.

Before you can start looking for information on an electronic database, you must decide what information you need! From this, you can decide on suitable words – called **key words** – that you will use for searching. You can then decide what sources are most likely to contain what you want. You must also be prepared to record what information you find. This might include printing it out, copying from a screen display or saving the information to a disk file.

Sometimes the information you need is not available just how you want it:

✪ There may be more information than you need, and you may need to **search** for what you really need from all that is available to you

✪ The information may not be in the order you want it, so you may need to **sort** the data into an order that suits you

Search techniques are covered in Chapter 2 on page 86:

✪ Using **relational operators** such as 'less than' ($<$) 'greater than' ($>$) and 'is equal to' ($=$)

✪ Using **logical operators** such as AND and OR

Combining simple searches to make more complex searches can save you time.

Activity 5.16

Gain access to an Internet site that offers books and CDs for sale and conduct searches to meet the needs of Jamil, Jon, Lesley and Archna:

★ **Jamil** is keen on books written by Wilbur Smith. He wants to buy another book by Wilbur Smith. What titles written by Wilbur Smith are available? Just use the surname Smith in your first search. How many matches does this give you. Is the information useful? How many matches do you find if you use the full name?

★ **Jon** is a James Bond fan. Caroline wants to buy him a book or a CD. Find out what books and CDs are available for sale that might make a good present.

★ **Lesley** has bought a juice machine, but she has no idea what mix of fruits or vegetables would make a tasty and nutritious drink. Lesley wants to spend less than £10 on a book of recipes. Find out what recipe books are available on juicing.

★ **Archna** is interested in alternative medicines and therapies, such as reflexology. She is interested in music CDs that would be good to listen to while relaxing. Find out what CDs might suit Archna.

Use the information you have collected to explain how to narrow down searches, using complex searches.

Now conduct a search for a book or CD on a topic that particularly interests you. Write down what key words you used, and list the matches that your search gave.

You might search the amazon.co.uk website for this kind of information. You might also search for information on CDs that are available to buy on the Internet.

Using other sources of information

There are other sources of information apart from paper-based and ICT-based sources. You can find information by doing a survey or making measurements and recording the data.

> You could conduct a survey to find the number of different plants growing in a hedgerow and information gathered to make weather forecasts.

People are also valuable sources of information.

> You could talk to older people or people from another country to find out about their customs or the ways things used to be done, e.g. at the beginning of the last century. Things such as the words and tunes of old folk songs may never have been written down.

Many organisations have an interest in gathering information about people. This information might be used to help in the design of products or services. Information about their habits, purchasing patterns, likes and dislikes can also be very valuable.

> In trying to find cures for diseases, it may be useful to look for links between habits and disease, such as smoking and lung cancer.

Gathering information by survey, measurement or testing

Gathering information by survey, measurement or testing is time-consuming. If you collect data by conducting a survey, taking measurements or testing, you must ensure that you follow some basic rules. Otherwise, the information you collect may not prove useful and you will have wasted your time.

Surveys

A **survey** is used to find information by sampling a population. The population might be people, e.g. all the people who live in Northumberland. The term **population** is also used to describe any complete set, e.g. the set of all DVD players sold in the UK in the year 2000.

A **sample** is then a subset of the population, used to test something about the population.

> A subset of the population of people in Northumberland might be 1000 people chosen randomly from a Northumberland telephone directory.

> A subset of the DVD players sold in the UK in the year 2000 might be those sold during January 2000.

A survey uses the sample to find out information and then to draw the conclusion that the same results apply to the whole population.

What population is surveyed depends on what questions you are trying to answer. How many of the population are included in the sample depends on your resources. If you had time, you might ask the entire population. If not, you might have to restrict your survey to a few.

It is important that the **sample size** is large enough. Otherwise, it is not reasonable to assume that the same results apply to the whole population.

The sample should also be representative of the population, so that if any factors may bias the opinions or information found, this is reflected in the sample. So, if the population of people in Northumberland is to be sampled, the sample should include roughly the same proportion of men and women as the whole population.

Measurement

When taking measurements, you should consider what units are sensible and how accurate your measurements can be. Table 5.1 gives some examples. You may also need to work with a partner, one of you to measure and the other to write the measurements down.

Experiment/survey	Measurement method	Accuracy
Compare hand span with height to see if there is any link between the two	Tape measure	To nearest 5 mm
To find the traffic volume passing the school gates between 8 and 9.30 am	Counter, tally chart	Whole numbers

Table 5.1 *Examples of measurements*

You may need to design a data collection form, e.g. if tallying the different types of vehicle passing your school it would make sense to have one section per type of vehicle.

Exercise 5.7

Think of some more situations where you would take measurements. For each one, answer these questions:

★ What would you use to make the measurement?
★ How would you record the measurement?
★ How accurate would you hope to be?

Copy Table 5.1 and extend it to include your examples.

Testing

You may decide to collect data about reaction times, or how far people can jump, or how long it takes for a hot liquid to cool down, or how long a hot fluid stays hot in a vacuum flask.

You may need to take measurements or calculate a score, but you also need to decide on the test, and what your 'rules' will be.

As with measurements, you may need to design a data collection form to record the results of your testing.

Exercise 5.8

Think of some more situations where you would perform testing. For each one, answer these questions:

★ How many tests will you carry out?
★ Who or what will you test?
★ What will be considered a pass? What will not pass your test?

Obtaining information from individuals

If you want to obtain information from individuals, you have two main choices: using a questionnaire or interviewing. Both of these provide you with an opportunity to practise key skills in communication.

- ✪ **Interviewing** is very time-consuming but may be the best way of collecting in-depth information, especially about people's opinions

- ✪ **Questionnaires** limit the responses that the person can give, but sometimes this is a very useful way of collecting information, e.g. for application forms

Sometimes interviewing is linked to a questionnaire, especially if the structure of the questions is very complex.

Exercise 5.9

Think of some situations where you would use a questionnaire. For each one, answer these questions:

★ What questions would you include on the questionnaire?
★ How many individuals would you ask to complete a questionnaire?
★ How would you process the replies?
★ How would you present your results?

One alternative is to observe the individual. **Observation** is used when the activity has to continue, or needs to be seen to be understood.

When conducting a survey of traffic passing a school, there is no need to stop the traffic! Information about the number of vehicles and the type of vehicle can be obtained just by watching them go by.

The Data Protection Act

The Data Protection Act may apply to information held about a person. Information about the Data Protection Act is given in the Good Working Practice Guide on page 424.

In collecting data from people, you should be aware of their rights:

- ✪ You should only collect information that is directly related to your purpose

- ✪ The person giving the information should volunteer it, knowing full well what you plan to do with the information

- ✪ You are not permitted to disclose confidential information to someone else

It is also polite to thank people who provide you with information.

Information in organisations

Organisations range in size from a single self-employed person to giant multinational commercial companies. Types of organisation include shops, manufacturers, banks, schools and hospitals. The people in all these organisations depend on a wide range of different information to keep the organisation working well.

Every organisation will hold information on its employees, its customers and its suppliers, and any regulations that must be followed, e.g. taxation rules. Some organisations may have information on their competitors and on potential customers. Exactly what other information an organisation needs depends on the goods or service that it sells or provides.

Generally, information used by organisations can be separated into three groups:

✪ **That coming in from outside**

✪ **Internal or operational information**

✪ **That going out**

See Chapter 1 for information about standard documents such as business letters and invoices.

Information coming in from outside may be obtained from many sources, e.g. telephone calls, orders from customers, regulations. Prospective employees may complete application forms, customers complete sales order forms, suppliers send product catalogues, and trade magazines are published.

Chris Lane

The reception staff are kept very busy answering incoming telephone calls. Members telephone to book tennis courts, to book a place on a studio class and to arrange an appointment in the Beauty Room.

Just how useful different **sources of information** are to the organisation depends on how up to date the sources are, how relevant the information is to the organisation and how easy it is to obtain the information.

Operational information is private to a company, e.g. sales and income forecasts, instructions to staff, reports. This kind of information is generated by people in the company to be used by other people in the same organisation. This information is confidential to the organisation.

George Honour

George takes great care that the products sold in his butcher's shop are of the highest quality. All meat is kept in a huge walk-in refrigerated storeroom so that it is in the best condition for sale. To ensure that he complies with health regulations, he has several forms that he uses to record information about deliveries of meat made to his shop, such as the temperature of the delivery van. He also records the temperature in his refrigerated storeroom regularly.

He has details of the recipes used to make the many varieties of sausage on sale and the burgers that he makes. To comply with safety regulations, he also has an accident book. All this is operational information.

All organisations need to send information to people outside the organisation, e.g. customers, suppliers, regulatory bodies. These **communications** may be in the form of written documents, e.g. letters, invoices, advertisements. Many communications use telephone links. Some organisations have a web page and may use e-mail for communication with other organisations. E-commerce may be used to place and accept orders, and payments may be made electronically by BACS.

Collecting information on a subject

Having studied sources of information, you must decide on a subject of interest for which you will search for information. The subject could be one related to a company that wants to sell goods, to a product manufacturer or to a provider of some service.

> A company could be thinking of entering the market to sell a service to owners of camping and caravan sites in Europe. The company would want to know, for each country, how many sites there are, the size of the sites, how long the camping/caravanning season is, and a great deal of other information. The company would analyse the information to decide whether or not to go ahead with its sales plans.

You could also choose to investigate a subject of personal interest.

> When you complete your studies, you may be thinking about working abroad for a while to improve your language skills and to take the opportunity to travel. You may need to find out about organisations that place students overseas, and you may also want to investigate travel options. You will need to think about how you will finance your visit, finding out about exchange rates, local employment rates of pay and the cost of rented housing.

Whatever your choice, it must be possible to collect information from a number of different types of source, including paper-based, ICT-based and at least one other.

Plan an investigation into your chosen subject, and make notes for your information pack:

★ Describe clearly the purpose of the investigation and the information you require

★ Make a list of where you think the information may be obtained

★ Explain the methods you will use to search for information

You will need to check with your teacher that your plan matches the requirements of this unit. You will be given a deadline to meet, and you must make sure that your plan allows you enough time to meet this deadline.

Carry out your investigation:

★ Make effective use of sort and search criteria in your use of database and Internet sources of information

★ Use simple search criteria to restrict and control the search for information

★ Work with different information sources in an efficient and effective way

> *Make notes on everything you do. You will need this as evidence of your investigation.*

It is important to write notes to describe the work you have done to find and record information. From your notes, it should be clear that you have a good understanding of a variety of different sources of information and the techniques used to access and extract the required information. This should include the identification of additional sources that may have helped you.

Activity 5.19

Document your investigation. Organise and present the notes so that the information is easy to find and understand.

Keep records and copies of all the information you find and how you found it. In particular, note the source of all information recorded so that someone else can trace the same information.

Annotate clearly the results of information searches and/or screen prints to describe how and why they were produced.

Include evidence to show you can work efficiently in identifying, selecting, rejecting and recording information from your selected sources. In particular, show how you checked that the information you found was accurate and valid, and what steps you took to keep backup copies.

Combine information from two or more sources and use it to draw conclusions not available from a single information source.

Before you hand in your portfolio material for assessment, ask yourself these questions:

★ Is it clear that there is an accurate match between the information extracted and the expressed needs?

★ Have you recorded the information in ways suited to its nature, e.g. using electronic files, paper copies, pictures, sound

continued

continued

recording, tables, graphs, charts or diagrams?

★ Have you presented your work in a logical order that allows the reader to follow the sequence of work and its results?

You might include a contents list and an index.

Revision questions

1. What is information overload? How can it be prevented?

2. What are key words? How are they used?

3. Explain what information is given in a dictionary.

4. How is an encyclopaedia different from a dictionary?

5. How is a thesaurus different from a dictionary?

6. Explain how the Dewey decimal system works.

7. Give three examples of tabular information that you have accessed.

8. Give three examples of graphical information that you have accessed.

9. What is viewdata?

10. What is a path name?

11. Give examples of Internet browsers and search engines that you have used.

12. Give one example of a relational operator and one example of a logical operator.

13. Explain the terms 'survey', 'sample' and 'population'.

14. In what circumstances would you use interviewing rather than questionnaires to collect information?

15. Give three examples of operational information.

Graphics

- Make use of software for creating graphics

- Use ICT to edit, change and create graphic images

- Understand and apply standards used in drawings

This unit also offers the opportunity to develop good working practices. Details about these, which apply to all units in this course, are on page 407 in the Good Working Practice Guide.

This chapter looks in detail at four topics.

✪ Types of image

✪ Graphics software tools and facilities

✪ Producing drawings (vector-based images)

✪ Producing photo and paint images (bitmap graphics), including scanned and photographed images, and clip art

Graphics that you prepare for this unit may provide evidence for presenting information, and may also be useful for any multimedia presentation, should you choose the multimedia optional unit.

Creating and editing images for a wide variety of commercial purposes is now most usually done using computer software. Vector-based software is the type most commonly used to create complex original images. Bitmap graphics programs are used extensively in the publishing industry to edit pictures scanned from colour photographs.

This chapter uses four case studies to illustrate the text:

✪ Bodylife

✪ Chris Lane Leisure Club

✪ Hawkes Design

✪ Penhaven Country House Hotel

Background information on these case studies is given in the Case Studies section on page xvii.

For all four of these organisations, images are an important part of their literature, and for Peter Hawkes his work.

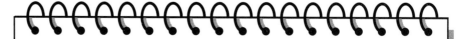

Bodylife

Bodylife magazine has many photos to illustrate the text. An example front cover is shown on page 32 in Chapter 1.

Chris Lane

Chris Lane's logo includes his signature, which suggests that he takes a close personal interest in his club. See examples of his logo in Chapter 1 on pages 10 and 12.

Hawkes Design

Peter Hawkes spends every day working on images. Details of the software he uses are given in Chapter 3 on page 165. Examples of his work appear in Chapter 1: see pages 6 and 17.

Penhaven Country House Hotel

Alan and Maxine are justly proud of their beautiful country house hotel. A photograph, taken from across the lawn and showing flowers in full bloom, is on the front page of their brochure. See Figure 6.1.

"Penhaven Country House Hotel"

Figure 6.1 *Penhaven Country House Hotel: front page of brochure*
Courtesy of Penhaven Country House Hotel

This unit may be assessed through an external assessment, or through your portfolio, depending on your awarding body. See the Examination Guide on page 450 for details of which units are assessed externally by the three awarding bodies: AQA, Edexcel and OCR.

Types of image

Images may be an important part of a document.

Graphic images are commonly used in company logos or simple sketches. They might involve bitmap or vector-graphic images drawn using a graphics software package, or they could be bitmaps of photographs produced by a scanner.

There are two different types of graphic image that you can create by using graphics software:

✪ bitmap images

✪ vector-based graphic images

Bitmap images

Bitmap images are called bitmap because bits of information (0 or 1) are used to map a picture.

Bitmap images are created with **paint** or **photo software**. Each bitmap image is made up of many dots, called **pixels**. These can be coloured or black-and-white (monochrome) dots.

Because bitmap images are composed of pixels, to store just one image you need a very large file (30 Mb for a 20 cm × 25 cm colour photo).

Bitmap images may include elements such as a line or a circle, but to edit these elements you have to edit the dots that form them.

Scanned images are saved as bitmap files. Scanning an image from paper provides a simple means of producing complex bitmap images.

Vector images

Vector images are based on the vectors that you will have learned about in maths. Vectors are pairs of numbers used to describe a movement from one position to another. From the origin to the point (2, 3), rather than going direct, you could move 2 units to the right (in the x direction) and 3 units up (in the y direction). A line starting at the point (2, 3) and going to the point (6, 4) can be described by the vector '4 to the right and 1 up'.

If you draw this line on a 4 $\times$ 6 grid and shade in the squares that would be the line, you have to shade in four squares. With bitmap graphics, Figure 6.2 shows that a 4 $\times$ 6 grid needs 24 bits of information to store the image. Notice that the bitmap image is very poor on this grid size. If the grid is enlarged by a scale factor of 4 (to give greater resolution), the image looks more like the line wanted but is still jagged. This enlarged image needs 16 $\times$ 24 bits, i.e. 384 bits! To create the effect of a line without steps, an even greater number of bits is needed to represent this simple line.

With vector-based graphics, this image can be stored as an identifier (to say it is a line rather than a rectangle or circle) and just four numbers: 2, 3, 4, 1 – which means 'start at point (2, 3) and move 4 right and 1 up'. Similarly, enough information to draw a circle can be stored as three numbers: the coordinates of its centre and a value for its radius. Storing so few numbers means that vector graphics need far less space in memory. Also, they can be drawn to any scale without loss of clarity. Scaling down does not result in jagged lines.

Vector images are created with **draw** or **CAD software**. Each vector image is made up of small elements, called **objects**, such as lines, circles and rectangles. These objects can be selected, moved and changed in size and appearance. To edit a vector-based image, you change the objects that form part of the image.

It is also useful to look at a complex vector image in **wireframe view**. This will show empty outlines of all the objects, including those that do not have an outline in normal view. This can be very useful to see objects that may have become hidden behind others.

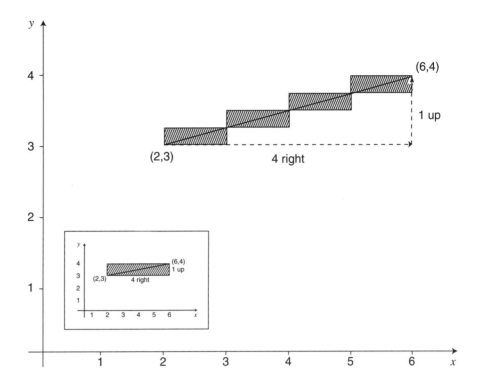

Figure 6.2 *Bitmap versus vector graphics*

Exercise 6.1

Make notes on the two types of graphic image and the differences between them.

Graphics software tools and facilities

Some software allows you to create and edit both bitmap and vector graphics. Your finished page may include both types of graphic.

You need to be able to identify the different types of graphics software. Some are common to all graphics software, some are mainly used for vector-based graphic images, and some are mainly used for bitmap images.

Tools common to all graphics software

Whether you are using vector-based or bitmap graphics software, you will be able to draw lines, circles, rectangles, freehand outlines and other shapes.

Lines have width and style. The **line width** is the thickness of the line. Line thickness is different from **line style**. The line style can be dotted, double and so on (Figure 6.3.)

Figure 6.3 *Different line thicknesses and styles*

**Activity
6.1**

Find out how to draw lines using both types of graphics software: vector and bitmap. What different line widths and line styles are available? Having drawn a line, how can you edit the line? Do you have to delete it and start again, or can you make changes?

Circles can also have **line width** and **line style**. They can be drawn with different line widths and line styles. Drawing the circle will not involve using a compass, and the end result will probably be much better than you might be able to do freehand. How you produce a circle depends on the graphics software package you are using. Probably, first you select 'circle' and decide where one point on the circumference, or where the centre, will be, and then you drag the cursor, using the mouse, until the circle is large enough (Figure 6.4).

Figure 6.4 *Circle styles*

Activity 6.2

Using both types of graphics software, find out how to draw a circle and what different widths and styles are available for drawing circles. Produce two A4 posters, one using vector-based software, the other using bitmap software. In each poster, include at least six different circles using different line widths and line styles to show your findings.

Activities 6.3 to 6.5 develop these posters further, but you may want to save each version and print them out at each stage so that you can use this as evidence in your portfolio.

Did You Know?

A rectangle with rounded corners is called a **soft box**

Rectangles may be drawn with lines: four lines joined at four right-angled corners. Each line can have its own width and style, but it would be more usual for all four to have the same width and style. We can then describe the line width and line style of the whole rectangle. Additional styles may also be used, e.g. a shadow effect to one side of the rectangle.

How you draw the rectangle depends on your graphics software package. Probably, you select 'rectangle', decide where one corner will be and then drag the cursor, using the mouse, to the diagonally opposite corner, until the rectangle is as large as you want. Rectangles usually have **square corners** (that is how you see them in a maths class). In graphics software, though, a 'friendlier' rectangle is often used – one with **rounded corners** (Figure 6.5).

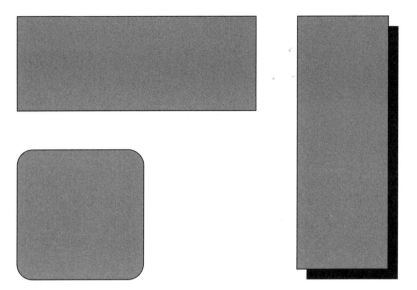

Figure 6.5 *Rectangle styles*

Activity 6.3

Using both types of graphics software, find out how to draw a rectangle.

★ What different widths and styles of line are available for drawing rectangles?

★ What different styles of corner are available?

Amend the posters you created in Activity 6.2 to include some rectangles and use a variety of styles.

Having drawn a diagram, your software will allow you to select component attributes such as fill colour, pattern, thickness and style. A shape (circle or rectangle) may be left empty, or it may be used to enclose a text message, or you may want to **fill** it with a colour or a pattern.

Fill options offered by graphics software packages vary, but usually there is a **palette** of colours and another of patterns to choose from. When you select a fill option, the area where your cursor currently points to changes – and this effect spreads outwards as far as the nearest boundary line. It is important that a shape you want to fill is 'closed', i.e. that there are no gaps in the lines forming the shape. Otherwise, choosing 'fill' results in your whole screen changing to the colour or pattern chosen!

What **colours** you use will depend on your printing facilities. If you do not have a colour printer, then you can only use shades of grey; these can be effective, but not as effective as a splash of colour. You can use coloured paper – for black-and-white or for colour printing.

How many colours you can use will also be affected by your printing facilities; you may be limited to a few colours or have a full palette of shades to choose from. Note that colour results in shades of grey on a printer that does not offer colour printing.

Activity 6.4

Using both types of graphics software, find out what different fill options are available. Amend your posters so that some shapes are filled. Use more than one pattern.

Find out what facilities you have for printing coloured graphic images. Find out how to print in colour rather than black and white. Find out how to use more than one colour at a time. Write notes so that someone new to your graphics software package would know what to do.

Revise your posters to show what colour facilities you have, and your ability to produce graphic images in colour.

Text is presented in a **style** and a certain **size**. Together, these attributes define the **font**. Use of fonts was covered in Chapter 1 (see page 16).

**Activity
6.5**

Using both types of graphics software, find out how to add text to your diagram.

Amend your posters to include some text labels describing the shapes and styles you have used. Draw a line from the label text to the feature it describes.

Add the name of the software package you used and your name in a larger and bolder font to your posters and print them out. File your posters in your portfolio.

Whichever type of graphics software you are using, there will be facilities for editing elements of drawings and images.

**Activity
6.6**

Using both types of graphics software, find out how to use each of these facilities:

cut	move	flip horizontal
copy	rotate	flip vertical

Make notes, especially where the method differs between the two types of software.

The term **image attributes** means the things that describe the graphic image. They include its height, width and the colours used.

- The **height** of a graphic image is the distance from the top to the bottom. It can be measured in centimetres or inches or in lines of the page. You might specify 'full page' or 'half page' as the height, or be more precise and say 5 cm.

⊕ The **width** of a graphic image is the distance from the left-hand side to the right-hand side. It will usually be measured in centimetres or inches (Figure 6.6).

The maximum height of a graphic image is fixed first by the length of the page you are printing it on. The maximum width of a graphic image is also limited by the page size. At most, it could be the width of the page (although you would normally avoid using the margins). However, you normally want to keep the dimensions of a graphic image in proportion, so the height tends to be decided first; the width then follows automatically.

How you control the **size** of a graphic image depends on your graphics software package. You may be able to specify exact measurements. You may be able to enlarge or reduce it to fit a frame in a page layout.

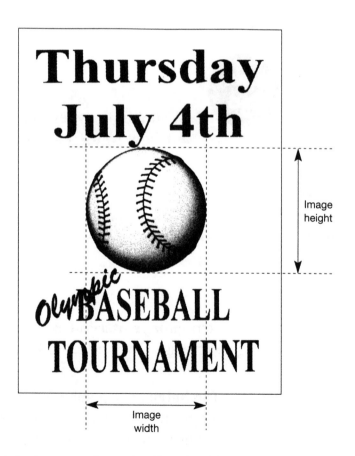

Figure 6.6 *Image attributes: height and width*

Activity 6.7

Find out how to control the size of a graphic image. Write notes so that someone new to your graphics software package would know what to do. Include diagrams in your explanation.

Tools and facilities used mainly with vector-based graphic images

Some tools are used mainly with vector-based graphic images, because the way they are processed is special.

Activity 6.8

You have already used vector-based software to draw simple shapes. Check that you can draw to scale, and that you know how to use the **grid snap** facility.

Explore other facilities that your vector-based software provides, and make notes.

Note the coordinates of the points at each end of a line. From this, calculate how long the line is and check this on your diagram.

> If you draw a triangle with a horizontal line of length 3 cm, and a 4 cm line at right angles to it, the hypotenuse (the longest side, opposite the right angle) of the triangle should be 5 cm in length.

If an image is produced using vector-based software, the parts of the image will be created as individual objects. These objects can then be **grouped** and treated as a single object.

Activity 6.9

Using vector-based graphics software, find out how to group and ungroup objects.

Explore the effect of the **move to back** and **move to front** options.

To find out how complex images are created, try to take apart a vector-based clip art graphic.

Start by ungrouping the picture to separate it into its individual objects – it may also be necessary to ungroup subgroups.

Then select and move the individual objects and change their positions in the layers of the image.

> Your teacher will be able to give you a complex image to work on.

Tools and facilities used mainly with bitmap graphic images

Bitmap images are created as elements that are combined in a single layer. The elements cannot be combined or moved separately.

Bitmap images are stored as pixels, so the way to change an image is to edit the pixels. To see each pixel, you need to **zoom** in on your image. You can then change the individual pixels.

Activity 6.10

Starting with a bitmap clip art or scanned image, make small changes to show that you can edit pixels.

You might add a moustache or glasses, or change the hairstyle of an image of yourself.

If you were *not* using an ICT system, what tools would you use to create special effects?

When drawing, you usually use a pen or pencil to make lines, which then form shapes. When painting, you may use a brush or a roller; this gives a different effect. If painting a large area, you might use a paint sprayer.

Graphics software usually offers the same three tools: **pencil**, **brush** and **spray**. Each one produces a different effect. You can also vary the width of your pencil, or your brush. You can then be quite precise if you want to, or create broad strokes if that is the effect you want.

The brush and spray options are linked to the colour and pattern palettes, so you can 'spray' a colour or pattern on to the screen.

Activity 6.11

Find out how to use the brush and spray options in your graphics software package.

Editing graphic images

You need to demonstrate that you can create and edit graphic images using both bitmap and vector-based graphics software. The editing tools that your graphics software provides are also used in other ICT activities, e.g. word processing, spreadsheets and databases:

cut	move	delete
copy	paste	insert

To **cut** or **crop** involves changing a graphic image to remove part of it. You may use an **eraser** tool to cut parts of a bitmap image. To **delete** involves removing the whole image.

Copy and move have the same meanings as in document processing. You use **copy** to repeat a graphic image or part of it; you use **move** to change the position of a graphic image or part of it.

The **paste** tool allows you to bring in graphic images that were cut (or copied) from elsewhere, possibly from a library of clip art or from some other graphic image you have drawn.

As with producing documents, when designing a graphic, you need to select a suitable page layout, including suitable margins, page orientation and page size. Refer to Chapter 1 for details of these.

Activity 6.12

You have already produced two A4 posters, one using bitmap graphics and the other using vector-based graphics software.

Look back to see if you have evidence that you can edit graphic images. If so, annotate your printouts to show which facilities you have used. If not, work on your posters to produce edited versions and annotate these.

Producing vector-based graphic images (drawings)

In real life, things are three-dimensional: a building, a car or a shirt.

To design a three-dimensional object, two-dimensional drawings are produced and recorded on a sheet of paper. These drawings show how to do something, how something will look, or they form a record of how something does look.

✪ Plans of a room, a workbench or the layout of a car park

✪ A drawing of how to make something, e.g. a bookcase, a fence panel, a desk or an item of clothing

✪ Diagrams such as maps, management charts or wiring layouts

Suppose you wanted to make a box. Initial ideas might be sketched, but drawings created for the production of items must be accurate and of the correct scale. The diagram must include information that shows the size of each part of the product. This would include the height, width and depth of the box.

Exercise 6.2

Draw a rough sketch of your classroom. If you had to draw an accurate plan of your classroom on a sheet of A4 paper, what scale should you use? What extra information should you show on your diagram?

There are three **object views**: plan, elevation and side view. The **plan view** looks at the object from above. The **elevation view** looks at it from the front. And the **side view** looks at it from the side. See Figure 6.7.

To show all the necessary information, and to produce a drawing from which someone can work accurately, you must be able to use the coordinates provided in the software to produce accurate scale drawings, and to use the facilities provided in the software to place these dimensions on the drawing correctly.

Dimensions are usually given in metric units (millimetres, centimetres, metres or kilometres), but some older plans may show Imperial units (inches, feet and yards). Angles are shown in degrees.

In explaining what **scale** you have used, you have a choice of ways to express this.

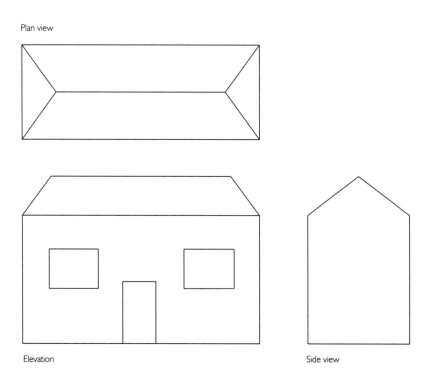

Plan view

Elevation

Side view

Figure 6.7   *Plan, elevation and side views of a house*

If you draw a plan with all dimensions half the actual size, you could write 'half size' or '1:2' or '1/2 full size'.

Most maps show the scale as a ratio, two numbers separated by a colon. The first number represents the plan, and the second number represent the real-world object. 1:25000 means that 1 cm on a map represents 25,000 cm in the real world.

There are some commonly accepted standards for constructing drawings. Special technical terms are used for different aspects of graphic images. There are three main **line types**:

✪ **Outlines** are shown as thick lines

✪ **Hidden features** are shown as dashed lines

✪ **Dimensions** are shown as thin lines

Activity 6.13

Look at several map books. What scale is used? How is the scale expressed?
Look at other examples of scale drawings. Identify the three views: plan, elevation and side.
Find examples of the three line types and note how dimensions are expressed.

For your portfolio, you need to produce images that show you can use both bitmap and vector-based graphics software. You will need to produce a set of documents that show your graphic skills.

Prepare a selection of documents that demonstrate your skills in using vector-based graphics software:

★ A plan view of a room, e.g. your bedroom
★ A drawing of a piece of furniture that is to be made by someone else, e.g. a bookcase
★ A map, e.g. how to get home from your school or college

Make sure that your selection of documents shows that you have good skills in using facilities such as scaling, mirroring, rotating, cloning, grouping, and so on.

If you are to be assessed externally, your awarding body will decide what you have to produce, and you will be told before your examination.

Producing bitmap graphic images (photo and paint images)

Apart from representing three-dimensional plans, two-dimensional drawings are also produced on paper to pass information to others, e.g. an advertisement or publicity poster for a sporting event, a sale or a play.

Some types of picture cannot be created using vector graphics. Too much detail is needed – at pixel level – so these are more easily created in a bitmap program.

If picture graphics are used with text for publicity posters, it is important that the page is planned to allow for both, and that you are accurate in the construction and organisation of elements. This is especially important where lines and shapes join or touch. Sometimes, if this not done carefully, one element can overflow into other areas, so that part of the text, or part of the diagram, is not shown fully.

Patterns involve a repetition of a design. Having designed the pattern, it is quite easy to repeat it to produce a sample of the material that might be used for wallpaper, curtains and matching seat covers.

Activity 6.15

You have already created and edited bitmap images to produce an A4 poster. In Activity 6.10 you also edited a clip art or scanned bitmap image. Check that you have evidence in your portfolio that you can produce and edit bitmap images, and that these are annotated with how you achieved the end result.

Rather than draw bitmap images, which takes a long time, you can scan images or use ready-made clip arts. If you have a digital camera, you can also load photos direct from the camera and incorporate them into documents.

Scanned images

Bitmap images are used a lot in the publishing industry to edit pictures scanned from colour photographs. It is possible to change the overall colour balance, remove blemishes and manipulate a scanned image in many ways.

A **scanner** is a piece of hardware that works in a similar way to a photocopier. But, unlike a photocopier, it copies images from paper and turns them into computer graphic files.

Activity 6.16

Scan in a drawing in black and white. Pixel edit the bitmap image to produce a colour version of the drawing.

It is possible to scan colour as well as black-and-white images. These files can be very large. When files are very large they are difficult for the computer to handle quickly. When handling large colour photographs, the computer may work very slowly because there are so many bitmap dots to deal with.

Bodylife

Bodylife staff spend most of their time talking to clients and contacts on the telephone. To introduce a personal note into the business, the Bodylife compliments slip includes a colour photograph of the person whose name appears on the slip. Figure 6.8 shows a picture of Nicky at Bodylife.

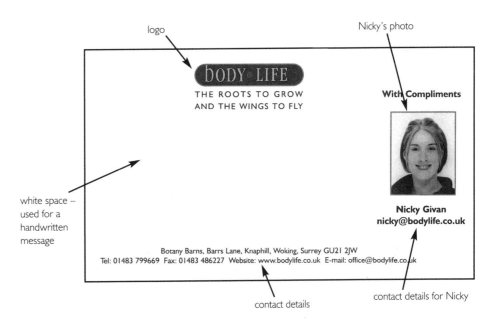

Figure 6.8 *Bodylife compliments slip*
Courtesy of Bodylife

Penhaven Country House Hotel

Penhaven's compliments slip includes a graphic image of a badger. Maxine and Alan encourage and protect the badgers that live in a wooded area within the hotel grounds. See Figure 6.9.

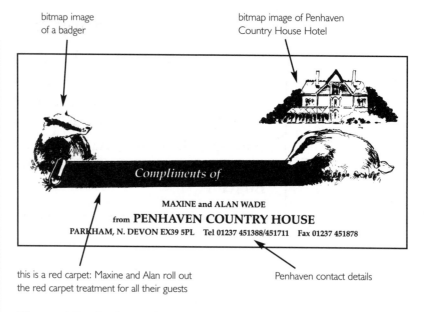

bitmap image of a badger

bitmap image of Penhaven Country House Hotel

this is a red carpet: Maxine and Alan roll out the red carpet treatment for all their guests

Penhaven contact details

Figure 6.9 *Penhaven Country House Hotel compliments slip*
Courtesy of Penhaven Country House Hotel

Clip art

It is possible to obtain disks and CD-ROMs that contain ready-made drawings and pictures. These drawings and pictures are called **clip art**. You can use clip art to improve the appearance of a presentation that you are making. You must be able to use bitmap and vector-based clip art to improve your work.

Most clip art is copyright free. However, some clip art has copyright protection, and you must obtain permission to use material that is protected by copyright.

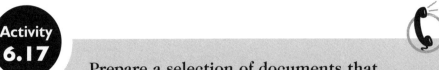

Activity 6.17

Prepare a selection of documents that demonstrate your skills in using bitmap graphics software:

★ A publicity poster for an event that combines clip art, scanned images and text

★ A wallpaper or fabric pattern

★ A collage or pattern including scanned images

> If you are to be assessed externally, your awarding body will decide what you have to produce, and you will be told before your examination.

Revision questions

1. Explain how bitmap images are stored.

2. Explain how vector images are stored.

3. What software is used to create and edit bitmap images? Give one example of software that you have used to edit a bitmap image.

4. What software is used to create and edit vector-based images? Give one example of software that you have used to edit a vector graphic image.

5. What is a pixel?

6. Give examples of different line styles.

7. What is a palette?

8. Give examples of image attributes.

9. Why would you need to use 'move to back' and 'move to front' ?

10. What is clip art?

11. Explain the difference between brush and spray.

12. What happens if you crop an image?

13. How are hidden features shown on a technical drawing? How are dimensions shown?

14. What is meant by plan, elevation and side views? What is a wireframe? What is meant by the term 'gridsnap'?

15. Explain how a scanner works. What kind of image does a scanner produce?

Multimedia

7

- Using multimedia computer systems

- Using multimedia creation software

- Making original presentations that include sound and images

- Appreciating the qualities of different types of multimedia presentation

Multimedia means 'many media'. The media in multimedia can be text, graphics, sound and video. Combining two or more of these media results in a multimedia presentation.

Multimedia is used for learning, for animation, for slide shows, for games and in web pages on the Internet. Commercially produced multimedia presentations are used for education, entertainment, advertising, and so on. Those used for advertising may be free, on CDs supplied with a computer magazine or on the Internet.

Multimedia tools have been developed, so now you can make exciting and attractive presentations too.

For this unit, you will create two multimedia presentations: one on your own and one as part of a team. However, you need to practise using the hardware involved and the various types of multimedia software before you will be ready to produce evidence for this unit. Therefore, your teacher may suggest that you create a team presentation to practise working together and to pick up some skills. Then you might create your own presentation, so that you feel quite competent before attempting the final two presentations: one on your own and one with a team.

This unit has close links with and builds on two other units: *Presenting Information* and *Graphics*. The images you create in the *Graphics* unit could be used in this unit. Also, since you will be working in a team for one of your presentations, you should read Chapter 9: *Working as Part of a Team*.

This unit will be assessed through your portfolio work only. The grade awarded will be your grade for the unit.

This chapter covers five topics:

❂ **Presentation techniques**

❂ **Accuracy and suitability**

❂ **Software**

❂ **Multimedia skills**

❂ **Planning techniques**

One case study is used to illustrate the text: the Met Office. Background information about this case study is given in the Case Studies section on page xxiii.

Presentation techniques

Chapter 1 concentrated on presenting information. With multimedia presentations, you need to present your message so that it is easy to understand. There are lots of ways you can achieve this:

- Using colour, shading and highlighting

- Using tables, bullet points and borders

- Using bitmap/vector and scanner/camera images

- Using clip art, drawings and charts

- Using scaling and spacing

- Using sounds

For consistency, you should choose an appropriate layout and style of presentation, and repeat elements such as logos or headers and footers.

The most important task in building an effective multimedia production is to hold the attention of the audience. In the early activity, you will be the audience. In later activities, you will be preparing multimedia presentations for other audiences, and it will be your task to keep your audience interested.

The Met Office

The Met Office provides information for the TV networks, which present weather forecasts to viewers. In newspapers, the weather news is presented as a map of the country with isobars showing the weather patterns.

On teletext screens, a text message is displayed that summarises the weather expected in various regions of the country. A graphic effect might show a sun or rain. Coloured text can also be used to attract attention.

On weather forecasts that accompany the news, a presentation can include satellite pictures to show cloud cover and wind direction. Symbols used to mean cloud, rain, snow and sunshine are placed on a background that represents the country. Arrows are used to show wind direction.

More recently, weather forecasts have included sequences, which show what weather is expected over the next few days. The Met Office website is at http://www.meto.gov.uk. It offers much more information, in an interactive way.

As a group, collect as many examples – and as many different types – of multimedia presentation as you can.

> Adverts in magazines may offer a free CD that you can send off for. Your school or college library may also have educational multimedia CDs.

Watch these presentations together and discuss which ones are good, and which are not. Individually, give each presentation a mark out of 10, and from this identify your top three presentations.
Compare your top three with those of others in your group.

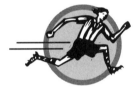

In your group, each one of you can decide whether a multimedia presentation is good or bad. Because it is your personal opinion, there may be disagreement within the group.

For an unbiased decision, you need to think about why you consider one presentation to be not so good and why another is better. To do this, you should think about the features of the presentation:

✪ What is the purpose of the presentation?

✪ Who is the intended audience?

✪ What components make up a multimedia presentation?

✪ What is the impact on the audience?

✪ Is the presentation appropriate and effective?

The aim or **purpose** of the presentation will have had an important bearing on how the material should be presented. Educational presentations should clearly and accurately present the material in detail. Multimedia presentations that are made for entertainment will present the material in an eye-catching and amusing way. Some educational presentations aim to entertain at the same time as teaching something – the balance between presenting detailed information and amusing the audience is more difficult to achieve.

Presentations are usually aimed at a particular **target audience**. Some are aimed at adults, others at children. Some are aimed at prospective customers of a product, or a service.

Some organisations display a presentation in their reception area so that visitors can learn about the company while they wait.

The Met Office

It is possible to visit the Met Office headquarters in Bracknell and see how the weather forecasters gather their information and transform it into the weather bulletins seen on television and in the newspapers. In the entrance hall, an interactive display explains how weather data is collected all over the world and combined to create weather forecasts.

Did You Know?

amazon.co.uk includes music clips of tracks from CDs that are for sale

Dating agencies make video clips of those looking for partners. These are then included in a database so that clients can view the ones that match their requirements.

Some estate agencies produce presentations of houses for sale so that interested buyers can view the properties without having to visit each one in person, and from that draw up a shortlist of properties they actually want to visit.

Each presentation is made from different elements, such as text, graphics, animation and sound. When designing your own presentation, you need to think about when one type of component is more suitable than another.

A multimedia training CD may include a section on 'trouble shooting – what to do when your printer jams'. A video clip or animation sequence of removing the paper that has jammed and restarting the printer, together with a voice track explaining each step, would be more effective than a still picture and a text description of how to do it.

There are lots of ways of communicating a message. The most straightforward technique, often used in multimedia educational and training presentations, is to give an explanation. Using this technique to sell a product may include listing the advantages of the product or service: it's the best, the cheapest, the fastest, the most powerful, the one that really works, etc.

This technique relies on the audience being interested enough to watch and listen, and take in the message. An alternative, more widely used, method is called the 'soft sell'. With this method, the product or service is linked with an image that may appeal to the audience. The audience is encouraged to link buying the product with an improved lifestyle, e.g. people who buy this product are better off, fashionable, popular, and so on.

Accuracy and suitability

The main purpose of a multimedia presentation is to communicate a message. In successful presentations, the message is communicated as effectively as possible.

What makes a presentation effective?

There a number of tactics that can be used to communicate a message:

✪ Shock or surprise your audience

✪ Amuse your audience

✪ Appeal to a particular audience

Shock tactics have been used for public information films about the dangers of taking drugs, smoking or drink-driving. By showing the effects of these things – personal stories from those who have suffered but survived, or the parents or friends of the people who have died – audiences may be shocked into taking these dangers more seriously.

Amusement is commonly found in TV advertisements. Most audiences enjoy watching the adverts that make them smile or laugh out loud. These adverts are more likely to be watched again and again, and this means that the product being advertised is remembered. It does not necessarily mean that people will buy it – or does it? At least by amusing the target audience the product might be looked on in a more favourable light.

Appealing to a particular audience makes a lot of sense. Television adverts are most often targeted to appeal to one particular group of people – the people who might buy the product.

Adverts for soft drinks or casual designer clothes are often targeted to appeal to young people.

Washing-powder adverts are often targeted at women, although they may feature other family members, e.g. children bringing home dirty sports kit.

Adverts for cars may be targeted at men, or at women, depending on the make of car.

Exercise 7.1

Think of some more examples of advertisements that are targeted at particular audiences. Notice adverts that are shown early in the morning, those shown during afternoon programmes and those shown in the evenings. What does this tell you about the products and about the audience that is expected to view television at these times?

Deciding who and what appears in the advertisement sets the scene for the target audience. A presentation about the problems of long-term care for the elderly might include video clips of interviews with doctors and patients rather than video clips of young and healthy people. A presentation about your college is more likely to include pictures of people at the school than in the local supermarket.

What are the factors of a successful presentation?

When looking at a presentation, trying to decide whether it gets its message across, you need to give reasons why it does or does not succeed. Using this knowledge, you will be able to create more effective and successful presentations of your own. There are a number of factors that you will want to consider:

- ✪ Content

- ✪ Pace

- ✪ Level of interaction

- ✪ Ease of use

- ✪ Layout

Exactly what is included in a presentation – the **content** or the quantity of information in text, pictures and sounds – should be just enough to inform the audience. Too much information may confuse or bore the audience. Not enough information may leave the audience dissatisfied.

The **pace** at which information is presented should be determined by what the audience needs to do with it. If they need to copy down a telephone number or an address, the information needs to remain long enough for them not to feel rushed but not so long that they lose interest. If information is presented too rapidly for the user to take it in, the message will not get across effectively.

The Met Office

In weather forecasts presented with the news on TV, the weather man or woman controls the pace of the presentation, using a button to call in the next 'slide'.

Interaction between the presentation and the audience is more likely to engage the attention of the audience and therefore communicate the message better. Where the information is presented in a passive way, without requiring any response from the audience, they are less likely to remember the message. If the audience is involved, e.g. clicking buttons or answering questions, they are more likely to remember the presentation.

> Tourist information boards offer an interactive presentation that can be used to help you to find out details of local facilities, e.g. hotels and theatres.

Ease of use is another important factor. A passive presentation may require no input from the audience; it is easy just to sit and watch. If there is some level of interaction, it is important that user instructions are provided. If the route through the presentation, and how to proceed, is too complex, an audience may give up trying to use the presentation and be left with a negative impression.

Last, but not least, the **layout** chosen for a presentation should be applied consistently. This then makes an impression on the audience, but in a subconscious way. A confused or inconsistent layout will be more noticeable and may give the audience a negative impression of the presentation.

Activity 7.2

As a group, brainstorm what you think makes a good multimedia presentation. Make a checklist of points that you will use to score presentations. Produce a form that you can use to evaluate multimedia presentations.

Brainstorming hints can be found in Chapter 4 (page 195).

The more multimedia presentations that you watch – with a critical eye, looking for good and bad points – the better you may become at designing your own presentations.

Activity 7.3

Choose two or three presentations that appeared in some of your groups' top five but not in everyone's top three. Watch the presentations as a group but, individually, give them scores out of five for each item on the checklist.

For some items on the checklist, you may use your first reactions to a presentation. For others, you may want to watch the presentation several times. Add up the scores and compare them with others in your group.

★ Can you reach agreement on what makes a good multimedia presentation?
★ Can you agree what makes a poor presentation?

Make notes on what you think makes a good presentation and what you need to avoid.

Deciding on the structure and content of the presentation can be the most difficult part of creating the presentation. By now, you will realise how important it is that your presentation uses language, images and sounds that match the needs of your audience and that are suited to your message. You need to make a choice that will get your message across to your target audience as effectively as possible. You must then practise combining these elements to create the right mood for your presentation. For this, you need software.

Software

Three main types of applications software are suitable for creating multimedia presentations:

✪ **Presentation software**

✪ **HTML web page software**

✪ **Multimedia authoring software**

Microsoft PowerPoint allows you to create a **slide show**.

Microsoft FrontPage allows you to create web pages and includes an HTML editor.

As with word-processing software, which offers similar facilities to those available with DTP software, the edges between these three types of software will become more blurred as newer versions become available.

Exercise 7.2

Resources for this unit should include suitable multimedia equipment to enable you to meet its requirements – such as audio recording equipment, a scanner and/or a digital camera – together with access to clip art and appropriate software for editing the media elements.
Find out what hardware and software resources are available for you to use for this unit.

If you have never used the hardware before, e.g. a digital camera, make time to find out how it works.

If you have never used some of the software before, watch a demonstration and make notes on the features available.

You must learn to create different types of multimedia presentation and then prepare at least two presentations: one using HTML web page software and the other demonstrating your ability to use one of the other two types of software.

Presentation software, such as Microsoft PowerPoint, lets you create presentations in the form of slide shows. A slide show comprises individual frames (called **slides**). The slides can be printed and used as OHTs (overhead transparencies), or put on to film. The presentation can be viewed on a PC screen or, for an effective presentation to a larger audience, the slides can be projected direct from the PC on to a white screen.

The Met Office

The Met Office has a multimedia presentation on the history of weather forecasting, which can be included in talks given to visitors to the Bracknell headquarters. The slides are projected on to a large screen, which everyone in the lecture hall can see. The speaker controls the slides from a PC.

Wizards are available so that you can select an overall style and also a general content. You can then enter text, and features included allow you to draw pictures, insert clip art and videos, create tables and bullet lists – all things you normally do with word-processing or graphics software.

When designing the sequence of slides, movement from screen to screen can be controlled manually, or you can automate this.

If you will be talking through the presentation of slides, the software can help you to plan the timing. You can rehearse what you will say. When you are ready to start, you can set a clock to start and the software then times you. From this, you can plan the overall time of the presentation. If it is too long, you will have to think about how you can cut it down to fit the available time. If it is too short, you can think about how you can include more information to fill all the time you have. If the presentation is to be automatic, you can set the time that each slide is to remain on view. How long will depend on the amount of information on the slide.

You may also include transition slides that control what appears between slides. The software provides a variety of options. Some transitions involve a 'fade' from one screen to the next; others give the impression of horizontal (or vertical) blinds closing on one slide and opening on the other. For consistency, you might use the same transition between each pair of screens. If you want the audience to see the transition, you can set the timing to 'slow'.

Presentation software provides facilities to keep notes on each slide and offers a variety of print options so that the audience can also be given a copy of the slides. This can save them taking notes during the presentation.

It should be easy to change the order the slides appear in your presentation, so you can create slides in whatever order that occurs to you and rearrange them into the most sensible order for the presentation. It should also be possible to hide slides, so that one set of slides can be used for more than one presentation. Hidden slides might also be useful if the presentation takes less time than you had planned. The hidden slides can be kept in reserve and used only if time allows.

Activity 7.4

Using presentation software, explore the features available. Watch any demonstration that is available and make notes.

Use this checklist to make sure that you fully understand how to produce a presentation using this particular type of software:

★ Design screen frames or pages
★ Use graphics, text and sound
★ Create presenter notes
★ Provide manual control of the display
★ Use automated timing for each frame
★ Use a variety of slide-frame transitions

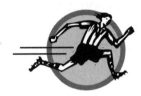

Did You Know?

More recent versions of Microsoft PowerPoint include options to introduce *animation effects* into a presentation

HTML or **hyperlink (web page) software** lets you do similar things to presentation software. The unit of information is called a **page** rather than a slide, but each page can contain the same kind of information as a slide: text, graphics, sound. In addition, you can allow **user interaction** and set up links between pages using **hyperlinks**.

Exercise 7.3

Check whether your presentation software provides enough facilities to be called HTML or hyperlink (web page) software.

Activity 7.5

Using HTML web page software, explore the features available. Watch any demonstration that is available and make notes.

Use this checklist to make sure that you fully understand how to produce a presentation using this particular type of software:

★ Design pages of information
★ Use graphics, text and sound
★ Use video or animation files
★ Enable user interaction
★ Set hyperlinks to display new pages
★ Access and modify HTML code

Multimedia authoring software is similar to HTML web page software, but instead of slides or pages, the unit of information is a **screen**, and you edit the program code (or **script**).

Exercise 7.4

Check whether your HTML web page software provides enough facilities to be called multimedia authoring software.

Using multimedia authoring software, explore the features available. Watch any demonstration that is available and make notes. Use this checklist to make sure that you fully understand how to produce a presentation using this particular type of software:

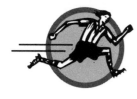

★ Design screen displays
★ Use graphics, text, sound and video
★ Animate images
★ Adjust the speed of display
★ Interact with users
★ Edit the program code (or script)

Multimedia skills

Many multimedia presentations are produced as a result of a group of people working together. You will work in a group to create at least one team presentation. When working with others in your team, everyone in the group should learn how to behave so that as a team you are successful:

- ✪ Agree responsibilities for a presentation

- ✪ Contribute constructively and productively

- ✪ Work to agreed deadlines

- ✪ Respond constructively to suggestions

- ✪ Offer helpful comments

- ✪ Listen to the opinions of others

Working as part of a team is covered in Chapter 9 in detail. Work done in preparing a multimedia presentation may provide useful evidence for that unit, and for your *Working with Others* key skills.

To create a multimedia presentation, the first step is to decide the **scope** of your presentation – what information your presentation is going to cover, and what you are going to exclude.

Activity 7.7

In a small group, brainstorm ideas for a multimedia presentation that you will produce as a team. Here are some ideas related to your school or college to get you started:

★ A slide show presentation of the staff in your school, grouped by department

★ An explanation of the courses available at your school or college, to be put on display during an open evening

★ A tour of your school or college, to be on show in the school entrance

Evaluate all the ideas and decide on a topic that appeals to everyone in the group. Make notes on what you have agreed.

> You may decide that one person in the team should be the scribe – the person to write down the ideas and to write up the notes from the meeting.

A **flowchart** can be used to show the route through the presentation and is particularly useful for presentations with multiple paths

The ideas you come up with at this stage need not be detailed. However, you should identify how the user will interact with the presentation and navigate through it, and what sort of 'story' the presentation will tell. Having decided on a general topic, you need to decide what you will include in your presentation, and for this you can use one or both of two tools: a **flowchart** and a **storyboard**.

If your team decides to produce information on the staff at your school or college, you may decide to use a slide show. The very first slide might show a picture of the school and an introductory paragraph explaining how many staff are currently employed. This first slide could lead to a slide showing an overview of the various departments. Then a series of slides – one per department – could show the staff in a department displayed as an organisation chart. Photos of individual heads of department could be shown at the top of each chart.

Figure 7.1 shows a flowchart and a storyboard for a presentation describing a school. Notice that the storyboard combines a diagram or picture of the slide or page with written details of the content:

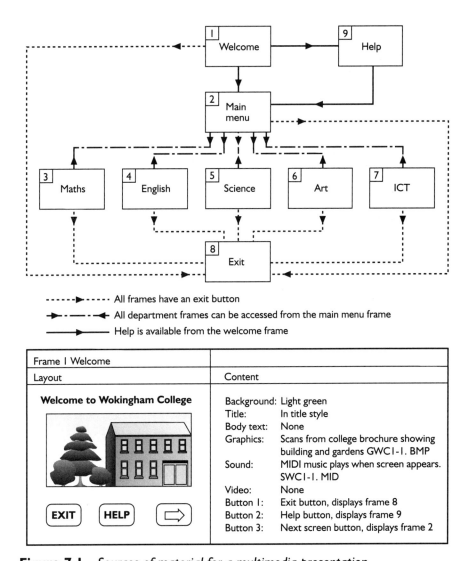

Figure 7.1 *Sources of material for a multimedia presentation*

✪ The diagram shows the individual elements and their approximate layout

✪ The written description provides details of the source and the content, including the effect of clicking on the buttons or hot spots

Each slide, page or screen in a presentation should carry a limited amount of information. The order of material on the screen must be logical, working top to bottom and left to right. Text and images should be large enough to be seen and read easily. Colour may be used to improve the design, but you should take care – too much colour may detract attention from the message.

Having decided on the content of your presentation, you need to identify where each piece of material will come from – the source of material.

Table 7.1 lists the variety of material you might decide to include in your presentation. Make sure that you have the necessary hardware before making final decisions on what you will include.

Content	Source
Text	You might create this yourself, or you might take it from material already available, e.g. a brochure
Clip art pictures	These are available as part of many software packages
Background pictures	These are available (copyright-free) as clip art
Photographs	You can take these yourself using a digital camera, or you could scan in photos taken on a standard camera
Spoken commentary	You will need to record this yourself
Background music	Some copyright-free music can be downloaded from the Internet, but music CDs are copyright, and you cannot use them without obtaining permission
Video clips	You could record these yourself if you have access to a camcorder

Table 7.1 *Sources of material for a multimedia presentation*

For your slide show of the staff in your school, you may be able to take photos using a digital camera.

Activity 7.8

As a group, produce a storyboard showing what your team presentation will include. For each item, give details of who will prepare it and the source of the information.

Agree a timetable for completing the presentation so that it can be finished before any deadline your teacher may set you.

You may decide that one of your team should be made responsible for checking progress, to make sure everyone in the team stays on schedule.

There are many places where you can find pictures, video clips and music, such as the Internet. You must note any **copyright restrictions**, since almost all commercially produced videos and music cannot legally be used in your presentation without the permission of the copyright holder. In most cases, if your presentation is to be used for financial gain, the copyright holder may give permission, but only on payment of a royalty charge. If your presentation is to be used as evidence in an examination situation, you may find that permission will be given without any charge.

In developing your first team multimedia presentation, you may use skills that you have already learned on this course:

- ✪ Scanning images and text

- ✪ Using pictures, drawings and clip art

- ✪ Using graphs and charts

You may also learn new skills:

- ✪ Using sound

- ✪ Setting the timing of frames or display

- ✪ Setting the speed of replay

- ✪ Selecting suitable transitions

- ✪ Sequencing sound, text and graphics

- ✪ Editing and modifying program code

- ✪ Providing for suitable user interaction

- ✪ Setting hyperlinks to navigate pages

It is unlikely that you'll master all these skills by producing just one multimedia presentation.

Activity 7.9

When you have completed your first team presentation, review how it went and identify what skills you learned as an individual. From the list above, identify any skills that you have yet to master and make a note to cover them in your next multimedia presentation.

Planning techniques

As with any project, planning can affect the quality of your finished work. It is important to allow time in your plan to watch the latest version of your presentation and to think about changes that may improve it.

Keeping a log of exactly how much time you spend on one presentation will help you to plan for the next one. If you make notes of what you achieve alongside 'clocking on' and 'clocking off' times, you'll soon be able to gauge how much more time you need to spend on a presentation.

> If one slide takes you 20 minutes to complete, and you plan to include twelve slides in your presentation, it is likely to take you 4 hours to produce all the slides. If each slide take you an hour to create – perhaps you should think about having fewer slides in your presentation!

Each new presentation that you create will give you more experience so that, eventually, you will be able to visualise the effect you want before you start. In this way, you will learn to plan the design of your productions.

It is important that you make notes:

✪ What you are setting out to do (your message)

✪ Your audience and their particular needs

✪ Material to be included in your presentation (sounds, words, images, video)

✪ Sketches outlining the content and operation of your presentation (a storyboard)

Your final presentation needs to be fully documented:

✪ Details of user requirements, i.e. the target audience

✪ Deadlines set by your teacher

✪ Planning notes, including a schedule and initial draft ideas, e.g. as a storyboard

✪ Details of individual responsibilities and group work

✪ Working drafts

✪ Working multimedia files

✪ Printed copy with annotation

✪ Clearly written user requirements and planning notes that define the presentation, including a storyboard, the individual and group responsibilities, the audience, and the sources of materials to be used

Activity 7.10

Plan and design your own multimedia presentation.
Produce a storyboard with a brief outline description of the content of each screen/page.
Use a flowchart to indicate the sequence of screens and the different routes for the user.

continued

continued

Make sure that your presentation covers your chosen topic in adequate detail.

Carry out your plans and show that you can work independently to produce your presentation to agreed deadlines.

In producing your multimedia presentation, make sure that you demonstrate your multimedia skills:

★ Using presentation techniques appropriately to combine a variety of textual, graphic and sound elements

★ Scanning images and text, editing sound and using graphics

★ Combining the elements of your presentation in an imaginative and smooth sequence

★ Managing the presentation appropriately – with suitable timing sequences and transitions between scenes, or hot spot links in an interactive presentation

★ Editing program code correctly to achieve a desired result – and producing annotated printed copy as evidence of this

Check that you have made good use of button, text and graphic hyperlinks between documents, files or sites so that your user can navigate your presentation where necessary.

Document your presentation and file this as evidence in your portfolio:

★ A storyboard that clearly defines the script, associates script with graphics used and defines timing and transitions

★ Clear, well-prepared and well-written notes, making appropriate use of technical language

continued

continued

To show that you have developed a good understanding of the different types of multimedia software, make comments on any problems experienced and possible improvements to your multimedia presentations.

Your evaluation should be clear and concise and make fluent use of technical language. It should also include the views of users.

Check that you have now covered the list of multimedia skills given on page 317. If there are any that you have not yet tackled, make a note to remember to include these in your next activity.

Check the accuracy of your work and keep backup copies of all files.

When you have completed a multimedia presentation on your own, you will be ready to contribute towards the team presentation that will be used as evidence for this unit.

Activity 7.11

Working as a team, use multimedia software to produce a team presentation. As a team, you must demonstrate good skills in planning, production and teamwork.

Decide on a plan and agree roles and responsibilities within the team.

Design your presentation to make good use of text, images, animation, sound and colour, and blend the different elements into an interesting, smooth sequence. Document your presentation fully, including your own contribution to the team effort.

Evaluate your presentation, making sure that this demonstrates your understanding of the function and purpose of the main features of multimedia presentations and the software used.

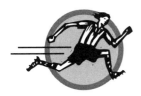

Revision questions

1.   What does multimedia mean?

2.   What is a target audience?

3.   In what ways can you achieve a consistent layout and style of presentation?

4.   Name three things that help to make a good multimedia presentation.

5.   Name three things to avoid when making presentations.

6.   Give two examples of how shock tactics might be used in a multimedia presentation.

7. Give two examples of advertisements that rely on humour.

8. Give two examples of multimedia presentations that appeal to a particular audience.

9. Explain how the pace of a presentation can be a factor in its success.

10. In what ways can the audience interact with a multimedia presentation?

11. Name three different types of applications software that are suitable for creating multimedia presentations and explain the difference between them.

12. Explain the difference between a slide, a page and a screen.

13. What is the purpose of a hyperlink?

14. What information is given in a storyboard?

15. What is HTML?

Preparing for Employment

8

● Look for jobs and training

● Choose a job or training that suits you

● Write a job or training application

● Prepare yourself for a job or training interview

This chapter looks in detail at four topics:

✪ Where to look for jobs or training opportunities

✪ Choosing suitable jobs or training

✪ Applying for jobs

✪ Preparing for an interview

Getting a job may seem impossible just now. Where you live, unemployment rates may be very high. You may be undecided about the kind of job you would be happy doing.

When you do get a job, it may not be great fun, working every day and having much less free time than you do while you are at school or college. One of the plus points is that you will have money to spend. You can look forward to some financial independence, spending your own money on the things you want. The bonus would be to get a job that you really enjoy, working with people like yourself and feeling enthusiastic about going to work each morning.

This unit gives you the chance to practise and prepare for all four stages of getting a job or training. You will investigate the different ways of looking for jobs or training and think about why a job or training suits you – and you it!

You will need to work out your strengths, skills and interests and to match them to the types of job or training that would suit you best.

If you are thinking about further training, your own careers adviser at your school or college will be able to help you to find the course that is right for you. At some point, though, you will need to think about getting a job. So the aim of this chapter is to present lots of ways of finding the right job, making sure you are the right person for that job and giving you practice in persuading the employer to select you as the ideal person for the job.

This chapter concentrates on two case studies: the Chris Lane Leisure Club and NCI. Background information about these organisations is given in the Case Studies section of this book, starting on page xvii.

Where to look for jobs or training opportunities

Having studied GNVQ ICT, you may be interested in finding a job which involves working with ICT. Employers who are likely to employ someone like you – with experience in ICT – fall into two main groups:

- ✪ **ICT users** – that's almost everyone nowadays and includes companies like Chris Lane

- ✪ **ICT suppliers** – the service providers (the help desk, service engineers, etc.) and the ICT producers, the technical whizz-kids who design hardware and write software, or supply hardware and software, like NCI

Exercise 8.1

Which of these two groups interests you more? Think about what it is that attracts you to it.

The list of people using ICT is almost endless: shops, factories, banks, booking agencies and many others.

Exercise 8.2

Think of some more examples of organisations that use ICT.
Which jobs in that organisation involve the greatest use of ICT?

In fact, it might be quicker to make a list of the people who do *not* use ICT. ICT is used for many different purposes:

✪ Processing documents, numerical data and graphics

✪ Creating, maintaining and interrogating databases

✪ Controlling production processes

For all these tasks, a knowledge of ICT is needed.

There are four main types of ICT supplier:

✪ Computer manufacturers

✪ Software producers

✪ Computer shops

✪ ICT maintenance and support agencies

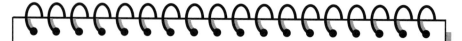

NCI

NCI is an example of an organisation that provides ICT maintenance and support for its clients.

Exercise 8.3

Think of some examples of organisations that are ICT suppliers. Are these organisations local to you, or would you have to travel – or even move – to be able to work for them?

In some parts of the UK, there is a greater opportunity to find work in organisations like these – not because unemployment is lower in these areas but because these types of organisation seem to develop close to each other.

Having identified the type of employer you may want to work for, there are still many different ways of looking for jobs or training:

✪ Looking at advertisements placed by employers seeking to recruit staff – you will find these in local and national newspapers, and in specialist magazines, and in workplaces and shop windows

✪ Visiting the professional advisers at a careers or job centre, or an employment or recruitment agency

✪ Asking employers themselves, usually through their personnel departments, about job vacancies by writing to them, telephoning or visiting a place of work

✪ Other informal sources, i.e. the grapevine

NCI

NCI does not advertise in specialist ICT papers. It tends to recruit its staff from personal contacts, i.e. using the grapevine.

Advertisements

One way of learning about the jobs available in an industry is to study the advertisements placed by employers looking for staff. There are several sources of advertisements:

- ✪ Local newspapers

- ✪ National press

- ✪ Computer press

- ✪ Internet

Local newspapers may be the best source of information about jobs if you want to work locally.

National newspapers may concentrate on vacancies in ICT on a particular day of the week.

Trade journals are sometimes sent free to professionals in the ICT industry, but mostly you will have to subscribe to them, i.e. pay for each issue.

Exercise 8.4

Make a list of national newspapers and find out if they concentrate on vacancies in ICT on a particular day of the week.

Exercise 8.5

Find out the names of publications in the computer press.

Activity 8.1

Working in small groups, study recent advertisements to identify some examples of ICT users and others of ICT suppliers. Cut out (or make a copy of) and keep the advertisements.

For each advert, note the date and source of the publication, so you know how old the information is when you next refer to it.

You might decide to pin the adverts on a noticeboard, or set up your own website to display this information.

The Internet is likely to be your easiest source of information about jobs and training opportunities.

Exercise 8.6

Search the net for websites that provide information about job vacancies.

Employers who need new staff usually place advertisements to attract applicants. Where they do this will depend on the type of job on offer and the type of people they want to recruit.

- ✪ Employers seeking highly trained and highly experienced staff might approach an agency and ask it to 'headhunt' the right person for the job

- ✪ Employers seeking well-qualified people for job vacancies all over the country might use advertisements in the national press

- ✪ Employers seeking people with special qualities might take an advertisement in a specialist magazine or trade journal or in a supplement of a national newspaper

- ✪ Employers seeking local staff might advertise through the local careers or job centre, or use a noticeboard outside their own building. Lots of supermarkets do this. Some companies advertise in local shop windows

Chris Lane

Chris Lane advertises for staff on a noticeboard in the entrance hall of the club (Figure 8.1). This means that prospective employees hear about the club through existing members, or may even be members themselves.

ARE YOU UNDERVALUED AT WORK?

What Do You Really Want From A Job?

Job Satisfaction	[ ]
Career Opportunities	[ ]
Empowerment	[ ]
Training & Development	[ ]
Challenges	[ ]
Fun Environment	[ ]
Added Perks & Benefits	[ ]
The Chance To Make A Difference	[ ]

If you ticked one or more of the above then we have the opportunities you are looking for. We require full time mature team players to $\underline{BE}$ the valuable 1st Impression to all our members. The post involves shifts and the starting salary of £11K + full club membership and additional perks & benefits. We are eager to meet you, so call us on 01483 722113 for an application form NOW!

ISN'T IT ABOUT TIME YOU GOT
WHAT YOU DESERVE?

Figure 8.1   *Chris Lane advertisement*
Courtesy of Chris Lane Family Leisure Club

Exercise 8.7

Think of some companies local to you that advertise job vacancies in the shop window, or on a display board near the entrance.

★ What information is given on these boards?
★ How frequently is the information updated?
★ How frequently would you have to look at the board to make sure you did not miss any opportunities?

Sometimes jobs are advertised internally to give existing staff the chance to seek promotion. People outside the company may not even be aware of these job opportunities.

Activity 8.2

Working in small groups, look again at the advertisements you have collected.

★ Which type of company placed these ads? An ICT user or a supplier?
★ What types of job vacancy do these organisations have?
★ Which ICT skills would the successful applicant need?
★ Where are the organisations located?
★ What qualifications do applicants need?

Careers or job centres; employment or recruitment agencies

Exercise 8.8

Find out the address and telephone number of your local careers office, job centre and at least two recruitment agencies.

Professional advisers earn their living by helping people to get a job. They include careers teachers, staff at job centres and employment agencies. These people deal with enquiries all day from people like you. They have all the necessary information at their fingertips:

✪ Details of local companies

✪ Contacts within those companies

✪ Details of further training courses that might help you to break into a particular line of work

You could consider registering with local employment or recruitment agencies. You might also talk to people with ICT qualifications who are already working in the ICT industry. They may be able to give you invaluable advice, and perhaps the names of some contacts in companies that might employ someone like you.

Direct contact with employers

You could contact employers by writing to them, telephoning or visiting the place of work. By keeping watch on which companies are recruiting, i.e. which ones are advertising for staff, you could contact them directly and say you are enquiring about other vacancies in their organisation.

You may persuade them to accept a copy of your CV to keep on file should a suitable vacancy arise. Certainly, you may find that they appreciate how keen you are to obtain a job. If they decide to interview you for a vacancy, it may save them the costs of advertising.

In the first instance, you might contact the personnel department, but you might also try the ICT department. When you telephone a company, speak to the switchboard operator and ask who you should speak to about vacancies. Ask for the name of the person in charge of recruitment, and then ask to be put through to them. Make a note of their name and be sure to make every effort to impress them when you do get through.

For this method, you need lots of perseverance. It is like looking for a needle in a haystack – a job in a company that has not advertised a vacancy. But if you decide that you like the way a company works, it is worth approaching it. For every ten refusals, you might get someone to put your CV on file. For every ten CVs you send, you might get one interview. For every ten interviews, you might get one offer of a job. Then all your hard work will have been worth it.

Choosing suitable jobs or training

Before you can decide whether to apply for a job, you need to know all about it. There are many useful **sources** of advice and information.

- ✪ **Careers advisers** – these people will have more information to give you and may be specially trained to advise on careers

- ✪ **Reference materials** – many books have been written offering job advice, and some include details of courses on offer or organisations to contact; you might also use a careers program on a computer or use the Internet

- ✪ **Other informed sources** – such as staff in schools, people in industry involved in schools–industry link work and personnel staff in industry

So there is a range of people and resources that you can use to help you find out about and choose suitable jobs and training:

- ✪ You could talk to a careers adviser or teacher, to friends and family

- ✪ You could visit a local careers office or library, a careers or job centre

- ✪ You could use a careers program on a computer, or the Internet

- ✪ You could observe and talk to people in the workplace or at the local chamber of commerce, or gain work experience, paid or voluntary

You should always be willing to listen to others. People of all ages – younger and older – will have had different experiences from you, and hearing about their experiences may help you. It will be up to you to listen to everyone's views and decide whose advice helps you the most.

You will hear people say: 'It's not what you know. It's who you know that counts.' Another favourite is: 'I was in the right place at the right time.' If you think you don't know anyone who counts, or you feel you are the one in the wrong place at the wrong time, this news is not encouraging.

However, you may be surprised what contacts you do have. Through family and friends, you may know someone who knows someone, who knows someone, who knows someone who can help. The trick is to let friends and family know that you are looking for work in a particular area, and to behave in such a way that they would be pleased to pass your name on. It is unlikely that you will receive any help from these **informal contacts** if people worry about you letting them down.

While on a work placement, it makes sense to talk to other people working with you to find out more about their job and their working environment. If you watch them, you will learn more about what they do and how much they enjoy their work. Just taking part in a work experience scheme will provide you with opportunities to make useful contacts.

If you have decided that your next move is into further training, your careers teacher will be able to point you in the right direction. Even if you decide that further training is best for you, at some point you'll need to think about getting a job. So the rest of this chapter focuses on jobs and how to find the one that suits you.

What jobs are available?

Many jobs have been lost though the introduction of computerised techniques. At the same time, new jobs have been created, many of them providing ICT services:

- ✪ User support

- ✪ System maintenance

- ✪ Hardware and software maintenance

- ✪ Servicing and repair

- ✪ Network management

- ✪ Database management

Exercise 8.9

Do any of these types of job appeal to you? If so, why? If not, why not?

The manufacture of the products themselves has also generated new job opportunities:

- ✪ ICT systems design

- ✪ Software production

- ✪ Manufacture

- ✪ Publishing

There are also job opportunities with the growth of the Internet, e.g. in designing web pages.

In the ICT industry there are many different types of job. Not all the jobs advertised will suit you if you are looking for a first job. In fact, you may find that hardly any of them seem to suit you at all! This may be because you have been looking in the wrong place, i.e. the wrong newspapers.

Here is a list of some job titles, which might suit you as a first job.

1. Computer operator
2. Junior programmer
3. Computer service engineer
4. Data preparation clerk
5. Technical support staff
6. Software support staff

Chris Lane

Chris Lane employs some people straight from school or college. ICT skills are considered important for all posts in Chris Lane but, along with these, you need to have the right personality to work in a team where there is lots of face-to-face contact with members.

Activity 8.3

Working in a small group, look again at your collection of advertisements.

Find examples of advertisements for a variety of jobs. Have you a cross-section of jobs: with companies using ICT and those with ICT suppliers?

Make a note of any companies that were advertising for applicants with little or no experience.

> You might decide to write to these employers to ask about possible vacancies for when your course ends, about training opportunities they might offer and to find out exactly what qualifications they expect from applicants.

When thinking about your first job, you should consider which jobs will offer you further progress.

Some job titles include the words 'junior' or 'senior' to show that, with experience, there is an opportunity to advance to jobs with more responsibility (and more pay).

If you wanted to work for a large company, you would be advised to apply for posts in smaller companies (which might take on college leavers) and gain some experience before approaching larger companies.

What does the job involve?

One way to find out what jobs may suit you is to investigate what is involved in the job.

Exercise 8.10

Re-read all the advertisements you have collected and try to decide what each job actually involves.

All jobs in an industry will be in a 'pecking order'. Usually, everyone starts at the bottom and slowly – or quickly – works their way up the ladder of success. Having extra qualifications may mean that you can jump a few rungs on the ladder, although you will have spent time gaining your qualifications. Someone with on-the-job experience but fewer qualifications may also make good progress. A lot depends on the type of job you are doing and how you approach your work.

One important measure of a job is the salary it offers. Some jobs offer a 'negotiable' salary. This means that the prospective employer may measure you by what you've earned to date, rather than what the job on offer demands from you.

Most people spend two-thirds of their time awake. When you do start work, the time spent at work – and travelling to and from work – can be as much as 70 per cent of your waking day. If you work a five-day week and count weekends as free time, this can come close to 50 per cent of your total available time. It will be very important to find a job that you like. Otherwise, half your life may be spent doing something you do not enjoy.

How can you decide what type of job will suit you? From a prospective employer's point of view, you might also consider what it is about you that might suit the job on offer.

There are three main things to consider:

- ✪ Your own circumstances

- ✪ Your interests

- ✪ The opportunities available

Activity 8.4

Working in a small group, classify the advertisements you have collected so far, by salary offered. Also note the previous experience, or qualifications required, for each job.

> You could put all the data you are collecting into a spreadsheet or database. It would then be easier to sort the adverts (for example, into salary order) or to calculate the average salary for a particular level of work.

Matching your own circumstances

You could start with some self-evaluation, by making a list to describe yourself. Be honest about your good points and your faults.

Activity 8.5

Write down eight things about yourself that you might be proud to tell a prospective employer.
Write down four things that you might not want that employer to know.

Compare your list with the checklist below. Did you consider any of these points to be important?

- ✪ What age are you? Are you married? Do you have any children – or other dependants – to support?

- ✪ What qualifications do you have? Would you be willing to do more training to gain more qualifications?

- ✪ What work experience do you have? Do you have any references from previous employers?

- ✪ Where do you live? Do you live at home with your parents? Do you live in rented accommodation, or in your own home? Would you be willing to move to get a job?

- ✪ Do you have your own transport? Do you have a clean driving licence? How would you get to and from work?

○ How do you look? Are you careful about your appearance? Do you have clothes that would be good enough to wear to an interview? Do you have clothes that would be suitable to wear to work?

○ How are you with people? Do you feel confident when meeting people for the first time? Are you good at remembering the names of people you meet?

○ Do you plan things? Are you organised – a natural list writer? Are you always on time?

○ Is your handwriting neat and legible? Are you good on the telephone? Can you leave a sensible message on an answering machine?

○ How good are you working with ICT?

Hopefully, this last question will be one to which you can give a definite positive answer. What about the others? Are there things you need to improve on to increase your chances of getting a job?

Exercise 8.11

Look back at your list of eight good things and four not-so-good things from Activity 8.5.

★ Can you add more good things to say about yourself?

★ Are there things you will need to work on to make yourself more attractive to a prospective employer?

Before you decide to apply for a job, you must check that you would be prepared to do whatever is involved.

✪ When would you be required to work? Does it involve shift working?

✪ Would you need to wear a special uniform or outfit?

✪ Would you need to do further training, say one day a week at college?

✪ Would you need to travel away from home?

✪ Where would you work? In a quiet office? In a busy, noisy office? With lots of other people? On your own? Indoors? Outdoors?

If the job involves some condition that would make you unhappy, then the long-term prospects of doing that job would not be good. Instead, try to find work that suits you – or think about changing your approach to what you do or do not like doing.

Chris Lane

The Chris Lane clubhouse is open from 6.30 am until 11 pm, seven days a week – except Christmas Day and Boxing Day! Most staff work on a shift rota system so that, for example, the reception desk, the gym and the bar/restaurant areas are staffed at all times.

Exercise 8.12

What conditions would appeal to you?
What conditions do you think you would not be willing to accept?
Make a list, so that you can use it later to decide whether to apply for a particular job.

Tasks of a job

Each day, most of your time will be spent 'doing the job'.

✪ What tasks will it involve?

✪ Will there be lots of paperwork?

✪ Will you be sat in front of a workstation all day?

✪ How will your time be spent? On the telephone? Making calls? Receiving calls?

✪ Will you be doing the same thing all day, or will there be some variety in your work?

NCI

As a newcomer at NCI, most of the time you might work at head office constructing PCs. Occasionally, though, you may need to answer the telephone and take messages. Very occasionally, you might be asked to collect equipment that needs to be fixed and then returned to the client.

However, this may be exactly the kind of job you would enjoy. One of its recent recruits, straight from school, had this to say: 'I'm mad on computers and I got this job through a friend. They are quite a small company and everyone is very friendly. I help to build computers. I've learned so much since I joined that I could build my own one now!'

It is important that you realise the pressures that might build up if presented with working conditions that are too stressful for you. While you might not recognise it, your body soon starts to show symptoms of stress: headaches or migraines, falling prey to colds, back pain.

Be honest with yourself about what you enjoy doing and what irritates you. Aim to find the type of work that will let you perform well, not get you down.

Exercise 8.13

What types of task appeal to you? What things do you not like doing?
Make a list, so that you can use it later to decide whether to apply for a particular job.

Responsibilities of a job

When you first start work, it is unlikely that you will be given responsibility for other people. However, you may be given responsibility for certain tasks in the office:

✪ It may be your job to answer the telephone and pass the call on to someone else, or if they are out, to take a message

✪ It may be your job to welcome visitors, to take their coat and fetch them a cup of coffee

✪ It may be your job to write up a list of all outgoing mail, to stick the stamps on the envelopes and take the mail to the local post office

✪ It may be your job to file all correspondence, or send faxes, or do the photocopying for everyone else in the office

When you start, you may feel that these tasks – including making tea for everyone – means that you are being used as a dogsbody. You may feel that you can do more but that you are not being given the opportunity to use your skills.

You need to be patient. These tasks may seem lowly, but the smooth running of an office involves many such tasks and, to start with, you will be given very easy things to do. Make a success of working with the other people in the office – learn how to get on with them and learn from them.

Your talent will show through, and then you may be given more responsibility. At all times, you will need to prove yourself. You cannot expect your employer to know what you are capable of straight away, or to risk giving you tasks that you might fail to complete satisfactorily – that could result in problems for the company and an embarrassment for you. Remember: learn to walk before you run.

Activity 8.6

Plan and carry out an investigation into ways of finding jobs suited to your interests and abilities.

Collect information from more than one place on a job that interests you.

Keep an accurate record of the information you collect and where you found it.

Match the kinds of skills and qualifications you have, or expect to have by the end of your course, to your chosen job. Explain why the job you select is suitable for you.

Make sure that you show independence in your approach to your work, make a realistic plan of how you will collect the information you need and use technical language correctly.

Check that your plan is working and make changes as necessary.

This activity might serve as evidence for Unit 5, Using Information Resources.

Applying for jobs

There are definite stages in the recruitment process.

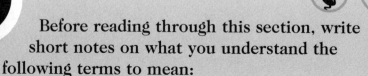

Activity 8.7

Before reading through this section, write short notes on what you understand the following terms to mean:

job vacancy	interview
appointment	advertisement
job description	selection
record of achievement	application
job offer	shortlist

When you have finished this section, look back and see how close you were.

The job description

The employer sets out a **job description** of the vacancy. This is a written description of the tasks and responsibilities of the person taking on the job. It may include details such as conditions of working (i.e. hours of working), holiday arrangements, place of work, persons immediately above or below this job position, and so on.

The advertisement

Usually, an **advertisement** is placed. This will invite suitable applicants to apply for the job. The advertisement should include several details:

- ✪ The name of the employer

- ✪ The place of work

- ✪ The type of work, or job title

- ✪ Some idea about pay and conditions

- ✪ Details of how to apply, e.g. an address or telephone number and a person to contact

Exercise 8.14

Look back at the advertisements you have collected so far. Do they all include the types of information listed above?
For each advertisement, would you know what information to send, where to send it and to whom it should be addressed?

Applying for the job

Applicants apply for the job. They may write a **letter of application** to the company and enclose a copy of their **CV**.

The employer may expect to receive many applications for one post. To ensure that they have exactly the information they require, each applicant may be sent an **application form**. This questionnaire has to be completed and sent back to the company before the application will be considered any further. Often the application form duplicates information already given on the CV, but you must complete it to make the job of selecting (and rejecting) applicants easier for the employer.

Activity 8.8

Do this activity with a partner.

Each of you write a letter of application for one of the jobs you have seen advertised. (If you have not yet seen a job advertisement that you would apply for, imagine that you have the required qualifications for one.)

> A letter of application should include at least six sentences and use standard style conventions. Refer to Chapter 1 for information about letter style.

Produce your letter of application in your own handwriting.

Swap letters and consider whether you would be impressed enough to invite this applicant for interview.

Discuss ways of improving the letter.

Letters of application are covered in more detail later.

Shortlisting and the interview process

The employer has to decide who to interview – a **shortlist** of applicants is drawn up.

Some applications will be rejected straight away because their qualifications do not match the job description. Some will be rejected because the company has a limit on the number of people it is willing to interview (for cost and/or time reasons).

It is at this stage that the overall effect of your **application form**, your **CV** and your covering **letter of application** will be all-important. The time spent deciding whether to put your application into the 'yes' or 'no' pile may be only a matter of seconds. After you are put into the 'no' pile, you will have lost your chance to impress that particular employer. It is therefore very important that everything you send is of the highest quality in appearance and content.

Exercise 8.15

Have another look at your CV and your letter of application. Have you included all relevant details? Would you be one of the shortlisted applicants? If not, what can you do to improve your chances of success?

A shortlist of applicants will be invited for **interview**. How the interview takes place will vary from employer to employer. Some large organisations offer an open day for a large number of potential recruits. This involves a talk from a senior manager, a tour of the offices and probably handing out some literature to answer any questions the applicants might have. Some applicants will then decide that they do not want to work for the company and **deselect** themselves. This makes the next stage of interviewing less time-consuming for the employer. They have only applicants who are keen to work for them.

Most interviews involve a **selection panel** – it may be one person or perhaps two or three people – who will meet each applicant, look through the information received to date and then ask more questions to help them to decide who should be offered the job.

Chris Lane

Prospective employees at Chris Lane have to attend at least three interviews before they can join the Green Team. First they are interviewed by the head of department (HOD), who checks that they have the necessary skills for the particular vacancy. If the HOD is happy for them to join the section, the next interview is with the head of training, Simon Thorpe. This interview is to check that they will fit into a teamworking environment. Finally, prospective staff are interviewed by Chris Lane, just to make sure that they have the sparkle that all people who work for Chris Lane need. This interview should be a formality – no one who passes the earlier interviews should 'fail' this final one. It is more of an opportunity for Chris to welcome new staff to the team personally. Figure 8.2 shows the new recruit checklist, which is used to track applications and to record the results of the interview process.

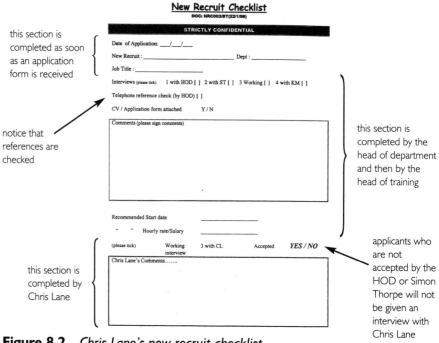

Figure 8.2 *Chris Lane's new recruit checklist*
Courtesy of Chris Lane Family Leisure Club

It is said that people make up their minds about someone they meet within the first few seconds, sometimes even before that person speaks. Good interviewers will be aware of this, but if you use those first few seconds well you may have won half the interview battle before you have even sat down. If you manage to disappoint the interviewer in the same few seconds, you will have difficulty winning back their confidence.

Activity 8.9

Working with a partner, role play the first few minutes of an interview.

Practise saying two or three sentences in reply to the question: 'Tell me something about yourself.' See how soon you can interest the interviewer with facts about yourself.

Selection and appointment

Once all the interviews have taken place, the **selection panel** will meet to discuss all the applicants and to decide who, if anyone, is to be offered the post. This may happen straight away, or there may be a delay if information still has to arrive, e.g. references from previous employers.

The successful applicant will be offered the post. This may be a verbal communication, but it should be followed up by a formal letter offering the post. The applicant then needs to accept the post in writing. Final details on a starting date and the salary will be agreed at this stage. The applicant has then been appointed.

**Activity
8.10**

Draw a diagram to show the events involved in recruiting new staff.

Use colour to show where you, the applicant, have an opportunity to impress the prospective employer.

Notice the stages at which you may be rejected, and make notes on how you can avoid this.

Personal information

When you apply for a job, you need to give the employer as much useful information as possible about yourself. Employers like to know why you have applied to them for a particular job or training, and what skills and interests you have that might make you suitable for the vacancy. This information will help the employer to decide whether to offer you a job. Most of this information is written down, on your **CV (curriculum vitae)** or on an **application form** (Figure 8.3).

To give the best possible impression, write as clearly as possible on an application form and prepare your CV using a word processor. These details should be included on your CV:

✪ Personal details, such as your name and address

✪ Courses followed and qualifications gained

✪ Skills, such as keyboard skills

✪ Personal qualities, such as being on time and being reliable

✪ Experience and achievements gained through work and training

Front

**Employment
Application
Form**

Reverse

Please indicate why you feel you would be suitable for this position

Date ____/____/____

Address _____

_____

_____

_____

Post Code _____

Title _____

Surname _____

First Name _____

Date of Birth ____/____/____

Gender _____

Telephone _____

Position applied for _____

Prepared to work ☐ Full time   ☐ Part time

Available to take up employment (date) _____

Applicants are requested to tick the relevant boxes to enable the Club to monitor its equal opportunity policy. This information is used for no other purpose and will be treated as confidential.

White ☐   Black-Caribbean ☐   Black-African ☐   Black- other ☐   (please specify) _____

Indian ☐   Pakistani ☐   Bangladesh ☐   Chinese ☐   Other ☐   (please specify) _____

Previous Employment - please start with your most recent employment and work backwards

Employer name & address	Dates (From - To)	Duties / Responsibilities

Reference
Please give the names of two referees that have known you in a work environment that we may contact.
(Please add a third referee if applying for a position working with children)

Name _____   Name _____

Address _____   Address _____

_____   _____

_____   _____

Telephone _____   Telephone _____

Relationship to applicant _____   Relationship to applicant _____

Recruitment Policy
It is the Club's policy to employ the best qualified personnel and provide equal opportunity for the advancement of employees including promotion and training and not to discriminate against any person because of colour, race, national origin, sex or marital status.
I authorise the Club to obtain references to support this application and release the Club and referees from any liability caused by giving and receiving information.
Declaration: I confirm that the information given on this form, is to the best of my knowledge, true and complete. Any false statement may be sufficient cause for rejection or, if employed, dismissal.

Signature _____   Date ____/____/____

Figure 8.3   *Blank application form (Chris Lane): you must give two references and all your information must be true, otherwise you could be dismissed*
Courtesy of Chris Lane Family Leisure Club

✪ Other achievements with your family and friends, such as looking after younger brothers and sisters

✪ Leisure activities, such as playing in a local football team

✪ Ambitions and goals – where you see yourself this time next year, or in five years time

This information is called **personal information**.

Activity 8.11

Prepare an outline CV, using the headings listed above.

> If you prepare your CV on a word-processing package, you can amend it until you are happy with what it says. Later, you can amend it to keep it up to date.

Personal details

The basic details will be your name, address, age and sex (whether you are male or female).

Activity 8.12

Complete the personal details section of your CV. Make sure that the layout of the material is pleasing to the eye.

> Make sure that you have made no spelling or keying errors. The spell-checker will not know if your surname is correct!

Courses followed and qualifications gained

Most jobs now require the applicant to have some qualifications. These can be split into two categories: vocational and academic.

Vocational qualifications, which include GNVQs and NVQs, cover the types of task you will do every day at work. Here are some examples of vocational qualifications:

OCR Basic Skills Using ICT	RSA CLAIT (Computer Literacy and Information Technology)
IT Key Skills Level I	RSA II Keyboarding
OCR Preparing for Employment	RSA II Databases

Exercise 8.16

What vocational qualifications do you expect to have when you finish your course of study? Make sure that you include this information in your CV.

Academic qualifications include GCSEs and GCE A/AS qualifications. These are not directly related to a particular job. They might be studied at school or college before taking a job or higher education. Here are some academic qualifications:

GCSE English	GCSE French
GCSE Science	GCSE History

Exercise 8.17

What academic qualifications do you expect to have when you finish your course of study? Make sure that you include expected grades for each academic qualification on your CV.

When you know your results, you can update your CV.

It is important to list subjects studied as well as qualifications achieved. Include details of the length of the course and where you were studying.

List your subjects in an order – your favourite subjects first, or in order of how well you have done, or in alphabetical order. At an interview, you may be asked to talk about the subjects you have studied, and you may find this list useful as a prompt. It would be embarrassing if you could not remember which subjects you had been studying!

You may be asked to prove what qualifications you have achieved. It will be important to keep all your examination certificates in a safe place. Do not send original certificates to a prospective employer; a photocopy could be sent in the post, and you could show them the original, if asked, at an interview.

All the information included in your CV so far is factual. Be sure that what you write is true. If you are offered a job based on this information and then later the employer finds out it is not true, you could be dismissed.

Complete some more sections of your CV and print out a draft.

In small groups, read over each other's CVs. Has anyone missed out any information?

On your own, decide how you can improve your CV. Make these changes and print out a fresh version.

Skills

All jobs need certain skills. Your first job will need few skills, but as you progress to more senior posts, more skills will be needed. Job skills fall into two types: vocational skills and key skills.

Vocational skills are the skills that are linked to the actual job:

- The ability to use a keyboard or mouse

- The experience of using a word-processing package

- The experience of using a DTP (desktop publishing) package

- The ability to customise applications programs

Exercise 8.18

What vocational skills have you acquired? Make sure that you have included these on your CV.

Key skills are useful for most jobs and include these abilities:

- ✪ To think for yourself
- ✪ To work without supervision
- ✪ To work in a team
- ✪ To work with numbers
- ✪ To solve problems
- ✪ To communicate your ideas to others
- ✪ To remember names and other important facts
- ✪ To work to a deadline

Chris Lane

Skills expected of sports staff at Chris Lane are proficiency at sports, e.g. tennis skills or gym work. All staff at Chris Lane are expected to be presentable, have an outgoing friendly personality, have ICT skills and be able to work in a team.

Did You Know?

Some of these skills – such as team-working – are tested in your optional units. Others may be included in part of your key skills qualifications

You may have studied first aid or other useful skills at evening classes. Remember to include all the skills you have to offer. Use this checklist to help you:

- ✪ Key skills (in communications and application of number)
- ✪ Driving (a clean licence is important)
- ✪ First aid

- A special skill, e.g. speaking a foreign language, or sign language

- Duke of Edinburgh scheme or similar awards

NCI

If you have a clean driving licence, you would be more useful to NCI. You could be asked to collect equipment and return it to clients' premises.

Personal qualities

You may decide to write a paragraph to describe yourself. This information might be included on your CV or in a letter of application enclosed with the CV. Here is a checklist of questions you may want to consider:

- Are you always on time?

- Do you take care of your appearance?

- Can you get on well with others?

- Can you communicate your ideas to others?

- Are you polite?

- Are you friendly?

- Are you enthusiastic?

- Are you keen to learn new things?

- Can others rely on you?

If you are called for an interview, some of these personal qualities will be noted by your interviewer. Be sure to describe yourself honestly. The interviewer may notice if you behave differently from the impression given in your written application, and this will give reason to doubt you.

Activity 8.14

Work with a friend on this activity.

Each of you write a paragraph about yourself, ready to include in your CV or an application letter. Swap paragraphs and see if you agree with what has been written.

Talk about what else you might write and then produce a revised version.

Produce your draft paragraph using a word processor. Print it in double-line spacing. It will then be easier for you to edit. Later, you could cut and paste it into your CV or letter of application.

Experience and achievements

You might not appreciate how valuable work experience is until you find that a prospective employer is impressed with what you have done. The teacher responsible for gaining a work placement should have tried to match you with your intended career path. If you enjoyed the work experience, you may have decided to follow that career path. More importantly, it may have helped you to decide what you did not like about certain working conditions, or opened your eyes as to what work is really like. Your prospective employer will know that you have already had a taste of work, and that is a good sign.

You may also have experienced particular tasks that will fall within your new job specification. This will help you to settle in more quickly.

Chris Lane

Chris Lane provides work placements for ten local students every year. Each student spends one full week at the club, usually during February, June or July. After an introduction and tour of the club, students work in every department for a short while. By the end of their week, students appreciate exactly what working at the club would entail.

NCI

It is rare for NCI to be able to offer work experience placements for UK students. However, it does accept overseas students who are already proficient in ICT skills but who want to improve their English. These students work for NCI for about three months before returning to their own countries.

If you are good at languages but would like to improve your spoken French or German, for example, you might consider trying to get work in France or Germany using your ICT skills.

Activity 8.15

Write short notes on your experience and achievements gained through work and training. Include relevant dates and times spent in training or on work experience. Include this information on your CV.

When applicants are called for interview, the interviewer uses a list of questions to find out more information about the applicant.

Chris Lane

Here are some of the questions and prompts used at the start of an interview for reception staff:

★ Have you been to the club before? What is your impression of it?

★ Have you worked on reception before?

NCI

Here are some of the questions and prompts used at the start of an interview for technicians:

★ Tell me something about yourself

★ Tell me about any experience you have in building PCs

Take turns to do this activity with a partner. One person plays the part of an interviewer and, looking at the CV of the other, says: 'Tell me some more about your work experience.'
The interviewee has to reply and within a few sentences impress the interviewer.
Can you remember what you have written on the CV? Can you add more details that will interest the prospective employer and impress them with what you have learned through work experience?

> If you can, video these mini-interviews. You can then see how well you perform.

Remember to mention other achievements, even if they didn't give you a special qualification. Your hobbies and interests tell a prospective employer a lot about you.

Faced with as many as ten CVs, all from people with the required qualifications, the employer can then only look at extracurricular activities – what you do in your spare time. Employers are more likely to be interested in someone who has outside interests. These help you to get on with other people who already work for the company.

If you list your interests as 'watching TV', you will have this in common with millions of TV viewers, but it does suggest that you spend your time being entertained rather than meeting people and sharing some interest.

At the other extreme, if you say that your main interest is 'dancing in clubs', the prospective employer will wonder if your social life will interfere with normal working hours. Will you be fresh for work every Monday morning?

Most employers will be glad to see that you are involved in some sporting activity – doing rather than watching – because this suggests a healthier lifestyle. So, how do you spend your leisure time?

✪ Do you help out, e.g. with a youth club, a guide or scout group? Or do you have younger brothers and sisters to look after?

✪ Do you do any voluntary work, e.g. through your church or a local hospital?

✪ Did you get involved in school plays or musical productions?

✪ Do you belong to any teams or clubs, e.g. football?

Have you taken on any special responsibilities?

✪ Were you a prefect at school?

✪ Are you the secretary or treasurer of any clubs?

NCI

NCI would be interested if you had taken part in an after-hours computer club at your school or college.

The importance of leisure activities should not be overlooked when writing your CV.

Activity 8.17

Write a paragraph describing your leisure interests to complete your CV. Print out a good copy.

Show it to friends and teachers, who may be able to offer advice as to how you could improve it. Listen to what they have to say and make any alterations that you think will help.

Proof-read your CV before printing the final copy.

Finally, think carefully about your ambitions and goals. An employer who knows your ambitions may well help you to achieve your goal. Don't worry if your main goal is to earn lots of money. Most employers see this as a plus point. It means that you are motivated to work hard, especially if the wages you earn will depend on your own efforts.

Ways of presenting yourself

You have several opportunities to present yourself to a prospective employer. To begin with, you may telephone to enquire about the vacancy.

In some advertisements, companies ask you to ring them. Smaller companies especially may ask you to ring; they will not expect to receive too many telephone calls and can use your call as a way of eliminating unsuitable applicants.

Other companies do expect you to write to them. For large organisations, which may expect a greater response from their advertisement, it is better for them not to ask you to ring – they might be inundated by callers. Instead, they will eliminate unsuitable applicants when the letters of application are received.

Some companies work through agencies, and you may not be able to tell who the employer will be from the information in the advertisement.

If an advert asks you to ring for more information, remember to have all you need in front of you before starting to dial:

✪ A copy of the advertisement

✪ A note of any questions you want to ask, e.g. the starting date, the place where you would have to work

✪ A notepad to write down details, e.g. who to speak to, their extension number

✪ A pen or pencil

Also, make sure you know your own details. You may be asked to give a contact telephone number and your address. Do you know your own postcode?

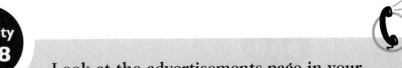

Activity 8.18

Look at the advertisements page in your local paper. Identify who you should contact if you were interested in applying for a job. Should you telephone, or should you write to the company?

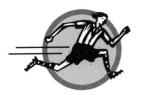

Most people spend hours on the telephone nowadays, so you might think that telephoning a company should not be a difficult task. However, it may not be as simple as you think.

Activity 8.19

Whether or not you have telephoned a company before, it may be advisable to have some practice:

★ Decide what you are going to say and write a script

★ Practise with a friend going through your script and amend your script if need be

★ Practise while holding a telephone receiver. (This may seem unnecessary, but you may find just holding the telephone makes you panic. It may stop your brain working and prevent you speaking)

★ Tape record your conversation. How do you sound? Confident? Nervous?

When you feel you have practised enough, select three adverts from your local paper, telephone the companies and enquire about the jobs they are advertising.

If you are really interested in any of the jobs, you can follow them through. If you are not interested, you need not do anything after the first telephone call, but at least you will have made contact with a local company.

The next stage may require some of these actions from you:

✪ Writing a letter of application

✪ Filling in an application form

✪ Presenting your CV

✪ Presenting your record of achievement, e.g. the National Record of Achievement

All these are written forms of communication. Your CV should be complete by now. You will also have your record of achievement, which you will have prepared over a period of time. The other two are now considered in detail.

Writing a letter of application

The letter of application is the first real chance that an employer has of learning about you – and your first main chance to be rejected. Make sure that your letter impresses the employer – otherwise you will get no further with your application.

Some employers insist that you handwrite the letter. Others will accept a typed or word-processed letter of application. Make sure that you present your letter in the way you are asked. The letter can be quite short but must include some essential information:

✪ **Your full name and address, and telephone number**

✪ **The contact details of the employer – use the correct title and full address as given in the advertisement**

✪ **The job you are applying for – the company may have placed many advertisements and have several vacant posts, so don't leave it guessing**

If your handwriting is not very neat, or you find it difficult to think what to write, prepare a draft version first and then copy it neatly. Make sure that the paper you write on is clean and uncrumpled. Take care with your envelope too; a coffee stain or your cat's footprint on the envelope will not impress the employer!

Activity 8.20

Refer back to the letters of application written in Activity 8.8.

★ Compare your letter with those written by others in your class.

★ Which letters were the most impressive? Why?

Rewrite your letter, incorporating improvements.

Filling in an application form

To be invited for interview, it will be important for you to impress the employer with your application form. The application form may be a general form used by the company for all posts or a particular one designed for the vacant post.

If it is a general form, you may feel that some of the questions are not relevant to you. Answer them anyway, as best you can. You may also feel that a general form does not provide enough space for you to tell the employer exactly what you want them to know about you. If so, write any additional information in a covering letter (which may be your letter of application).

Before you start writing on the application form, think carefully about what you are going to write. You do not want to make a mistake! You could photocopy the form and fill in the photocopy as practice. Then you could carefully copy your responses on to the real application form, as neatly as possible.

When you send the application form, address it to the correct person and remember to put a stamp on the envelope. No stamp equals no interview!

When the employer receives the form, several things will determine whether you are invited for an interview. Apart from the other applicants who may outshine you, your own application will be important.

- ✪ What were the initial impressions of the envelope, the application form and anything extra you sent?

- ✪ Was your handwriting neat and legible?

- ✪ When you completed the form, did you answer all the questions?

- ✪ Does the information on your form match what is needed for the post? (This is considered in more detail on page 382)

Finally, if you are successful in being called for interview, you will have the opportunity to present yourself personally. The impression you give visually, and the way you conduct yourself during the interview, will be judged.

You may think that qualifications are the important deciding factor when selecting an applicant for a job. This is so, but when faced with several applicants, all with the same qualifications, how can an employer make a choice?

NCI

Although qualifications, especially industry qualifications, are important, the management team at NCI is more interested in recruiting staff who are well motivated and who will work in a team environment.

The impression you give at an interview will be important. During the interview, the employer will be making notes. After all the interviews, these notes will help the employer to decide which of the applicants should be offered the post. Again, you are probably in competition with other applicants. If others performed better than you during their interview, this may prevent you being offered a job.

These are the kinds of thing the interviewer will remember about you:

- Were you confident? Were you overconfident?

- Did you look the part? Were you dressed appropriately for an interview?

- Did you answer the questions in a friendly and yet respectful way?

- Did you have some relevant questions besides the length of the lunch break and the number of holidays?

If you are not yet actively looking for work, or ready to apply for higher education courses, interviews may seem a long way off. So for now, just think about it.

Exercise 8.19

Look back at all your notes from this chapter. Are there any ways in which you can improve your presentation?

- ★ Can you improve your CV?
- ★ Are you happy with your letter of application?
- ★ Do you need more interview practice?
- ★ Talk to your teacher/tutor if you feel you need help.

Activity 8.21

For a job vacancy that you have identified, apply for the job by presenting clear and accurate information about yourself to the employer.

Include personal information that is relevant to the job, using at least a letter of application together with your CV and/or an application form. Decide which parts of your application were well presented and suggest practical ways of improving other parts of your application.

> Make sure that you explain clearly in the application how your interests and experience relate to the job description.

As well as looking at written information provided by the applicant, employers may use other **selection methods**:

✪ They may carry out a formal interview in the workplace, at the careers or job centre, or over the telephone

✪ They may ask the applicant to perform a task related to the job, such as typing a letter

✪ They may organise an informal chat or tour of the workplace

Work in a group for this role play activity.
Two or three people are needed for the
selection panel. One person (take it in turns) is
the interviewee. Others observe and make notes
on what is said and done.

Set the selection panel behind a long table with
one chair in front for the interviewee. Ask the
interviewee to wait outside the door (an imaginary
one, if necessary) until invited in. Watch the
interviewee walk in, sit down and answer the first
few questions. Include statements like:

★ Did you find us all right?

★ Tell me some more about yourself.

★ What makes you think you would be
   suitable for this job?

Watch the interviewee for subconscious movements:
fiddling with hair, chewing nails, fidgeting – these all
indicate nervousness and can be negative signs.

★ How well does the interviewee inform the
   panel of plus points?

★ How quickly does he or she impress the
   panel?

★ Does the interviewee do anything that
   would not impress the panel?

Limit each interview to five minutes.

It helps if you can video the whole interview
and then look back over everyone's
performance. The first time you see yourself
on video may not be a pleasant experience,
but this activity gives exceptionally good
practice for any real interview.

Practising interview techniques with your friends is a good idea. However, you will be given a mock interview as part of your assessment. Evidence of your performance will then be produced for your portfolio. Your teacher will let you know when your mock interview will take place.

After the interview, try to identify what went well and what went badly. You can then make practical suggestions as to how you could improve your performance.

If you are successful in getting a real interview, this can be used as evidence instead.

Preparing for an interview

Most employers expect you to attend an interview before you can be offered a job. Some organisations hold group interviews to reduce the number of applicants who are to be invited for an individual interview. Group interviews are discussed in Chapter 9 on page 403.

It is important that you prepare for an interview. It is difficult enough to get to the point of being offered an interview, so do not throw this opportunity away by failing to be prepared.

✪ **What will you wear? How will you look?**

✪ **How will you get to the interview? Have you checked the route and allowed yourself plenty of time?**

✪ **Who will you be seeing? How will you greet the interviewer?**

✪ **What messages will your body language convey during the interview?**

✪ **Do you have the confidence to speak clearly so that you can be understood?**

✪ **Will you be relaxed enough to be able to listen and respond appropriately to the interviewer?**

✪ **Have you thought through what you want to say? Will you be able to provide information that is relevant, thoughtful and truthful?**

Apart from having practice in general interview techniques, you should prepare yourself for each particular job.

Activity 8.23

Find out as much as you can about the company:

> Investigating the company may provide evidence for Unit 5, Using Information Resources.

★ How big is the company? How many people does it employ? What are your prospects for promotion?

★ What goods does it produce or sell? Or does it provide a service?

★ Who are its customers?

★ Where are its offices? Does it have connections overseas?

★ Why do you want to work for it? What is it about the company that attracts you?

> Companies House has a website that allows you to find out information on all registered companies.

Having fully investigated the company, you should prepare yourself for the actual interview:

✪ What questions do you want to ask the interviewer?

✪ Are there any details you need to know about this particular job?

✪ What qualifications and skills will you have to offer?

Remember to be polite and show respect for all the people you meet. Even if you are not offered this job, if you present yourself well, your interviewer might remember you for a different job another time.

By now you should have more idea of what you might want to do when you finish this course. At least you may be clearer about what you do not want to do, or what you will not be able to do without further qualifications.

Revision questions

1. Suggest three places where you could look for a job in ICT.

2. List five things that you should include on your CV.

3. What work does a data preparation clerk do?

4. What work do software support staff do?

5. What is a pecking order?

6. What information is included in a job specification?

7. What is the difference between a letter of application and an application form?

8. What is a shortlist?

9. What is a selection panel?

10. What is the difference between vocational and academic qualifications?

11. List five key skills.

12. List five personal qualities that employers look for in a new recruit.

13. Before telephoning to enquire about a job vacancy, what should you do?

14. What information should you include in a letter of application?

15. What advice would you give someone who is preparing for an interview?

Working as Part of a Team

9

- Choosing an activity and identifying the aims

- Planning a team activity, identifying the roles and responsibilities of team members

- Carrying out an activity

- Reviewing an activity to find out how the team worked

Almost all jobs involve working as part of a team. This chapter will help you to develop teamwork skills. It is important that you can work well as a team member because you are likely to do at least part of your work as a member of a team.

This chapter looks in detail at four topics:

- ✪ Choosing a team activity

- ✪ Planning as a team

- ✪ Working as a team

- ✪ Reviewing teamwork

You may be able to achieve this unit at the same time as completing another vocational unit. This unit can also help you to produce evidence for the key skills unit *Working with Others*. This unit is common to other Foundation GNVQs, so you could work as a team with friends who are studying other subjects:

Business

Land and environment

Construction and the built environment

Leisure and tourism

Engineering

Manufacturing

Health and social care

Retail and distributive services

Hospitality and catering

Science

This unit is assessed through your portfolio work. The grade on that assessment will be your grade for the unit.

Brainstorming

You will probably have already experienced teamwork elsewhere in this course. You will have worked in small groups to collect information and to prepare for activities.

Brainstorming – a method of generating ideas in a group – is an important element of this unit, and teamwork is a necessary part of any brainstorming session. If you have experienced difficulties during brainstorming sessions, it may be because the group is not acting as a team. If you can answer yes to any of the statements on this checklist, your team needs to think again about the rules of brainstorming (see page 196):

✪ The sessions go on for too long

✪ The person who is supposed to write down all the ideas only notes the ones he/she agrees with

- The flipchart is no longer used, so it is difficult to see what ideas have been suggested so far. I have to take my own notes, which distracts my attention

- Team members try to evaluate ideas during the brainstorming session

- Some team members are very critical of the ideas of others in the group. This means that some people are less willing to voice their ideas

- One particular person seems to think that he/she is the 'expert'

- We seem to talk more about solutions to the problem rather than the causes of the problem

- Our team leader is not good at chairing the meeting. Everyone talks at once sometimes

- We often have arguments, and voices are raised

Your team

Deciding who is in your team – and who you will work with – may be done by your teacher. You might think that you prefer to work with people you already know well, and with whom you are friends. However, your choice of teammates – with you – may not make a good team.

When you are planning a social outing, e.g. at the weekend, you choose to go with people you like and get on with. When putting together a team to work on a project, it is not so important that people get on. Sometimes it actually helps if there is some friction in the team. If used well, this friction can make people try harder to make a success of the project. However, it is important that everyone can make a contribution and that everyone agrees with the end goal – success for everyone involved.

Exercise 9.1

Think of some teams that work well. How can you explain their success? Good management? Good people in the team?
Think of some teams that have not worked well. What caused their problems? Could the problems have been avoided?

If you were selecting a team to play a sports fixture, you would choose each player partly for their individual skills and partly for their ability as a team player.

So what does makes a good team? What skills can an individual team member contribute? And what makes a good team player? A team needs lots of different skills, and it can be counterproductive for members to have exactly the same skills.

Activity 9.1

In a small group, hold a brainstorming session to create a list of the team skills that you think are important. Present your list of team skills to the other groups in your class, and share ideas.

Remind yourselves of the rules of brainstorming (page 196 in Chapter 4) and avoid the pitfalls listed on the previous page.

Obviously, there can be only one **leader** of the team. The team leader may be someone who is thought to be the cleverest person in the group. Others may then follow the leader, trying to do their best to match his or her talents. Or the leader may be someone who is good at getting on with everyone and has a knack for getting the best out of people. This type of team leader may pull the team together, and the end result may be good. It is rare for a leader to be both extra clever and good with people, but your team may be lucky. Whatever talents you team leader has, all team members should support the leader, recognising their good points and working with them rather than against them.

Team members are just as important as the leader, maybe more so. Some team members may be brilliant at coming up with ideas and have lots of energy at the start of a project. Others may be thought of as plodders, but they will be the team members who work steadily on the project and make sure things are finished off properly. Some team members may be very neat – others may be known for losing things. Choosing the right person for the right job in a team is very important!

Exercise 9.2

Using the combined list of team skills, tick the skills that you think you have. Be honest with yourself!

★ What skills do you lack?
★ Who else in your class has the skills you lack?

Even when the team is put together, deciding who does what in a team can be a major problem. Some tasks may be seen as more important than others, and some team members may be reluctant to accept what they see as the lesser tasks. The team leader needs to make everyone on the team feel equally important.

Forming, storming, norming, performing

Any team or group of people that has to work together usually goes through four stages: forming, storming, norming and performing.

Forming describes the very early stage of a group. People with different experiences come together and take a little time before they can work together effectively. To begin with, everyone may be holding back their real feelings, waiting to see what others in the group will do. During the **forming** stage, the team will be defining goals, getting to know each other and sizing up the situation. It is a time when rules are defined, and some team members may be testing the ground rules. There is often uncertainty and confusion.

The forming stage does not last long before the **storming** stage starts – a time when real feelings surface and disagreements appear. There can be hostility and tension. There may be a challenge to the leadership of the team, quite a lot of resistance to suggestions made, and subgroups or cliques may form. Some team members may enjoy this stage, but for most people it can be a difficult time.

However, once the air has cleared and everyone understands the others in the team, the **norming** process begins. During the norming stage, there is an acceptance of the leader of the group and agreement about what should be happening. Trust forms between team members, and they learn to rely on each other. **Cooperation** and a sense of togetherness grows. Standards are agreed, and individual members feel happy with their role in the group.

Having grown through the three stages of forming, storming and norming, a team moves into the **performing** stage. This is when it can really work well. There is an openness between team members. There is flexibility in the team, with people willing to take on tasks and responsibilities. Everyone is helpful to others and supportive. At this stage, the team can expect to enjoy success.

Forming

Storming

Norming

Performing

It may be difficult for you, as an individual in a team, to see how effective your team is and where it is in the forming–storming–norming–performing process.

Figure 9.1 shows a checklist of questions you can ask about your team (or other teams).

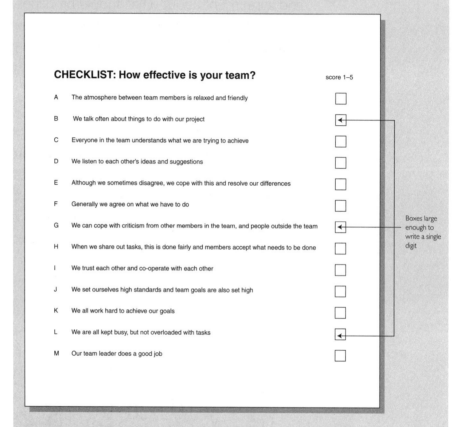

CHECKLIST: How effective is your team?   score 1–5

A   The atmosphere between team members is relaxed and friendly

B   We talk often about things to do with our project

C   Everyone in the team understands what we are trying to achieve

D   We listen to each other's ideas and suggestions

E   Although we sometimes disagree, we cope with this and resolve our differences

F   Generally we agree on what we have to do

G   We can cope with criticism from other members in the team, and people outside the team

H   When we share out tasks, this is done fairly and members accept what needs to be done

I   We trust each other and co-operate with each other

J   We set ourselves high standards and team goals are also set high

K   We all work hard to achieve our goals

L   We are all kept busy, but not overloaded with tasks

M   Our team leader does a good job

Boxes large enough to write a single digit

Figure 9.1   *How effective is your team?*

When your team is underway, look at this list and give each statement a score from 1 to 5:

1   means strongly disagree

2   means disagree

3   means neither agree nor disagree

continued

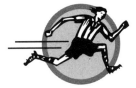

continued

4   means agree

5   means strongly agree

Then add up the score. The higher the score, the more effective your team is.

For the things on the list to which you gave a low score, talk to others in the team to see if you can improve the situation.

Repeat this activity later on and see how your team has changed.

If things start to go wrong, you may feel that you are in the wrong team or that the success of your own work is being held back by others, or that you cannot work at the levels others seem to expect of you. If this happens, you should talk to others in your team. They may be feeling the same way. Unless you explain how you feel, they may not realise what is getting you down. Between you, you should try to resolve the problem. To start with, try to solve your problems without seeking your teacher's help. Bringing in someone outside the team can work against team spirit. In the long run, the team will benefit if you can resolve all problems without involving others.

Once your team has been chosen, you need to get started on your team activity.

Choosing a team activity

The first step is to decide on what your team is going to do. Your teacher will be able to help you with suggestions, but if your team can suggest an activity that interests you all, this will be helpful and your team may feel more committed to the activity.

If your team includes people from different courses, you will need to try to find a project that is vocationally relevant to everyone in the team. This may seem impossible at first, but actually there are lots of activities that pull together people from different subjects.

> A social event for elderly people could involve health and social care students planning some recreational activities, business students organising finance and fund-raising, and hospitality and catering students planning, preparing and delivering the refreshments.

If the activity involves outsiders, e.g. a children's party, it is important to ensure that the rights and needs of those outsiders are respected and that significant outsiders are involved in the planning process. For this, you may find the knowledge of team members on other courses – and their teachers – very useful.

Here are some ideas for activities:

- ✪ A party for children or elderly people, e.g. at Christmas

- ✪ A visit to a theme park, e.g. the Millennium Dome

- ✪ Producing a display for prospective students, e.g. for an open evening

- ✪ Fund-raising for a charity of your choice, e.g. for Red Nose Day

Hold a team meeting to choose an activity that is related to the vocational area of every team member. Have a brainstorming session to create ideas for your team activity. Decide if the team activity is to involve other people.

Decide what the team aims to achieve in the team activity. Make sure that all the team members understand what the aims are.

> Appoint one team member to keep a record of team discussions and decisions made.

You will need to keep a record of **your contribution** to the team activity so that your teacher can assess your individual performance. You need to keep a log or diary of the time you spend on the activity and to file a copy of all notes made at meetings. Your teacher will tell you how your performance will be assessed and any recording systems that may be used.

For example, your teacher may sit in on a meeting as an observer, to see how your team performs, and to see how each individual in the team contributes to the discussion. If this happens, try not to include the teacher in making decisions – treat him or her as an observer and try to behave in the same way as you would if you were not being observed. Your teacher will then see how your team actually performs.

Your team may also decide to take photographs, or make video or audio tapes to show what your activity involved. For example, if you hold a party, photos of everyone enjoying themselves and the team hard at work in the kitchen would say more than any written record of the event. You may also receive thank-you letters from the people who attended the party, which can be used as evidence of the success of the activity.

Planning as a team

For any event to be a success, it must be planned carefully. This does not ensure success, but lack of planning can certainly contribute towards disaster. Planning involves thinking about what needs to be done and deciding how best to do it. It includes thinking about what might go wrong and taking steps to avoid problems.

The importance of planning and the steps and techniques involved in planning are covered in Chapter 4 (page 210). Planning as a team is very similar, except that the activity is large enough to need several people to achieve it, and coordinating several people is generally much more tricky than just coordinating yourself.

The team will need to analyse the activity, break it down into manageable sections and allocate individual responsibilities. Having completed this, each team member will be able to define his or her own role and may identify criteria for determining success.

Activity 9.4

Arrange a team meeting to discuss your team activity:

★ Decide and agree what needs to be done and who will do it

★ Identify when each task needs to be done and agree target dates for completion

★ Identify the resources needed, including money, people, materials, equipment and information

★ Identify things that might go wrong and think about what can be done to avoid problems

★ Decide how the team can check progress and monitor each team member's contribution

★ Agree regular meeting times and ways of communicating between team members

You may decide that one team member needs to keep track of the plan. He or she could create a Gantt chart (see page 213) and colour code tasks according to which team member is responsible.

Each team member has to be committed to the overall team objective but also has to show individual contributions to the team activity, so at this point everyone should know what the team expects of them.

Think carefully about the discussions that you have had so far with other team members. As a record for your portfolio, write a description of the activity that your team has chosen. Write at least three sentences, including the main aims of the activity, and how the team chose the activity. Include a copy of the agreed plan in your portfolio, but write your own description of how the activity was planned.

Refer to notes taken at the meetings and from these identify exactly what your contribution will be.

Plan your own work within the team activity and include this plan in your portfolio. Check that your plan is achievable. Do you have enough time to complete your tasks by the deadlines?

Check you have all the resources you need. Book time to use computers or to meet with people if this is one of your tasks.

Identify how you make sure of success in this activity. Write a mission statement starting 'My contribution will be successful if. . .' and put this in your portfolio.

> During the activity, you can refer back to your mission statement to check that you are still on course for success.

Planning will happen at the start of an activity, but it is important to review progress and monitor the plan. The best-laid plans can quite easily go wrong, and you may need to revise them later. In your plan, include times to meet to check that the tasks will be finished by the agreed deadlines and to revise the plan if it is not working. The use of **team reviews** throughout the activity will also allow you to generate evidence towards communication key skills.

Activity 9.6

Each time your team holds a review meeting, as a group, look at the plan and check that each task has been completed satisfactorily. Identify any tasks that are running late and decide how you can revise the plan so that when these tasks are completed, the overall activity is still achievable within the timescales and will meet the final deadline.

Discuss any problems that have arisen. In deciding how to cope with these, consider all the possible solutions and reject any unrealistic ones in favour of those that can be achieved realistically.

Make a record of discussions and any revisions to your team plan.

> Make sure that review meetings are held in the right spirit. Everyone should contribute to the discussion, and everyone should listen to others and communicate well with them.

Individually, file a copy of the record and revised plan and make notes that comment on how well you have worked to date. Repeat Activity 9.1 and record how well you think the team has worked together.

Working as a team

Most events are organised by teams. This is because each event is made up of a number of activities that need to be carried out. To be successful, it is important that the people in the team really do work as a team. Energy spent arguing or working against the interests of the whole team is wasted energy. So what makes a successful team?

Exercise 9.3

Compare the list generated in Activity 9.1 with this list:

★ Team members work together
★ They offer ideas and listen to the ideas of other team members
★ All team members work to achieve the same goal and understand what the goal is
★ Each team member takes on a role in the team that matches their skills, knowledge and qualities
★ All team members recognise when they need help and contact the appropriate person

Does this describe your team? If not, what can be done to improve things?

In any team, individual team members have different roles and responsibilities.

Check this list. Do you pull your weight in the team?

- ★ Communicating with other team members using verbal, non-verbal and listening skills
- ★ Understanding and working to the team aims
- ★ Supporting other team members by providing helpful feedback
- ★ Knowing when you or other members of your team need help and how to contact the appropriate person
- ★ Keeping other team members informed of problems and solutions
- ★ Carrying out your team role according to the plan

Remember that your success in this unit depends on your approach to teamwork as well as on the success of your team's chosen activity. Make sure you contribute fully to your team. If everyone in your team takes the same approach, your team activity is almost guaranteed to succeed.

Reviewing teamwork

Once an activity is over, it is important to look back – individually and as a team – to review the whole activity and think about how things went.

If things went wrong, you should try to decide why. If something went wrong, what you learn from it can help you to improve your performance next time. There is no point in making the same mistakes again.

If the activity went well, you can use the same methods again. There is no point in trying to reinvent the wheel.

Exercise 9.5

Look back at your notes on the activity and then answer these questions:

★ Did your team meet its aims? If so, what do you think made it a success? If not, what do you think went wrong?

★ Did your individual plan work? If not, how would you do things differently another time?

★ Did the overall team plan work? If not, how could this have been avoided?

★ How well did you carry out your role as a team member? Did you support others in your team, giving guidance when needed and encouragement to fellow team members? Could you have been a better team member? If so, how would you achieve this?

★ How well did others perform in the team? What suggestions would you make to them?

Make notes to use in the team review of the activity and to keep as a record in your portfolio.

Activity 9.7

As a team, review your team activity and answer these questions:

★ What went well?
★ What did not go well?
★ How well did individuals in the team carry out their roles?
★ How well did your team members work as a team?
★ How could the team have worked together better?
★ How did teamwork help in the activity?

Individually, write your report for your portfolio. Record your own contribution to the team activity, the contribution of other team members, your review of the team activity and your evaluation of the success or otherwise of it.

There may be situations where you are in a team without realising it. One situation, where it is important that you do realise your role in a team is the **group interview**.

Some organisations arrange for group interviews before inviting some applicants to individual interviews. This can be particularly useful when a vacancy attracts a lot of interest – it may not be practical to interview every applicant. Instead, all applicants are invited to attend 'an informal group interview'. You may think that you are being given the opportunity to find out about the organisation. In fact, the interviewers will be watching you to see how you behave in a group situation:

✪ You may be kept waiting, just to see how you cope with minor irritations

✪ You may be asked to take part in a role play activity to see how you cope with more stressful situations

✪ You may be asked to give an impromptu talk on an amusing topic to assess your sense of humour and to see how confident you are giving a talk to a group of strangers

To break the ice, an interviewer may ask each of you to say a few words about yourself. One way is to ask each person in turn, going systematically round the room. Apart from the first person, everyone else can decide what to say based on what has been said already. Another way is to let the applicants volunteer the information, in any order. Would you be the first to speak? Or would you be the last? What would you say?

This **ice-breaker activity** also provides an interviewer with the opportunity to test your listening skills. You could be asked to describe other applicants – would you be able to remember their names and some other details about them all?

An interviewer will sometimes say something to provoke controversy:

✪ Do you dominate the conversation? This may be because you are very confident – maybe too confident – or it may show how nervous you are

✪ Are you the quietest person in the group? This may be because you are very shy, or it may be that you are listening to everyone else before making your contribution

Some interviews include a group task – a practical activity that has to be solved as a team. Your contribution to the team effort will be noted:

✪ Were you the person in the group who assumed the role of leader?

- ✪ Were you one of the people who came up with ideas?

- ✪ Were you the person who came up with the best ideas?

- ✪ How did you contribute to the group task?

- ✪ Did you fail to contribute to the group task?

A trained interviewer will also notice things about you that you may not be aware of:

- ✪ When you arrived, did you choose to sit near the front, or did you go straight to a seat in the back row?

- ✪ How did you interact with other applicants?

- ✪ What does your body language say about you?

The more practice you have had in working with others in a team, the more likely you will be able to cope with group interviews.

Revision questions

1. Give three examples of situations where teamworking is found.

2. Give one example of a team that is particularly successful. Why is that team successful?

3. Give one example of a team that has been unsuccessful. Explain why the team was unsuccessful.

4. What makes a good team?

5. How should teams be chosen?

6. Suggest five rules for a brainstorming session.

7. What skills should a team leader have?

8. Explain the terms 'forming', 'storming', 'norming' and 'performing'.

9. Explain how important planning is to any team activity.

10. What recording methods are useful for planning?

11. What recording methods are useful for team meetings?

12. Suggest four advantages of working in a team.

13. Suggest two disadvantages of working in a team.

14. How can communication skills be used to make a team more effective?

15. What other skills are useful in a team?

Good Working Practice Guide

Before IT systems, computers and word-processing packages were ever invented, typists had to type very carefully. If they made a mistake, they would have to retype a letter. With a word processing package, however, you can **edit** your document. What does this mean?

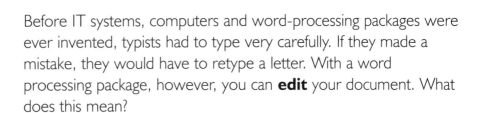

- ✪ You can change your mind about what you want to say

- ✪ You can think of a better way of saying something

- ✪ You can correct any keying errors

- ✪ You can check your spelling

- ✪ You can make sure the finished document is perfect before printing the copy on paper

It was thought that the introduction of word-processing packages would create the **paperless** office. Instead, users tend to print out many draft copies before they are satisfied with the finished document. The end result may be better, but we often use a lot of paper in the process.

The type of information kept on an IT system and possibly transmitted to other users is subject to laws, for instance the

control of pornography. Unfortunately, computers make the spread of this information easier and detection quite difficult. Also, information may be sensitive, e.g. medical records or financial details. If hackers gain access to computer files through a network, confidentiality may be lost. Commerce on the Internet has already introduced some questions that need to be resolved: which country's trading standards should apply if you buy something over the net? How safe is it to pay for goods using a credit card?

Many laws have been introduced, not least to try to combat computer-based crime:

○ **Computer Misuse Act 1990**

○ **Copyright, Designs and Patents Act 1998**

○ **Obscene Publications Act 1990**

Although you do not need to learn about all these laws, you should be aware of two important pieces of legislation:

○ **Health and safety** issues (see page 421)

○ **Data Protection Act** (see page 424)

and other good working practice expected of you during your practical work.

For your work to progress smoothly, you can help yourself by adopting standard ways of working. This can also help you to work well with others. In several units, standard ways of working are listed, e.g. the unit on presenting information. You must apply these techniques to *all* of your ICT work.

Standard ways of working

Many organisations have rules and guidelines to help people work effectively and to avoid problems. These 'standard ways of working' are particularly important for people working with information technology, and there are many reasons for having them. The most important is that information in ICT systems can be easily lost or misused:

❂ Unauthorised persons may gain access to confidential information

❂ People may copy original work and present it as their own

❂ Information presented professionally may be believed, even though it may be inaccurate

Things can often go wrong:

❂ The computer crashes when you are halfway through keying in some new text

❂ A floppy disk is corrupted so that you cannot access any of its files

❂ Paper files can be mislaid

❂ The operator miskeys while keying

❂ The wrong disk or tape is used

❂ The hardware malfunctions

❂ The power fails

Various **equipment faults** can happen with the hardware (e.g. the screen) or with the medium (e.g. the disk or tape). It is important to keep equipment and surfaces free of dust, and to store tapes and disks in sleeves or covers. It is important to store consumables in a cool, dry and dust-free environment, and to replace them correctly. A paper jam when your deadline is fast approaching will not help!

Loss of information can be damaging for the user. They can be embarrassed and might lose customers. At worst, a business may fail.

By adopting good working practices, you can minimise the disruptions that these sorts of problems cause.

Most good working practices are based on common sense. Others show that you have thought about the possible consequences of your actions. The ones that most people remember are the ones they learned when things went wrong!

- ❂ If you print before you save a document, and the computer crashes due to some memory problem while printing, you will have lost any changes you made to file since you last saved it. The sensible thing is always to save a document before printing

- ❂ If you set up headers or footers to show the path name of the document, at a later date you'll be able to find the file again

- ❂ If you number the pages of a document that has more than a couple of pages, there will be no chance of confusion, e.g. if the document is dropped and the pages scatter

- ❂ If you take a backup copy of your files, when one floppy disk lets you down, you have a backup copy you can use instead

Often there is no single 'right' way of doing something. To select a function, e.g. 'copy', you could move the cursor to a toolbar and click on the 'copy' icon, or you could use a right click followed by selecting on the special menu that appears for you. Which method you use depends on how confident you are in using the software.

You can become better at using the software if you take the time to read through the help notes. On-line help often includes demonstrations. These may take a short time to follow through, but you may learn useful tricks that will save you time later. Rather than limiting yourself to the few things you have already learned and use regularly, take time to explore what other facilities the software offers. In the long run, this can save you a lot of time.

Most of the things that go wrong while working on a computer are your own fault:

✪ Overwriting a document by accident

✪ Deleting a file, or some text, by accident

One obvious statement: it is important to think before doing anything! If you are not sure about how successful your next move will be, save your document before you attempt to make difficult changes. Then, if need be, you can retrieve the previous version of the document. Alternatively, remember that the undo button will reverse your previous actions.

The undo button cannot undo everything you do. For example, the undo button is no help with the overwriting of a document if you have already clicked on 'Okay'.

Taking advice from others

It is very difficult to find everything out for yourself, without the help of others. Your teacher will provide a lot of help and information about how to do things on your IT system and use the software available to you. In addition, you can use other sources of information:

✪ Manuals

✪ On-line help

✪ Magazine articles from the computer press

- Television programmes about using IT

- CD-ROMs in your library

- Information on the Internet

It is important that you know how to use on-line help. Often you need to know something in the middle of preparing a document while at a workstation. If you can use the on-line help, you can usually find the answer to your problem very quickly, and without interrupting anyone else.

Proof-reading

Organisations may produce hundreds of letters or reports each day. Many of the staff will spend nearly all of their working day preparing documents. A major part of their work may be in proof-reading drafts of documents.

So that people can work together on documents, it is important to understand and use a standard convention for the proof-reading symbols. BS 5261 Part 2 1976 is the standard that most publishers and typesetters use.

Copies of the standard can be obtained by post from BSI Sales, Linford Wood, Milton Keynes MK14 6LE; Telefax: 01908 320856.

File names

When you create a document, you must invent a name for it for storage purposes. Then, next time you need the document, you ask for the file by name.

There are restrictions on the names that you can use, and it is advisable to think carefully before choosing a name. There may also be a limit on the number of characters that you can use.

Choosing file names is not a bit like choosing passwords! Passwords have to be kept secret, so you try to think of a word that you can remember, that is special to you *and* that no one else might guess. File names are no secret, but you must be able to remember what you called your document. Otherwise, you might never find it again!

Choose names that make sense. Meaningful file names that make the file contents obvious are best.

Managing your work

The way you manage your ICT work is important. Here are some of the things that you should do to manage your work:

- ✪ Plan your work to produce what is required to given deadlines

- ✪ Use standard formats

- ✪ Enter information so that you can easily make changes, e.g. using spaces, tabs and indents correctly to ensure consistent layout

- ✪ Edit and save work regularly

- ✪ Make dated backup copies of your work, giving an idea of sequence

- ✪ When you are using any information that has been collected using secondary research, check it for validity and cross-reference with other books to ensure that it is correct

- ✪ Keep a log of your work, especially any ICT problems you meet and how you solve them

Keeping information secure

Protecting information from loss or misuse is essential in ICT. You must learn the particular importance of keeping information secure (e.g. from theft, loss, viruses and fire), protecting confidentiality and respecting copyright.

Having data on an IT system rather than in paper files has advantages and disadvantages:

✪ Lots of data can be stored on a single floppy disk

✪ The data is more easily moved and removed (e.g. stolen)

✪ If linked via networks, access is quite easy

Physical control includes locking doors, storing data in safes and issuing ID cards to users

Logical control includes using a password system and setting different access levels for different members of staff

To improve **security**, two types of control can be used: **physical control** and **logical control**.

Viruses can damage the files on an ICT system. To avoid introducing **viruses**, some simple precautions can be taken:

✪ Install virus-checking software, which checks all files as they are opened, on the system

✪ Do not open files from sources that are unknown to you, e.g. sent over the Internet as attached files

It is important to have adequate **fire protection**. Fires can start from cables and connectors that are not electrically sound. It is also unwise to overload sockets.

People or companies may wish to keep information **confidential** so that others do not know about it. You must learn to keep this type of information secure and not pass it on to others (e.g. preventing illegal access to medical or criminal records).

Password systems aim to restrict access to data. These **password systems** are fine so long as you keep your password secret. Surveys on choices of passwords show that most people choose obvious ones, which are easy for friends to guess: the name of their pet, or a favourite place. With more and more people using Internet cafes, it is quite easy to watch someone entering a password and then use this to gain access to files and information that are private to that person. One way to avoid this problem is to change your password regularly. Then you have to remember what the current one is!

A computer program, words, pictures and graphic images may belong to other people. The people who created or own this material have **copyright**, and you must not use their work without their permission. If you do, you are breaking the law. You must understand and respect copyright law. Where you do use information created by others and have obtained their permission, it is important that you acknowledge the source by using an appropriate reference or listing it in a bibliography.

If work stored on an ICT system is lost, it is important that there is another file that can be used in its place. You will need to understand and use suitable security procedures when using IT systems:

✪ Making backup copies of your work

✪ Keeping dated backup copies of files on another disk and in another location

✪ Saving work regularly, and using different file names

Making **backup copies** involves saving a copy of the data to a safe place. Do it regularly, e.g. daily, so that, if there is any problem, you can retrieve your data from the backup copy. To avoid loss by fire or theft, backup copies are usually stored away from the IT system, e.g. in a fireproof safe or in another building.

Working safely

The ICT working environment is relatively safe. However, there are risks that should be minimised and hazards that can – and should – be avoided:

- ✪ Obstacles, e.g. in doorways, which people may trip over or bump into and be bruised

- ✪ Obstacles on fire exit routes, which may prevent people escaping if there is a fire

Most computers are powered by mains electricity, which introduces more potential hazards:

- ✪ Tripping over cables

- ✪ Static electricity build-up

- ✪ Screen glare

Hazards exist only because not enough care is taken to keep the workplace safe. They must be prevented, though, under the Health and Safety at Work Act.

Risks usually result in stress on the worker. This could result in their needing time off work to recover, or that they can no longer do the job properly. Risks cannot always be eliminated, but they can – and should – be reduced.

The user, i.e. the operator, must be protected from potential danger. Seating is very important. Poor seating can result in poor posture and cause back problems, and many more working hours are lost due to illnesses such as RSI (repetitive strain injury). RSI is a painful complaint that can make continuing work impossible for sufferers. Usually, it attacks the wrist or arm of people who have used a keyboard or mouse for a long time.

Ergonomics studies the relationship between people and their environment. Many different things can be adjusted to make the operator as comfortable as possible, and many risks can be minimised by studying the ergonomics of the workplace. This means looking at many things that affect the worker:

- ✪ How you are seated – the height of the seat and the desk, the angle of the seating, the height of your desk

- ✪ How conveniently the desk is set up – whether you can reach everything you need without stretching too far – the keyboard and screen position

- ✪ Lighting – whether this is good enough for you to read without straining your eyes. Fitting anti-glare screens can prevent eye strain

- ✪ Background noise – whether this allows you to think clearly while working

You should be aware that a comfortable working position is important to avoid physical stress, eye strain or safety hazards. This may include avoiding long periods of continuous VDU work by having brief rest periods and having a surrounding area that includes near and distant objects that the eyes can focus on.

Do's and don'ts

- ✪ **Do** plan your work to produce what is required to given deadlines

- ✪ **Do** make a backup of your work. Label your backup with the date

- ✪ **Do** keep backup copies of files on another disk and in another location

- ✪ **Do** keep previous drafts of documents, filed in date order and giving an idea of sequence. Then you can always look back if you need to

- ✪ **Do** keep a log to provide a record of what has happened, especially what has gone wrong

- ✪ **Do** proof-read your database and spreadsheet information to ensure accuracy

✪ **Do** save work regularly using different file names

✪ **Do** proof-read all documents before printing out the final copy

✪ **Do** evaluate your work and suggest how it might be improved

✪ **Do** keep information free from viruses

✪ **Do** respect confidentiality

✪ **Do** respect copyright

✪ **Don't** disconnect or connect equipment without first isolating the power source

✪ **Don't** eat or drink while working at a PC. Wash your hands after eating sticky or greasy foods – the remains of a jam doughnut can glue up a keyboard

Health and safety issues

Health and Safety at Work etc. Act (1974)

The basis of health and safety (H&S) law in Britain is the Health and Safety at Work etc. Act (1974). This Act sets out the general duties that employers have towards employees and members of the public. It also explains the duties that employees have to themselves and to each other.

Risk assessment

The main requirement on employers is to carry out a risk assessment. Employers with five or more employees have to record the significant findings of the risk assessment. Risk assessment should be straightforward for a typical office. It should only be complicated if it deals with serious hazards such as those in a nuclear power station, a chemical plant or laboratory, or on an oil rig. Besides carrying out a risk assessment, employers have other responsibilities:

✪ **To make arrangements for implementing the health and safety measures identified as necessary by the risk assessment**

✪ **To appoint competent people (often themselves or company colleagues) to help them to implement the arrangements**

✪ **To set up emergency procedures**

✪ **To provide clear information and training to employees**

✪ **To work together with other employers sharing the same workplace**

The Health and Safety Commission (HSC) produces guidance, approved codes of practice (ACOPs) and regulations.

The Health and Safety Executive (HSE) publishes guidance on a range of subjects, specific to the H&S problems of an industry or of a particular process used in a number of industries, for three main reasons:

✪ To interpret – helping people to understand what the law says – including, for example, how requirements based on EC directives fit with those under the Health and Safety at Work Act

✪ To help people to comply with the law

✪ To give technical advice

Following guidance is not compulsory, and employers are free to take other action. However, if they do follow guidance, they will normally be doing enough to comply with the law. The HSC/HSE aims to keep guidance up to date because as technologies change, risks – and the measures needed to address them – change too.

ACOPs offer practical examples of good practice. If regulations use words like 'suitable and sufficient', an ACOP can illustrate what this requires in particular circumstances. ACOPs have a special legal status. If employers are prosecuted for a breach of H&S law, and it is proved that they have not followed the relevant provisions of the ACOP, a court can find them at fault unless they can show that they have complied with the law in some other way.

Regulations are law, approved by Parliament. The Health and Safety at Work Act, and general duties in the management regulations, are goal-setting and leave employers freedom to decide how to control risks that they identify. Guidance and ACOPs give advice, but employers are free to take other measures provided they do what is reasonably practicable. However, some risks are so great, or the proper control measures so costly, that it would not be appropriate to leave employers discretion in deciding what to do about them. Regulations identify these risks and set out specific action that must be taken.

Some regulations apply across *all* companies e.g. the Display Screen Equipment Regulations apply wherever VDUs are used. Other regulations apply to hazards unique to specific industries, such as mining or nuclear safety law. Besides the Health and Safety at Work Act itself, these regulations apply across the full range of workplaces.

For your own safety, and that of others around you, you should make sure you follow all safety procedures adopted by your employer, your college or school. Visit the HSE website at http://www.hse.gov.uk for more information – many documents are available for downloading as Adobe Acrobat files.

Data Protection Act (DPA)

Computers are in use throughout society – collecting, storing and distributing information (processing). Much of that information is about living people (personal data). The DPA places obligations on those who record and use personal data (data users). They must be open about the use (through the data protection register) and follow sound and proper practices (the data protection principles).

The DPA also gives rights to individuals about whom information is recorded (data subjects). They may find out information about themselves, challenge it, have it corrected or erased if appropriate, and claim compensation in certain circumstances.

The Data Protection Registrar has many duties:

✪ **Establishing and maintaining a register of data users and computer bureaux and making it publicly available**

✪ **Promoting compliance with the data protection principles**

✪ **Encouraging, where appropriate, the development of codes of practice to help data users to comply with the principles**

✪ **Considering complaints about breaches of the principles of the Act and, where appropriate, prosecuting offenders or serving notices**

The DPA only applies to automatically processed information. It does not cover information that is held and processed manually – for example, in ordinary paper files. Not all computerised information is covered by the DPA, only that relating to living individuals. So, for example, it does not cover information that relates only to a company or an organisation.

Anyone who holds personal information about living individuals on computer must register unless covered by one of the exemptions provided by the DPA. To register as a data user, information has to be supplied for inclusion in the register:

✪ The name and address of the data user

✪ A description of the purposes for which personal data are used

✪ The type of personal data held

✪ Where the personal data are obtained

✪ To whom they will be disclosed

✪ A list of any countries outside the UK to which they may be transferred

Once a data user has registered, he or she must act only within the terms of his or her register entry. Not to do so is an offence. A data user can apply to the registrar to alter his or her register entry at any time. It is an offence to fail to register or to provide false information to the registrar.

Once registered, data users must comply with the principles in relation to the personal data held:

✪ Personal data shall be collected and processed fairly and lawfully

✪ Personal data shall be held only for specified and lawful purposes

✪ Personal data shall be used only for those purposes and only disclosed to those people described in the register entry

✪ Personal data shall be adequate, relevant and not excessive in relation to the purposes for which they are held

- ✪ Personal data shall be accurate and, where necessary, kept up to date

- ✪ Personal data shall be held no longer than is necessary for the registered purpose

- ✪ Personal data shall be protected by proper security

However, the registrar cannot enforce the principles against unregistered data users.

The **rights of the individual**: an individual is entitled to be supplied by a data user with a copy of any personal data held about him or her – the 'subject access' right. Individuals may write direct to the user for their data, or they may consult the register to obtain more details about the user.

Data users may charge up to £10 for meeting each request, but some may decide to charge less, or nothing at all. They have up to 40 days in which to provide the data from the date of receiving adequate information to help them locate the data or identify the individual making the request. If the data are not provided within the 40 days, the individual concerned can complain to the registrar or apply to the courts for an order that the data user should provide access.

There are several exemptions from the DPA. Manually held information, e.g. in card indexes or paper files, is not covered. Otherwise, the exemptions from the need to register are extremely narrow. They cover only the simplest tasks in the following areas: calculating pay and pensions, keeping accounts or records of purchases or sales, distributing articles or information (mailing lists), and preparing text documents. Most businesses find it difficult to meet and stay within the limits imposed by these exemptions and find it safer to register.

So people and organisations who hold personal information about living individuals on computer probably need to register under the DPA. No matter how unimportant this information may appear, the fact that it is on computer almost certainly makes the data user liable for registration.

Where personal data are exempt from the whole of the DPA, those data need not be registered, there is no right of subject access and the registrar and courts have no powers regarding this personal data. Some exemptions are unconditional, for example where national security is involved, or where an individual holds personal data for recreational purposes or for managing his own personal, family or household affairs. Other exemptions are conditional. For example, exemptions exist for unincorporated members' clubs and mailing lists. In the case of all the conditional exemptions, the data may not be disclosed without the consent of the individual to whom the data relate. Limited disclosures are permitted for the payroll, pensions and accounts exemptions without the consent of the individual.

There are also a number of exemptions from the need to provide information under the subject access provisions of the DPA. For example, personal information may be withheld where this would be likely to prejudice the prevention or detection of crime; the apprehension or prosecution of offenders; or the assessment or collection of any tax or duty.

Decisions to withhold information under these exemptions can be challenged by the registrar on receipt of a complaint from a member of the public.

More detailed information on all aspects of the Data Protection Act is contained in *The Guidelines*, a free publication available from the registrar's office.

Portfolio Guide

Your portfolio should contain all the evidence collected as you work through the units. For two of your units the assessment is by external testing, but material in your portfolio may well be needed to show your achievement in key skills. It therefore makes sense to keep a portfolio of all your work for all your units, even the two that are not portfolio-assessed.

To decide what material you need to produce and put in your portfolio, look at the assessment grid at the end of each unit specification. Your portfolio must contain at least the minimum stated in the first column of the 'Assessment evidence' section of each unit.

The assessment evidence section tells you exactly what type of evidence you need to produce – e.g. lists, notes, records, summary – to show what depth of work is needed, and you need to check that you have met this level of presentation.

- ✪ **Lists** are simply a series of brief comments on the main points

- ✪ **Notes** are more than just a list. For each item, you may write a paragraph of information. You may write notes when preparing for a task. They may include draft ideas, initial plans and drawings, and so on

✪ A **record** is an account of the activity that is being assessed. It could be a written record, including tables of data, a checklist of activities, and so on. You decide exactly what to include after discussion with your teacher

✪ A **report** is a finished piece of work that brings together lots of ideas and information

✪ A **summary** is a short account, similar to a record, but it should not include all your working papers

For some activities, your teacher will watch you working and then write an assessment of your performance. In some situations, another person, e.g. your supervisor in a work placement, may observe you.

With a presentation, you will present your finished work to an audience (maybe only to your teacher), but your portfolio evidence might include a taped recording or a video together with the material (e.g. OHTs or slides) that you used. Your teacher will be responsible for agreeing that you used a good standard of English during your presentation, and that your manner and tone were suitable for your audience.

For the tested units, the assessment grid does say what you have to produce, but your awarding body will specify the precise requirement in pre-release material given to you some time before the examination. See the Examination Guide on page 447.

Performance when doing assignments

Teachers can most easily assess the quality of your work by watching you when you do assignments, and by looking at what you produce for your portfolio. When you prepare for a task and are identifying sources of information, your teacher may consider these questions:

✪ **Were you usually told what tasks needed to be done and then had to be guided through them?**

✪ **Were you able to decide what steps you needed to take, and did you arrange the tasks into a sensible order, setting your own timescale?**

✪ **Did you use sources of information suggested by your teacher, and were you able to select and use the relevant information from these sources?**

✪ **Were you able to understand what the task involved without any guidance from your teacher?**

✪ **Did you understand what information was required, and did you look for extra sources of information as well as investigating those suggested by your teacher?**

The more independent you are, the higher your grade should be.

Similarly, the more care you take over planning and monitoring your work, the more likely you are to be successful, and the higher your grade should be. During every task, check that your original plan is working by monitoring and reviewing your progress. You should recognise that the planning may need changing. Sometimes, through no fault of your own, the plan does not work:

- ✪ Computers crash

- ✪ Books and other sources may not be available

- ✪ People that you have arranged to meet may fall ill and have to postpone your appointment

Even if things do not go wrong, you should be able to show that you have checked progress regularly against the original plan.

The quality of your work is also very important:

- ✪ At **pass level**, you should be able to demonstrate a basic understanding of the knowledge and skills required, but you may not be able to make connections between different aspects of your work. You should be able to use the normal ICT terminology but may need some help from your teacher

- ✪ At **merit level**, you should be able to make connections between different aspects of your work and demonstrate a clear understanding. Your use of ICT terminology should be accurate, and your written work should show confidence in the expression of your ideas

- ✪ At **distinction level**, you will have a clear understanding of the knowledge and skills required. You will use your personal experience to draw conclusions or suggest alternative courses of action

At the end of each assignment, all students are expected to be able to describe what they felt went well and what went badly. Evaluating your work is an important part of improving your own performance – one of the six key skills.

- ✪ Distinction-level students are able to learn from what they have done to date. They learn from any mistakes and build on success

- ✪ Pass-level students will be saying, 'Oh! that went wrong last time!'

So, while doing practice or real assignments, remember that if you perform well, you may be awarded a higher grade for this work. Here are some of the things your teacher will be checking when awarding a grade:

- ✪ Have you shown independence in your approach to your work?

- ✪ Have you completed the work to given deadlines?

- ✪ Have you planned your work effectively?

- ✪ Have you selected and used relevant information to help you meet your purposes?

- ✪ Have you used technical language correctly?

- ✪ Have you reviewed your work?

When assessing your portfolio, your teacher is looking for the right quality and quantity of work. He or she will first look to see that you have covered everything by checking that you have covered all items listed in the various columns of the 'Assessment evidence' chart. Work of a high quality may earn you a higher grade, so your teacher will be looking at all the columns of the chart.

What are the general 'rules' that allow your teacher to decide on your grade? This depends on the unit – and is detailed in the section called 'Assessment strategies'. Although this section is written for your teacher, you should read it carefully. Then you'll know how your work will be viewed by your teacher.

Generally speaking, the teacher will try to distinguish between students and award grades so that the higher grades are given to students who perform best. Make sure that you perform at your very best and you should achieve the highest grade possible for you.

Presenting information within a portfolio

It will help your teacher – and give extra information about your performance overall – if your portfolio is presented well. Chapter 1 covers Unit 1: *Presenting Information*. As a student on the Foundation GNVQ ICT course, you must be able to demonstrate that you can do this well!

You can handwrite your assignments, or you could use a word processor. If you handwrite your work, you will have to be very neat. If you make a mistake in your 'final' version, it will show and you may feel you have to write out a whole sheet again.

If you use a word processor, apart from showing IT key skills, you will have the benefits of using IT:

✪ You can edit your work until you are happy with it

✪ You can choose a style that reflects your own personality. You can choose a point size and a font that you like

✪ You can include clip art or other graphics, e.g. using WordArt, to improve the appearance of your portfolio material

For some assignments, you will have to use a computer. When doing assignments, most of your material will be produced on the computer.

The structure of your portfolio

There are a number of sections that your portfolio should include. This will demonstrate that you can structure material and present it in a sensible way. The main sections are listed here, but you can choose your own sections if you prefer:

✪ Front cover

✪ Contents list

✪ Assignment material

✪ Appendices

You may also have checklist sheets supplied by your teacher. These may be used to refer to where key skills are demonstrated. In addition, you may have material that confirms that your teacher saw you present some information, or has discussed your material with you.

Your name (and centre details) should appear at least once on the portfolio. For safety's sake, it would be good practice to include this information on every page. If you are using software, this is easily achieved by including this information in a header or footer.

It will be important that your contents list matches whatever you have included in the rest of your portfolio. Although it appears at the very start of your portfolio, it is one of the last pages you can complete. However, if you produce it using a word processor you can prepare a contents page at the very beginning and update it every time you add some material to your portfolio. Then it will be one less job to do when you are rushing to meet the final deadline.

In this book, the pages run from 1 to 458, and the contents list (on page iii) shows the starting page numbers for each chapter. For your portfolio, it may be easier to number the sections and then, within each section, number the pages by section. This numbering method is often used in manuals and means that extra sections can be added at any time without it upsetting the page numbering too much.

For the material produced when doing assignments, plus any material produced when doing activities, it probably makes sense to present the material in the same order as you completed the work. For each assignment, make sure you show clearly what the assignment is called, and what it covers. It may be possible to use material produced in another course as evidence of your ICT skills. It will help your teacher if you write clearly on each assignment which unit (and course) the assignment refers to.

Sometimes it make sense to move some material to an appendix. This shortens a section, and yet the material is available if the reader wants to look at it. So, for example, lengthy tables or diagrams or copies of original source materials may be put into an appendix.

You can also list your references in an appendix. It is important to include all your references: the books, magazines and CD-ROMs you used to find information for your assignments.

While building your portfolio, leave yourself messages about things you still have to include. You could write these notes on your plan (which will provide evidence of the fact that you have been reviewing and monitoring your plan) – or put Post-it notes on pages that still have work to be done, or write yourself a checklist, which you can then tick off as you complete the work.

Moderation and internal assessment

Your portfolio material is first marked by a teacher, and marking is then standardised internally by specially trained staff at your school or college.

The teachers must be able to verify that the work submitted by you is your own work. This does not prevent groups of students working together in the initial stages, but it is important to ensure that your individual contribution is clearly identified separately from that of any group in which you work.

When all portfolios have been internally standardised, data about your portfolio – and all the other students on your course – is then submitted to the awarding body by a specified date, after which postal moderation takes place in accordance with the awarding body's procedures and the code of practice.

Detailed arrangements for moderation are forwarded to all schools and colleges before the start of the course, so your teacher should be able to tell you when your deadlines will be.

Key Skills Guide

All jobs need certain skills. Your first job will need few skills, but as you progress to more senior posts, more skills are needed. Job skills fall into two types: vocational skills and key skills.

Vocational skills are the skills that are linked to the actual job:

✪ The ability to use a keyboard or mouse

✪ The experience of using a word-processing package

✪ The experience of using a DTP (desktop publishing) package

✪ The ability to install software and to customise applications programs

You will learn vocational skills while following this course, and, in doing so, will need to use key skills.

Key skills are not specific to a subject like ICT. Instead, they are useful for most jobs and include these abilities:

✪ To think for yourself

✪ To work without supervision

- ✪ To work in a team

- ✪ To work with numbers

- ✪ To solve problems

- ✪ To communicate your ideas to others

- ✪ To remember names and other important facts

- ✪ To work to a deadline

So key skills can help you to improve your own learning and performance in education and training, work and life in general.

- ✪ **In your learning**, key skills help you to focus on what and how you are learning. In this way, while reviewing your progress, you can get better results

- ✪ **In your career**, key skills enable you to be flexible in whatever kind of work you do. Employers look for key skills when recruiting and promoting people. In particular, your ability to work well in a team, and your motivation to learn, will be of interest to your interviewer. These skills are relevant to all levels of an organisation, including self-employment

- ✪ **In your personal life**, key skills can help you to organise yourself, manage your money, handle information and get on with others

Key skills qualifications are available in three main areas:

- ✪ Communication

- ✪ Application of number

- ✪ Information technology

There are three other key skills areas – the 'wider' key skills:

- ✪ Working with others

- ✪ Improving own learning and performance

- ✪ Problem solving

These last three key skills will become essential for success in your course. Many activities are based on teamwork, and employers are particularly interested in your ability to work well in a team. The 'Working with others' key skills specification also includes working on your own though! Employers are looking for staff who can work unsupervised and who are motivated not only to get a job but also to improve their own learning by attending courses and learning as much as possible while working.

Key skills awards are available in each of these six areas at levels 1, 2, 3 and 4. At level 5, a single unit combines communication skills with the skills of working with others, improving own learning and performance, and problem solving.

As you move up the levels, you are expected to take more responsibility for decisions on how you use your skills to suit different tasks, problems and situations. Students working at levels 1 and 2 work with straightforward subjects and materials, in routine situations. Students at higher levels deal with complex subjects and activities that are more demanding. At the higher levels, planning is very important. Students at levels 3 and 4 need to think about how to tackle tasks, what resources they will need and how to check their own work.

To achieve this qualification, you must demonstrate your skills through a portfolio of evidence. This evidence should not involve you in a lot of extra work. Instead, you should be able to collect evidence from your day-to-day studies, work or other activities and an appropriate form of independent assessment. As well as producing a portfolio of evidence, you will also have to pass an externally set test for each key skill.

Key skills signposting

In the Foundation GNVQ course, you have the opportunity to learn, practice and gather evidence of all six key skills.

In each unit of the specification for the Foundation GNVQ in ICT, there is a section called 'Guidance on key skills'. This highlights the most relevant key skills opportunities available for that particular unit. Key skills and vocational achievement are interdependent, and the guidance section shows how vocational and key skills achievement can be successfully combined.

Guidance is referenced in two ways: keys to attainment and signposts. The two sections should be used together – they are intended to complement each other.

- ✪ **Keys to attainment** are key skills that you should achieve at the same time as you meet the vocational requirements of the unit. They are central to your vocational achievement — they really are the 'key skills' needed to ensure your success.

- ✪ **Signposting** shows opportunities that can be incorporated into the learning process. However, they might not be achieved at the same time as producing evidence of your vocational skills. These signposts point to naturally occurring opportunities for the development of key skills, so it may make sense to go a bit further in your studies to produce evidence that meets key skills requirements, on top of your vocational evidence.

The 'Guidance on key skills' section of every unit contains suggestions of opportunities to meet key skills in that unit. For some aspects of key skills, you need to produce more than one example as evidence, so it is important to concentrate on the keys to attainments because these offer the best opportunities to achieve key skills in your vocational work.

The three compulsory units should provide you with all the

opportunities you need, but there are also opportunities in the optional units. In choosing your mix of units, you will need to ensure that key skills evidence can also be produced without having to do lots of extra work.

To help you, the three awarding bodies include grids in their specifications showing which key skills match which of their units. In this book, each activity includes an indication of what key skills may be useful, and this may also help you to decide where your evidence of key skills will naturally arise. You (with the help of your teacher) will then need to decide how and when you will produce all the evidence required to meet the key skills specifications. It is quite possible that you may need to develop additional evidence elsewhere – even another course – to meet all requirements of the key skills specifications.

Note that, not surprisingly, information technology key skills (level 1) are automatically included in the units covered for Foundation GNVQ ICT. So you do not need anything extra to achieve key skills in IT, unless you are aiming for key skills at level 2 or higher. However, you do have to take the external assessment test!

Key skills terms

The key skills specifications use terms in a special way:

✪ **Evidence** is what you produce to prove that you have the key skills required, e.g. things you have made, written work, artwork and diagrams, photos, audio/video recordings, printouts, together with records from your assessor and others who have seen your work

✪ **Portfolio** is where you collect and organise evidence for assessment. Your portfolio should include a contents page to show where evidence for each part of the unit(s) can be found. For more details on how to prepare your portfolio, see the Portfolio Guide on page 429

It is possible – and it makes sense – to use some evidence for more than one key skill, e.g. a printout of text and images, such as graphs and charts, may provide valuable evidence of written communication skills as well as presenting findings in application of number and IT. The subject content and the material you use will be mostly straightforward, but it may sometimes be complex.

✪ **Straightforward** subjects and materials are the ones that you meet most often in your work, studies or other activities. Content is presented in a direct way so that it easy to identify the main points. The sentence structures are simple, and the vocabulary will be familiar to you

✪ **Complex** subjects and materials present a number of ideas: some abstract ideas, some very detailed concepts and some requiring you to deal with sensitive issues. The relationship between ideas and any lines of reasoning may not be immediately clear. You may need to understand specialised vocabulary, and complicated sentence structures may be used

During your Foundation GNVQ course, you may use and prepare **extended documents**. These include textbooks like this one, newspaper reports, articles on the Internet and essays that you write – anything that has more than three pages. Such documents may relate to straightforward or complex subjects. They may include images such as diagrams, pictures and charts.

Any activity that includes a number of related tasks, where the results of one task then affect how you carry out the remaining tasks, is called a **substantial activity**. For the key skill application of number, a substantial activity may involve obtaining and interpreting information, using this information to carry out calculations and then explaining how the results of your calculations meet the purpose of the activity.

How to read a key skills unit

Each key skills specification document is presented as a folded sheet of A3 paper with four sides of A4 printing. It covers one level of one key skill area, e.g. application of number, level 1. It is important to read the whole specification, not just a single part of it – because all four pages present a different view of the key skill, and you need to see it from all angles.

What is this unit about? On the front cover, the first section outlines the unit. Check that you have the correct key skills specification, at the right level. The specification documents look very similar, so it is easy to be looking at the wrong level.

How do I use the information in this unit? A second section on the front cover shows the other three pages – parts A, B and C of the specification – and explains the purpose of each section:

✪ **Part A: What you need to know** lists what you need to learn and practise to feel confident about applying the key skill in your studies, work or other aspects of your life. Check whether you know how to do these things and think about the opportunities you might have for showing these skills. Some topics may be familiar to you, and you may feel confident that you can produce evidence to prove this. For other topics, you may have some learning to do, and you may need practice before you are ready for assessment.

✪ **Part B: What you must do** has a numbered list of the key skills you must show. The numbers in the list are used as signposts in other examination specifications. For each numbered item, there is then a bullet list of evidence that you must produce. All your work for this section has to be assessed. You must have evidence that you can do *all* the things listed in the bullet points.

✪ **Part C: Guidance** describes some activities that you might like to use to develop and show your key skill, and some ideas on the sort of activities that could be suitable. It also contains examples of the sort of evidence you could produce to prove you have the skills required.

Examination of key skills

External moderation will be used to check how well you have demonstrated your key skills in your portfolio material. More details on how to present your portfolio are given in the Portfolio Guide on page 429.

Tests for key skills are being developed while this book is being written, so it is not possible to say, at this time, exactly what form the examinations will take.

However, material will be made available later this year (2000), and teachers and students alike will then be able to access this information via the Internet.

Examination Guide

For the Foundation GNVQ in Information and Communication Technology, there are three **compulsory units**:

- ✪ Presenting information

- ✪ Handling information

- ✪ Hardware and software

Two different awards are available:

- ✪ **For the three-unit award – the Part One Foundation GNVQ award – you study only the three compulsory units**

- ✪ **For the six-unit award – the Foundation GNVQ award – you study six units: the three compulsory units plus any three others chosen from optional units**

For some of the units, you will demonstrate your understanding by your portfolio material; for other units, you will be assessed externally. However, the balance of portfolio to externally assessed units means that most of your work will be assessed as you work through the course (continuous assessment).

Each unit, whether assessed by portfolio or external assessment, is individually graded, and points will be awarded for each unit on a scale of 0–16:

✪ 0–6 below pass

0 = did not submit any work

1 = did not achieve any of the pass-grade criteria

2 = achieves only one pass-grade criterion

3 = achieves less then half of the pass-grade criteria

4 = achieves half of the pass-grade criteria

5 = achieves more than half of the pass-grade criteria

6 = just below pass grade

✪ 7–9 pass

7 = achieves pass-grade criteria

8 = comfortably achieves pass-grade criteria

9 = a good pass just below merit grade

✪ 10–12 merit

10 = achieves merit-grade criteria

11 = comfortably achieves merit-grade criteria

12 = a good merit just below distinction grade

✪ 13–16 distinction

13 = achieves distinction-grade criteria

14 = comfortably achieves distinction-grade criteria

15 = a good distinction-grade achievement

16 = an excellent distinction-grade achievment

For tested units, your grade will reflect how many marks you earned in the test. For portfolio-assessed material, the mark awarded will take into account the extent to which the evidence matches both the unit pass standards, represented by the set of criteria in the pass column of the grid, and the grading standards, represented progressively by the criteria in the merit and distinction columns.

Then, a single grade (pass, merit or distinction) is decided on a points basis to reflect your performance over all your units; this single grade is then your 'final' grade for the Foundation GNVQ (as with GCSEs) and can be used for entry to higher education on the usual points basis.

For the six-unit Foundation GNVQ, your final grade will depend on this final score:

✪ 0–41 below pass

✪ 42–59 pass

✪ 60–77 merit

✪ 78–96 distinction

When you have completed the work for a single unit, you should be ready to sit the external test.

Tests and assignments are scheduled to take place at set times of the year, after you have worked on a particular unit. It does not matter what order you take the external tests, because each unit is available for assessment in both testing sessions: January and June. The important thing is to make sure that you are confident that you have covered all the material for the unit *before* you sit the test.

According to the unit, and your awarding body, you may be expected to do an assignment, or perhaps some preparatory work, before sitting the written test.

Although your choice of units may result in more externally tested units, two is the minimum number of externally assessed units for the six-unit Foundation GNVQ.

The written tests – one per tested unit – last 90 minutes each. You write your answers in a booklet in the spaces provided.

Sample papers, which you can use as a mock examinations for the tests, are available on the web. The revision questions given at the end of each chapter will also provide you with some practice.

Which units are externally tested?

This table shows each chapter in this book and the numbering of units for each awarding body. The unit numbers for those units that are assessed externally are shown in bold.

Chapter	Title	OCR	AQA	Edexcel
1	Presenting information	1	1	**1**
2	Handling information	2	2	2
3	Hardware and software	**3**	**3**	3
4	Design project	4	5	4
5	Using information resources	5	6	**5**
6	Graphics	**6**	**4**	6
7	Multimedia	7	7	7
8	Preparing for employment	8	8	8
9	Working as part of a team	9	9	9

Abbreviations

AOB	any other business
ATM	automatic teller machine
BACS	bankers automated clearing services
BIOS	basic input/output system
bps	bits per second
CAD	computer-aided design
CPU	central processing unit
CTRL	control (key)
CV	curriculum vitae
dpi	dots per inch
DOS	disk operating system
DTP	desktop publishing
DVD	digital versatile disk
EFT	electronic funds transfer
EFTPOS	electronic funds transfer at point of sale
ESC	escape (key)
EU	European Union
fax	facsimile
GCSE	General Certificate of Secondary Education
Gb	gigabyte
GIGO	garbage in, garbage out

GNVQ	General National Vocational Qualification
GPS	global positioning system
GUI	graphical user interface
HCI	human/computer interface
HTML	hypertext mark-up language
ID	identity
ICT	information and communication technology
ISA	industry-standard architecture
IT	information technology
Kb	kilobyte
LAN	local area network
Mb	megabyte
MHz	megahertz
NRA	National Record of Achievement
PAYE	pay as you earn
R&D	research and development
RAM	random-access memory
ROM	read-only memory
tab	tabulation
Tb	terabyte
TP	twisted pair
TV	television
UK	United Kingdom
URL	uniform resource locator (or a unique Internet address)
VAT	value-added tax
VDU	visual display unit
VR	virtual reality
WAN	wide area network
WIMP	window, icon, mouse, pointer
WORM	write once, read many
WWW	world wide web
WYSIWYG	what you see is what you get

Index